The Saddest Girl in the World

Cathy Glass

The Saddest Girl in the World

The true story of a neglected and isolated little girl
who just wanted to be loved

HarperElement
An Imprint of HarperCollins*Publishers*
77–85 Fulham Palace Road,
Hammersmith, London W6 8JB

www.harpercollins.co.uk

and *HarperElement* are trademarks of
HarperCollins*Publishers* Ltd

First published by HarperElement 2009

2

© Cathy Glass 2007

Cathy Glass asserts the moral right to
be identified as the author of this work

A catalogue record of this book
is available from the British Library

HB ISBN 978-0-00-728103-9
PB ISBN 978-0-00-728105-3

Printed and bound in Great Britain by
Clays Ltd, St Ives plc

FSC is a non-profit international organisation established to promote the responsible management of the world's forests. Products carrying the FSC label are independently certified to assure consumers that they come from forests that are managed to meet the social, economic and ecological needs of present and future generations.

Find out more about HarperCollins and the environment at
www.harpercollins.co.uk/green

Prologue

This is the story of Donna, who came to live with me when she was ten. At the time I had been fostering for eleven years, and it is set before I had fostered Jodie (*Damaged*) or Tayo (*Hidden*), and before I had fostered Lucy, whom I went on to adopt. When Donna arrived, my son Adrian was ten and my daughter Paula was six; the impact Donna had on our lives was enormous, and what she achieved has stayed with us.

Certain details, including names, places, and dates have been changed to protect the child.

The Saddest Girl in the World

Chapter One
Sibling Rivalry

I t was the third week in August, and Adrian, Paula and I were enjoying the long summer holidays, when the routine of school was as far behind us as it was in front. The weather was excellent and we were making the most of the long warm days, clear blue skies and the chance to spend some time together. Our previous foster child, Tina, had returned to live with her mother the week before and, although we had been sorry to see her go at the end of her six-month stay with us, we were happy for her. Her mother had sorted out her life and removed herself from a highly abusive partner. Although they would still be monitored by the social services, their future looked very positive. Tina's mother wanted to do what was best for her daughter and appeared to have just lost her way for a while – mother and daughter clearly loved each other.

I wasn't expecting to have another foster child placed with me until the start of the new school term in September. August is considered a 'quiet time' for the Looked After Children's teams at the social services, not because children aren't being abused or families aren't in crises, but simply because no one knows about them. It is a sad fact that once children return to school in September teachers start to see bruises on children, hear them talk of being left home alone or not being fed, or note that a child appears withdrawn, upset and uncared for, and then they raise their concerns. One of the busiest times for the Looked After Children's team and foster carers is late September and October, and also sadly after Christmas, when the strain on a dysfunctional family of being thrust together for a whole week finally takes its toll.

It was with some surprise, therefore, that having come in from the garden, where I had been hanging out the washing, to answer the phone, I heard Jill's voice. Jill was my support social worker from Homefinders Fostering Agency, the agency for whom I fostered.

'Hi, Cathy,' Jill said in her usual bright tone. 'Enjoying the sun?'

'Absolutely. Did you have a good holiday?'

'Yes, thanks. Crete was lovely, although two days back and I'm ready for another holiday.'

'Is the agency busy, then?' I asked, surprised.

'No, but I'm in the office alone this week. Rose and Mike are both away.' Jill paused, and I waited, for I doubted she had phoned simply to ask if I was enjoying the sun or lament the passing of her holiday. I was right. 'Cathy, I've just had a phone call from a social worker, Edna Smith. She's lovely, a real treasure, and she is looking to move a child – Donna, who was brought into care at the end of July. I immediately thought of you.'

I gave a small laugh of acknowledgement, for without doubt this prefaced trouble. A child who had to be moved from her carer after three weeks suggested the child had been acting out and playing up big time, to the point where the carer could no longer cope.

'What has she done?' I asked.

It was Jill's turn to give a small laugh. 'I'm not really sure, and neither is Edna. All the carers are saying is that Donna doesn't get along with her two younger brothers. The three of them were placed together.'

'That doesn't sound like much of a reason for moving her,' I said. Children are only moved from a foster home when it is absolutely essential and the placement has irretrievably broken down, for clearly it is very unsettling for a child to move home.

'No, that's what I said, and Edna feels the same. Edna is on her way to visit the carers now and see what's going on. Hopefully she'll be able to smooth things over, but is it OK if I give her your number so that she can call you direct if she needs to?'

'Yes, of course,' I said. 'I'll be in until lunchtime, and then I thought I would take Adrian and Paula to the park. I'll have my mobile with me, so give Edna both numbers. I assume that even if Donna has to be moved there won't be a rush?'

'No, I shouldn't think so. And you're happy to take her, if necessary?'

'Yes. How old is she?'

'Ten, but I understand she is quite a big girl and looks and acts older than her years.'

'OK, no problem. Hopefully Edna can sort it out if it's only sibling rivalry, and Donna won't have to move.'

'Yes,' Jill agreed. 'Thanks. Enjoy the rest of your day.'

'And you.'

She sighed. 'At work?'

* * *

I returned to the garden to finish hanging out the washing. Adrian and Paula were in the garden, playing in the toy sandpit. While Paula was happy to sit at the edge of the sandpit and make little animal sand shapes with the plastic moulds, Adrian was busy transporting the sand with aid of a large plastic digger to various places on the lawn. There were now quite sizeable hills of sand dotted on the grass, as if some mischievous mole had been busy underground. I knew that the sand, now mixed with grass, would not be welcomed back into the sandpit by Paula, who liked the sand, as she did most things, clean.

'Try to keep the sand in the sandpit. Good boy,' I said to Adrian as I passed.

'I'm building a motorway,' he said. 'I'm going to need cement and water to mix with the sand, and then it will set hard into concrete.'

'Oh yes?' I asked doubtfully.

'It's to make the pillars that hold up the bridges on the motorway. Then I'm going to bury dead bodies in the cement in the pillar.'

'What?' I said. Paula looked up.

'They hide dead bodies in the cement,' Adrian confirmed.

'Whoever told you that?'

'Brad at school. He said the Mafia murder people who owe them money, and then put the dead bodies in the pillars on the motorway bridges. No one ever finds them.'

'Charming,' I said. 'Perhaps you could build a more traditional bridge without bodies. And preferably keeping the sand in the sandpit.'

'Look!' he continued, unperturbed. 'I've already buried one body.'

I paused from hanging up the washing as Adrian quickly demolished one of the molehills of sand with the digger to reveal a small doll caked in sand.

'That's mine!' Paula squealed. 'It's Topsy! You've taken her from my doll's house!' Her eyes immediately misted.

'Adrian,' I said, 'did you ask Paula if you could borrow Topsy and bury her in sand?'

'She's not hurt,' he said, brushing off the sand. 'Why's she such a baby?'

'I'm not a baby,' Paula wailed. 'You're rotten!'

'OK, OK,' I said. 'Enough. Adrian, clean up Topsy and give her back to Paula. And please ask your sister next time before you take her things. If you want to bury something, why not use your model dinosaurs? Dinosaurs are used to being buried: they've been at it for millions of years.'

'Cor, yes, that's cool,' Adrian said with renewed enthusiasm. 'I'll dig in the garden for dinosaur fossils!' On his hands and knees, he scooped Topsy up in the digger and deposited her in Paula's lap, and then headed for the freshly turned soil in a flowerbed that I had recently weeded. I thought that if Edna couldn't smooth over the sibling rivalry between Donna and her younger brothers and Donna did come to stay, she would be in very good company, and would soon feel most at home.

I made the three of us a sandwich lunch, which we ate in the garden under the shade of the tree; then I suggested to Adrian and Paula that we went to our local park for an hour or so. The park was about a ten-minute walk away, and Adrian wanted to take his bike and Paula her doll's pram. I asked Adrian to go to the shed at the bottom of the garden and get out the bike and doll's pram while I took in the dry washing and the lunch things, and closed the downstairs windows. Since my divorce, Adrian, in small ways, had become the man of the house, and although I would never have put on him or given him responsibility beyond his years, having little 'man' jobs to do had helped ease the blow of no longer having his father living with us, as did seeing him regularly.

It was quite safe for Adrian and Paula to go into the shed: anything dangerous like the shears, lawn feed and weedkiller was locked in a cupboard, and I had the key. Apart from being necessary for my own children's safety, this was an essential part of our 'safer caring policy', which was a document all foster carers had to draw up and follow, and detailed how the foster home was to be kept safe for everyone. Each year Jill, my support social worker, checked the house and garden for safety, as part of my annual review. The garden had to be enclosed by sturdy fencing, the side gate kept locked, drains covered and anything likely to be hazardous to children kept locked away. The safety checklist for the house itself grew each year. Apart from the obvious smoke alarms, stair gates (top and bottom) if toddlers were being fostered, the locked medicine cupboard high on the wall in the kitchen, and the plug covers or circuit breaker, there were also now less obvious requirements. The banister rails on the stairs had to be a set distance apart so that a small child couldn't get their head, arm or leg stuck in the gap; the glass in the French windows had had to be toughened in case a child ran or fell into them; and the thermostats on the radiators had to be set to a temperature that could never burn a young child's delicate skin. It is true to say that a foster carer's home is probably a lot safer than it would be if only the carer's own children were living there.

'And don't forget to close the shed door, please, Adrian,' I called after him. 'We don't want that cat getting in again.'

'Sure, Mum,' he returned, for he remembered, as I did, the horrendous smell that had greeted us last week after a tomcat had accidentally got locked in overnight; the smell still hadn't completely gone, even after all my swabbing with disinfectant.

'Sure, Mum,' Paula repeated, emulating Adrian, having forgiven him. I watched as Adrian stopped and waited for Paula to catch up. He held her hand and continued down the garden, protectively explaining to her that she could wait outside the shed while he got her pram so that she wouldn't have to encounter the big hairy spiders that lurked unseen inside. Ninety per cent of the time Adrian and Paula got along fine, but like all siblings occasionally they squabbled.

Half an hour later we were ready to go. The bike and doll's pram, which we had brought in through the house to save unpadlocking the side gate, were in the hall. I had my mobile and a bottle of water each for the children in my handbag, and my keys for chub-locking the front door were in my hand. Then Paula said she wanted to do a wee now because she didn't like the toilets in the park because of the spiders. Adrian and I waited in the hall while she went upstairs, and when she returned five minutes later we were finally ready for off. I opened the front door, Adrian manoeuvred his bike out over the step, and Paula and I were ready to follow with her doll's pram when the phone on the hall table started ringing.

'Adrian, just wait there a moment,' I called, and with Adrian paused in the front garden and Paula waiting for me to lift the pram over the step I picked up the phone. 'Hello?'

'Is that Cathy Glass?' It was a woman's voice with a mellow Scottish accent.

'Speaking.'

'Hello, Cathy. It's Edna Smith, Donna's social worker. I spoke to Jill earlier. I think you're expecting my call?'

'Oh yes, hello Edna. I'm sorry, can you just wait one moment please?' I covered the mouthpiece. 'It's a social worker,' I said to Adrian. 'Come back inside for a minute.' He left his bike on the front path and came in, while I helped Paula reverse her pram a little along the hall so that I could close the front door. 'I won't be long,' I said to the children. 'Go into the lounge and look at a book for a few minutes.' Adrian tutted but nevertheless nodded to Paula to follow him down the hall and into the lounge.

'Sorry, Edna,' I said, uncovering the mouthpiece. 'We were just going out.'

'I'm sorry. Are you sure it's all right to continue?'

'Yes, go ahead.' In truth, I could hardly say no.

'Cathy, I'm in the car now, with Donna. She's been a bit upset and I'm taking her for a drive. I had hoped to come and visit you, just for a few minutes?'

'Well, yes, OK. How far away are you?'

'About ten minutes. Would that be all right, Cathy?'

'Yes. We were only going to the park. We can go later.'

'Thank you. We won't stay long, but I do like to do an initial introductory visit before a move.' So Donna was being moved, I thought, and while I admired Edna's dedi-cation, for doubtless this unplanned visit had disrupted her schedule as it had ours, I just wished it could have waited for an hour until after our outing. 'I should like to move Donna to you this evening, Cathy,' Edna added, 'if that's all right with you and your family?'

Clearly the situation with Donna and her brothers had deteriorated badly since she had spoken to Jill. 'Yes, we'll see you shortly, then, Edna,' I confirmed.

'Thank you, Cathy.' She paused. 'And Cathy, you might find Donna is a bit upset, but normally she is a very pleasant child.'

'OK, Edna. We'll look forward to meeting her.'

I replaced the receiver and paused for a minute in the hall. Edna had clearly been guarded in what she had said, as Donna was in the car with her and able to hear every word. But the fact that everything was happening so quickly said it all. Jill had phoned only an hour and a half before, and since then Edna had seen the need to remove Donna from the foster home to diffuse the situation. And the way Edna had described Donna – 'a bit upset, but normally … a very pleasant child' – was a euphemism I had no difficulty in interpreting. It was a case of batten down the hatches and prepare for a storm.

Adrian and Paula had heard me finish on the phone and were coming from the lounge and down the hall, ready for our outing. 'Sorry,' I said. 'We'll have to go to the park a bit later. The social worker is bringing a girl to visit us in ten minutes. Sorry,' I said again. 'We'll go to the park just as soon as they've gone.'

Unsurprisingly they both pulled faces, Adrian more so. 'Now I've got to get my bike in again,' he grumbled.

'I'll do it,' I said. 'Then how about I get you both an ice cream from the freezer, and you can have it in the garden while I talk to the social worker?' Predictably this softened their disappointment. I pushed Paula's pram out of the way and into the front room, and then brought in Adrian's bike and put that in the front room too. I went through to the kitchen and took two Cornettos from the freezer, unwrapped them, and took a small bite from each before presenting them to the children in the lounge. They didn't comment – they were used to my habit of having a crafty bite. I opened the French windows and, while Adrian and Paula returned to the garden to eat their ice creams in the shade of the tree, I went quickly upstairs to check what, tonight, would be Donna's bedroom. Foster carers and their families get used to having their plans changed and being adaptable.

Chapter Two

So Dreadfully Sad

No sooner had I returned downstairs than the front door bell rang. Resisting the temptation to peek through the security spy-hole for a stolen glance at my expected visitors, I opened the door. Edna and Donna stood side by side in the porch, and my gaze went from Edna, to Donna. Two things immediately struck me about Donna: firstly that, as Edna has said, she was a big girl, not overweight but just tall for her age and well built, and secondly that she looked so dreadfully, dreadfully sad. Her big brown eyes were downcast and her shoulders were slumped forward as though she carried the weight of the world on them. Without doubt she was the saddest-looking child I had ever seen – fostered or otherwise.

'Come in,' I said, welcomingly and, smiling, I held the door wide open.

'Cathy, this is Donna,' Edna said in her sing-song Scottish accent.

I smiled again at Donna, who didn't look up. 'Hello, Donna,' I said brightly. 'It's nice to meet you.' She shuffled into the hall and found it impossible to even look up and acknowledge me. 'The lounge is straight ahead of you, down the hall,' I said to her, closing the front door behind us.

Donna waited in the hall, head down and arms hanging loosely at her side, until I led the way. 'This is nice, isn't it?' Edna said to Donna, trying to create a positive atmosphere. Donna still didn't say anything but followed Edna and me into the lounge. 'What a lovely room,' Edna tried again. 'And look at that beautiful garden. I can see swings at the bottom.'

The French windows were open and to most children it would have been an irresistible invitation to run off and play, happy for the chance to escape adult conversation, but Donna kept close to her social worker's side and didn't even look up.

'Would you like to go outside?' I asked Donna. 'My children, Adrian and Paula, are out there having an ice cream. Would you like an ice cream?' I looked at her: she was about five feet tall, only a few inches shorter than me, and her olive skin and dark brown hair suggested that one of her parents or grandparents was Afro-Caribbean. She had a lovely round face, but her expression was woeful and dejected; her face was blanked with sadness. I wanted to take her in my arms and give her a big hug.

'Would you like an ice cream?' Edna repeated. Donna hadn't answered me or even looked up to acknowledge my question.

She imperceptibly shook her head.

'Would you like to join Adrian and Paula in the garden for a few minutes, while I talk to Cathy?' Edna asked.

Donna gave the same slight shake of her head but said nothing. I knew that Edna would really have liked Donna to have gone into the garden so that she could discuss her situation candidly with me, which she clearly couldn't do if Donna was present. More details about Donna's family and what had brought her into care would follow with the placement forms Edna would bring with her when she moved Donna. But it would have been useful to have had some information now so that I could prepare better for Donna's arrival, anticipate some of the problems that might arise and generally better cater for her needs. Donna remained standing impassively beside Edna at the open French windows and didn't even raise her eyes to look out.

'Well, shall we sit down and have a chat?' I suggested. 'Then perhaps Donna might feel more at home. It is good to meet you, Donna,' I said again, and I lightly touched her arm. She moved away, as though recoiling from the touch. I thought this was one hurting child, and for the life of me I couldn't begin to imagine what 'sibling rivalry' had led to this; clearly there was more to it than the usual sibling strife.

'Yes, that's a good idea. Let's sit down,' Edna said encouragingly. I had taken an immediate liking to Edna. She was a homely middle-aged woman with short grey hair, and appeared to be one of the old-style 'hands-on' social workers who have no degree but years and years of practical experience. She sat on the sofa by the French windows, which had a good view of the garden, and Donna sat silently next to her.

'Can I get you both a drink?' I asked.

'Not for me, thanks, Cathy. I took Donna out for some lunch earlier. Donna, would you like a drink?' She turned sideways to look at her.

Donna gave that same small shake of the head without looking up.

'Not even an ice lolly?' I tried. 'You can eat it in here with us if you prefer?'

The same half-shake of the head and she didn't move her gaze from where it had settled on the carpet, a couple of feet in front of her. She was perched on the edge of the sofa, her shoulders hunched forward and her arms folded into her waist as though she was protecting herself.

'Perhaps later,' Edna said.

I nodded, and sat on the sofa opposite. 'It's a lovely day,' I offered.

'Isn't it just,' Edna agreed. 'Now, Cathy, I was explaining to Donna in the car that we are very lucky to have found you at such short notice. Donna has been rather unhappy where she has been staying. She came into care a month ago with her two younger brothers so that her mummy could have a chance to sort out a few things. Donna has an older sister, Chelsea, who is fourteen, and she is staying with mum at present until we find her a suitable foster placement.' Edna met my eyes with a pointed look and I knew that she had left more unsaid than said. With Donna present she wouldn't be going into all the details, but it crossed my mind that Chelsea might have refused to move. I doubted Edna would have taken three children into care and left the fourth at home, but at fourteen it was virtually impossible to move a child without their full cooperation, even if it was in their best interest.

'Donna goes to Belfont School,' Edna continued, 'which is about fifteen minutes from here.'

'Yes, I know the school,' I said. 'I had another child there once, some years ago.'

'Excellent.' Edna glanced at Donna, hoping for some enthusiasm, but Donna didn't even look up. 'Mrs Bristow is still the head there, and she has worked very closely with me. School doesn't start again until the fourth of

September and Donna will be in year five when she returns.' I did a quick calculation and realised that Donna was in a year below the one for her age. 'Donna likes school and is very keen to learn,' Edna continued positively. 'I am sure that once she is settled with you she will catch up very quickly. The school has a very good special needs department and Mrs Bristow is flexible regarding which year children are placed in.' From this I understood that Donna had learning difficulties and had probably (and sensibly) been placed out of the year for her age in order to better accommodate her learning needs. 'She has a good friend, Emily, who is in the same class,' Edna said, and she looked again at Donna in the hope of eliciting a positive response, but Donna remained hunched forward, arms folded and staring at the carpet.

'I'll look forward to meeting Emily,' I said brightly. 'And perhaps she would like to come here for tea some time?'

Edna and I both looked at Donna, but she remained impassive. Edna touched her arm. 'It's all right, Donna. You are doing very well.'

I looked at Donna and my heart went out to her: she appeared to be suffering so much, and in silence. I would have preferred her to have been angry, like so many of the children who had come to me. Shouting abuse and throwing things seemed a lot healthier than internalising all the pain, as Donna was. Huddled forward with her arms crossed, it was as though Donna was giving herself the hug of comfort she so badly needed. Again I felt the urge to go and sit beside her and hug her for all I was worth.

At that moment Adrian burst in through the open French windows, quickly followed by Paula. 'I've brought in my wrapper,' he said, offering the Cornetto wrapper; then he stopped as he saw Edna and Donna.

'Good boy,' I said. 'Adrian, this is Donna, who will be coming to stay with us, and this is her social worker, Edna.'

'Hello, Adrian,' Edna said with her warm smile, putting him immediately at ease.

'Hi,' he said.

'And you must be Paula?' Edna said.

Paula grinned sheepishly and gave me her Cornetto wrapper.

'How old are you?' Edna asked.

'I'm ten,' Adrian said, 'and she's six.'

'I'm six,' Paula said, feeling she was quite able to tell Edna how old she was herself. Donna still had her eyes trained on the floor; she hadn't even looked up as Adrian and Paula had bounced in.

'That's lovely, isn't it, Donna?' Edna said, trying again to engage Donna; then, addressing Adrian and Paula, 'Donna has two younger brothers, aged seven and six. It will be nice for her to have someone her own age to play with.' This clearly didn't impress Adrian, for at his age girls were something you dangled worms in front of to make them scream but didn't actually play with. And given the difference in size – Donna was a good four inches taller than Adrian – she would be more like an older sister than one of his peer group.

'You can play with me now,' Paula said, spying a golden opportunity for some girl company.

'That's a good idea,' Edna said to Paula. 'Although we won't be staying long – we've got a lot to do.' Placing her hand on Donna's arm again, Edna said, 'Donna, you go in

the garden with Paula for a few minutes, and then we will
show you around the house and go.'

I looked at Donna and wondered if she would follow
what had been an instruction from Edna rather than a
request. Edna, Adrian and Paula looked too.

'Come on,' Paula said. 'Come and play with me.' She
placed her little hand on the sleeve of Donna's T-shirt and
gave it a small tug. I noticed Donna didn't pull away.

'Go on, Donna,' Edna encouraged. 'A few minutes in the
garden and then we must go.'

'Come on, Donna,' Paula said again and she gave her T-
shirt another tug. 'You can push me on the swing.'

With her arms still folded across her waist and not
looking up, Donna slowly stood. She was like a little old
woman dragging herself to do the washing up rather than
a ten-year-old going to play in the garden.

'Good girl,' Edna said. We both watched as, with her
head lowered, Donna allowed Paula to gently ease her out
of the French windows and into the garden. Adrian
watched, mesmerised, and then looked at me questioningly.
I knew what he was thinking: children didn't usually have
this much trouble going into the garden to play.

'Donna is a bit upset,' I said to him. 'She'll be all right.
You can go and play too.'

He turned and went out, and Edna and I watched them
go down the garden. Adrian returned to his archaeological
pursuits in the sandpit while Paula, still holding Donna's
T-shirt, led her towards the swings.

'Paula will be fine with Donna,' Edna said, reading my
thoughts. 'Donna is good with little ones.' While I
hadn't thought that Donna would hit Paula, she was so
much bigger, and it had crossed my mind that all her

pent-up emotion could easily be released in any number of ways, including physical aggression. Edna gave a little sigh and returned to the sofa. I sat next to her so that I could keep an eye on what was happening down the garden.

'I've had a very busy morning,' Edna said. 'Mary and Ray, Donna's present carers, phoned me first thing and demanded that I remove Donna immediately. I've had to cancel all my appointments for the whole day to deal with this.'

I nodded. 'Donna seems very sad,' I said.

'Yes.' She gave another little sigh. 'Cathy, I really can't understand what has gone so badly wrong. All the carers are saying is that Donna is obsessively possessive with her brothers, Warren and Jason, and won't let Mary and Ray take care of them. Apparently they've had to physically remove her more than once from the room so that they could take care of the boys. Donna is a big girl and I understand there have been quite a few ugly scenes. Mary showed me a bruise on her arm, which she said Donna had done last night when she and Ray had tried to get her out of the bathroom so that the boys could be bathed. They are experienced carers, but feel they can't continue to look after Donna.'

I frowned, as puzzled as Edna was, for the description she had just given me of Donna hardly matched the silent withdrawn child who had slunk in unable even to look at me.

'The boys are staying with Mary and Ray for now,' Edna continued. 'They all go to the same school, so you will meet Ray and Mary when school returns. They are both full-time carers; Ray took early retirement. They are approved to look after three children and have done so in the past, very successfully, so I really don't know what's gone wrong here.'

Neither did I from what Edna was saying, but it wasn't my place to second guess or criticise. 'Looking after three children has probably been too much,' I said. 'It's a lot of work looking after one, let alone three, particularly when they have just come into care and are upset and still adjusting.'

Edna nodded thoughtfully and glanced down the garden, as I did. Donna was pushing Paula on the swing, but whereas Paula was in her element and squealing with delight, Donna appeared to be performing a mundane duty and was taking no enjoyment whatsoever in the task.

'Is Donna all right doing that?' I asked. 'She doesn't have to push Paula on the swing.'

'I'm sure she is fine, Cathy. She's showing no enthusiasm for anything at present.' Edna returned her gaze to me. 'I've been working with Donna's family for three years now. I have really tried to keep them together, but her mum just couldn't cope. I put in place all the support I could. I have even been going round to their home and helping to wash and iron the clothes, and clean the house, but by my next visit it's always filthy again. I had no alternative but to bring them into care.' Edna looked at me with deep regret and I knew she was taking it personally, feeling that she had failed in not keeping the family together, despite all her efforts. Edna was certainly one conscientious and dedicated social worker, and Donna was very lucky to have her.

'You obviously did all you could,' I offered. 'There can't be many who would have done all that,' and I meant it.

Edna looked at me. 'Donna's family has a long history with social services, and mum herself was in and out of care as a child. Donna's father is not supposed to be living at the family home but he was there only last week when I made a planned visit. The front door had been broken down and Rita, Donna's mum, said Mr Bajan, Donna's father, had smashed his way in. But he was sitting happily in a chair with a beer when I arrived and Rita wasn't exactly trying to get him out. I made arrangements to have the door repaired straight away, because there was no way they could secure the house and Chelsea is still living there.'

I nodded. 'What a worry for you!'

'Yes, it is. Chelsea hasn't been in school for months,' Edna continued, shaking her head sadly. 'And she told me that Mr Bajan hadn't been taking his medication again. He's been diagnosed as a paranoid schizophrenic, and if he doesn't take his medication he becomes very delusional and sometimes violent. I explained to him that he must keep taking it and that if he didn't I would have to have him sectioned again. He was very cooperative, but I don't suppose he will remember what I said. When he is taking the tablets he functions normally, and then because he feels better he thinks he doesn't need the tablets any more, he stops taking them, and becomes ill again.'

I thought what a lot Donna and her family had had to cope with, and I again glanced down the garden, where Donna was still laboriously pushing Paula on the swing.

'Donna's mum, Rita, has a drink problem,' Edna contin-ued, following my gaze, 'and possibly drug abuse, although we don't know for sure. The house is absolutely filthy, a health hazard, and I've had the council in a number of times to fumigate it. Rita can't keep it clean. I've shown her how to clean, many times, but there's always cat and dog mess on the floors, as they encourage strays in. Instead of clearing up the mess, they throw newspaper down to cover it. The whole house stinks. They have broken the new bath I had put in, and the cooker I gave Rita a grant for has never been connected. There is no sign of the table and chairs I had delivered, nor the beds I ordered. The children were sleeping on an old mattress – all of them on one. There's nothing on the floors but old newspaper, and most of the windows have been smashed at one time or another. Rita phones me each time one is broken and I have to make arrangements to have it repaired. There is never any food in the house, and Warren and Jason, Donna's brothers, were running riot on the estate. Neighbours have repeatedly complained about the family, and also about the screaming and shouting coming from the house when Mr Bajan is there.'

I nodded again, and we both looked down the garden, where Donna was still pushing Paula on the swing.

'Mr Bajan is Donna's father and also the father of Warren and Jason, according to the birth certificates, although I have my doubts,' Edna said. 'Chelsea has a different father who has never been named, but she looks like Donna – more than Donna looks like the boys. Mr Bajan has dual heritage and his mother is originally from Barbados. She lives on the same estate and has helped the family as much as she can. I asked her if she could look after the children, but at her age she didn't feel up to it, which is understandable. She's not in the best of health herself and goes back to visit her family in Barbados for some of the winter. She's a lovely lady, but like the rest of the family blames me for bringing the children into care.'

Edna paused and let out another sigh. 'But what could I do, Cathy? The family situation was getting worse, not better. When I first took Donna and her brothers into care they all had head lice, and fleas, and the two boys had worms. I told their mother and she just shrugged. I can't seem to get through to Rita.'

'So what are the long-term plans for the children?' I asked.

'We have ICOs' – Edna was referring to Interim Court Orders – 'for Donna and the boys. I'll apply to the court to renew them, and then see how it goes. Having the children taken into care might give Rita the wake-up call she needs to get herself on track. I hope so; otherwise I'll have no alternative but to apply for a Full Care Order and keep the children in long-term foster care. I'm sure Rita loves her children in her own way but she can't look after them or run a house. I wanted to remove Chelsea too, but she is refusing, and in some ways it's almost too late. Chelsea is rather a one for the boys, and mum can't see that it's wrong for a fourteen-year-old to be sleeping with her boyfriend. In fact Rita encourages it – she lets Chelsea's boyfriend sleep with her at their house and has put Chelsea on the pill. I've told Rita that under-age sex is illegal but she laughs. Rita was pregnant with Chelsea at fifteen and can't see anything wrong in it. She's spent most of her life having children – apart from Chelsea, Donna, and the boys she's had three miscarriages to my knowledge.'

I shuddered. 'How dreadfully sad.'

'It is. It would be best if Rita didn't have any more wee babies and I'm trying to persuade her to be sterilised, but I'm not getting anywhere at present. She has learning difficulties like Donna and Chelsea. Warren and Jason are quite bright – in fact Warren is very bright. He taught himself to read as soon as he started school and had access to books.'

'Really? That's amazing,' I said, impressed.

Edna nodded, and then looked at me carefully. 'You won't give up on Donna, will you, Cathy? She's a good kid really, and I don't know what's gone wrong.'

'No, of course I won't,' I reassured her. 'I'm sure she'll settle. I've taken an immediate liking to Donna and so has Paula by the look of it. ' We both glanced down the garden again. 'Although from what you've said Donna is going to miss her brothers,' I added.

'I think Donna is blaming herself for the three of them being taken in care,' Edna said. 'Donna was the one who looked after Warren and Jason, and tried to do the house-work. Chelsea was always out, and mum sleeps for most of the day when she's been drinking. But you can't expect a ten-year-old to bring up two children and run a house. Donna blames herself, and the rest of the family blame me. Rita hit me the last time I was there. I've told her if she does it again I'll call the police and have her arrested.' Not for the first time I wondered at the danger social workers were expected to place themselves in as a routine part of their jobs.

We both looked down the garden. Paula was off the swing now, talking to Donna, who was standing with her arms folded, head cocked slightly to one side. She had the stance of a mother listening to her child with assumed patience, rather than that of a ten-year-old.

'Donna and her brothers will be seeing their parents three times a week,' Edna said. 'Monday, Wednesday and

Friday, five to six thirty, although I've cancelled tonight's contact. I'm supervising the contact at our office in Brampton Road for now, until a space is free at the family centre. Do you know where that is?'

'Yes.' I nodded.

'Will you be able to take and collect Donna for contact?'

'Yes, I will.'

'Good. Thanks. Rita is angry but you shouldn't have to meet her. I'll bring the placement forms with me this evening when I move Donna. It's going to be after six o'clock by the time we arrive. Ray wants to be there when Donna leaves in case there is a problem. He doesn't finish work until five thirty. And Mary has asked that I keep Donna away for the afternoon. She said she will pack her things and have them ready for five thirty.' Edna sighed again. 'Donna will have to come with me to the office for the afternoon, and I'll find her some crayons and paper to keep her busy. Really, Cathy, she's a good girl.'

'I'm sure she is,' I said. 'It's a pity she can't come with us to the park this afternoon.' But we both knew that couldn't happen, as until all the placement forms had been signed that evening I was not officially Donna's foster carer.

'I think that's all then, Cathy,' Edna said. 'I can't think of anything else at present.'

'Food?' I asked. 'Does Donna have any special dietary requirements?'

'No, and she likes most things. There are no health concerns either. Well, not physical, at least.' I looked at her questioningly and she shrugged. 'Mary said she thought Donna was suffering from OCD.'

'OCD?' I asked.

'Obsessive Compulsive Disorder.'

'Oh, I see,' I said, surprised. 'Why does she think that?'

'Apparently she keeps washing her hands.' Edna gave one of her characteristic sighs. 'I don't know, Cathy. You seem pretty sensible. I'm sure you'll notice if there is anything untoward.'

'It's probably just nerves,' I offered.

'Yes. Anyway, we'll leave you to go to the park now. Thanks for taking Donna and sorry it's such short notice. I know I have to phone Jill and update her later.'

'Yes please. Would Donna like to look around the house before you go?'

Edna nodded. 'We'll give her a tour, but don't expect much in the way of response.'

'No,' I said, smiling. 'Don't worry. I'm sure she'll soon thaw out when she moves in.' Edna seemed to need more reassurance than I did, and I thought that over the three years she had worked with the family she had probably built up quite a bond with the children. She appeared to have a particularly soft spot for Donna, and I could see why: Donna was crying out for love and attention, although she didn't know it.

I stood and went to the French windows. 'Paula!' I called from the step. 'Donna has to go now.'

I saw Paula relay this to Donna, who was still standing, arms folded and head lowered, not looking at Paula. Donna didn't make a move, so I guessed Paula repeated it; then I watched as Paula slipped her hand into Donna's and began to lead her up the garden and towards the house. It was sad and almost comical to see little Paula in charge of, and leading, this big girl, and Donna walking a pace behind her, allowing herself to be led.

'Good girls,' I said, as they arrived.

Paula grinned but Donna kept her eyes down and carefully trained away from mine.

'Cathy is going to show us around now, Donna,' Edna said brightly. 'Then we must be going.'

'Can I come to show Donna around?' Paula asked.

'Yes, of course.' I smiled at her, and looked at Donna, but she didn't look up, and sidled closer to Edna, taking comfort in her familiar presence in what was for her an unfamiliar house. I could see that Donna thought a lot of Edna, as Edna did of Donna.

I gave them a quick tour of the downstairs of the house and pointed out where all the toys were. As we entered each room Edna said, 'This is nice, isn't it, Donna?' trying to spark some interest. Donna managed a small nod but nothing else, and I wasn't expecting any more, for clearly and unsurprisingly she was finding all this very difficult. She didn't raise her eyes high enough to see any of the rooms we went into. As we entered what was to be her bedroom and Edna said, 'This is nice, isn't it?' Donna managed a small grunt, and I thought for a second she was going to look up, but instead she snuggled closer to Edna, and it was left to Paula to comment on the view out of the bedroom window.

'Look, you can see the swings in the garden,' Paula called, going over to the window. 'And next door's garden. They've got children and they come round and play sometimes.'

Donna gave a small nod, but I thought she looked sadder than ever. I wondered if that was because she was going to have to settle into what would be her third bedroom in under a month; or perhaps it was because of the mention of 'children' and the realisation that she wouldn't be playing with her brothers on a daily basis.

'It will look lovely when you have your things in here, Donna,' Edna said encouragingly. Donna didn't say anything and Edna looked at me. 'Thank you for showing us around, Cathy. I think it's time we went now. We've got a lot to do.'

Edna led the way out of the bedroom with Donna at her heels, and Paula and me following. Paula tucked her hand into mine and gave it a squeeze; I looked at her.

'Doesn't she like her bedroom?' Paula asked quietly, but not quietly enough; I knew Donna had heard.

'Yes, but I'm sure it must seem very strange to begin with. You're lucky: you've never had to move. Don't worry, we'll soon make her feel welcome.'

Paula came with me to the front door to see Edna and Donna out. 'Say goodbye to Adrian for me,' Edna said. 'Donna and I will see you as soon after six o'clock as we can make it. Is that all right with you?'

'Yes. We'll be looking forward to it.'

'Bye, Donna,' Paula said as I opened the door and they stepped out. 'See you later.'

Edna looked back and smiled, but Donna kept going. Once they had disappeared along the pavement towards Edna's car, I closed the door and felt relief run through me. Although Donna wasn't the disruptive child I had thought she might be, kicking, screaming and shouting abuse, the weight of her unhappiness was so tangible it was as exhausting as any outward disturbing or challenging behaviour.

Paula followed me down the hall and towards the French windows to call Adrian in. 'Do you think Donna will want to play with me?' she asked.

'Yes, I am sure she will, love. She's a bit shy at present.'

'I'll make her happy playing with me,' she said. 'We can have lots of fun.'

I smiled and nodded, but I thought that it would be a long time before Donna had genuine and heartfelt fun, although she might well go through the motions and cooperate with Paula, as she had done when pushing the swing. Despite all Edna had told me about Donna's family, the circumstances for bringing her and her brothers into care and now moving her to me, I was really none the wiser as to why she was having to move and why she was so withdrawn. But one thing I was certain of was that Donna carried a heavy burden in her heart which she wasn't going to surrender easily.

Chapter Three

Donna

With Adrian pushing his bike along the pavement, and Paula her doll's pram, we made a somewhat faltering journey to our local park. I always insisted that Adrian wheel his bike until we were away from the road and in the safety of the park with its cycle paths. Paula stopped every so often to readjust the covers around the 'baby' in the pram, although in truth, and as Adrian pointed out with some relish, it was so hot that it hardly mattered that baby was uncovered as 'it' was hardly likely to catch cold.

'Not again,' Adrian lamented as our progress was once more interrupted by Paula stopping and seeing to baby. 'Give it to me,' he said at last, 'and I'll tie it to my handle-bars. Then we can get there.'

'It's not an it,' Paula said, rising to the bait.

But that was normal brother and sister teasing, and I thought a far cry from whatever had been happening between Donna and her brothers. As nothing Edna had said had explained how the situation between Donna and her brothers had deteriorated to the point of her having to move, I came back to the possibility it could be an excuse from her carers. Perhaps Mary and Ray hadn't been able to cope with having three children, all with very different needs and who would have been very unsettled, and as experienced carers they had felt unable to simply admit defeat and say they couldn't cope, and had seized upon some sibling jealousy to effect the move. I didn't blame them, although I hoped that Donna hadn't been aware that she was the 'culprit'; Edna had referred to the situation as Donna being 'upset', which shouldn't have left her feeling in any way guilty.

Once in the park, Adrian cycled up and down the cycle paths, aware that, as usual, he had to stay within sight of me. 'If you can see me, then I can see you,' I said to him as I said each time we brought his bike to the park. Even so, I had one eye on him while I pushed Paula on the swings and kept my other eye on 'the baby' in the pram as Paula had told me to.

I thought of Donna as Paula swung higher and higher in front of me with little whoops of glee at each of my pushes. I thought of Donna's profile as I had seen her at the bottom of our garden, slumped, dejected and going through the motions of entertaining Paula. I would have to make sure that Paula didn't 'put on' Donna, for I didn't want Donna to feel she *had* to entertain or play with Paula, or Adrian for that matter, although this was less likely. Something in Donna's compliance, her malleability, had suggested she was used to going along with others' wishes, possibly to keep the peace.

Paula swapped the swing for the see-saw, and I sat on one end and she on the other. As I dangled her little weight high in the air to her not-very-convincing squeals of 'Put me down', I felt a surge of hope and anticipation, an optimism. I was sure that when Donna came to stay with us, given the time and space, care and attention she clearly so badly needed, she would come out of her shell and make huge progress, and I could visualise her coming here to play. I also thought that Donna was going to be a lot easier to look after than some of the children I had fostered. She didn't come with behavioural difficulties – kicking or screaming abuse, for instance – and certainly wasn't hyperactive; and if Mary did have a bruise on her arm, I now smugly assumed it was because she and Ray had mishandled the situation when they had been trying to bath the boys. Had they allowed Donna to help a little, instead of trying to forcibly remove her from the bathroom, I was sure the whole episode could have been defused. Like so many situations with children, fostered or one's own, it was simply, I thought, a matter of handling the child correctly – giving choices and some responsibility, so that the child felt they had a say in their lives.

I had a lot to learn!

We ate at 5.00 p.m., earlier than usual, so that I could clear away and be ready for Donna's expected arrival soon after 6.00. We'd had chicken casserole and I had plated up some for Donna, which I would re-heat in the microwave if she was hungry. After she had spent the afternoon with Edna in her office they were returning to Mary and Ray's only to collect her belongings and say goodbye, so there was a good chance she wouldn't have had dinner. Children always feel better once they've eaten their first meal in the house, and spent their first night in their new bedroom. I had also bathed Paula early, and she was changed into her pyjamas; her usual bedtime was between 7.00 and 7.30, but that was when I would be directing my attention to Donna tonight. Adrian, at ten, was used to taking care of his own bath or shower, and could be left to get on with it – he didn't need or want me to be present any more.

At 6.00 p.m. the children's television programmes had finished; the French windows were still wide open on to the glorious summer evening and Adrian was sitting on the bench on the patio, playing with his hand-held Gameboy with Paula beside him, watching. I'd told Paula that she could go outside again, but as she'd had her bath I didn't want her playing in the sandpit and in need of another bath. I was sitting on the sofa by the French windows with the television on, vaguely watching the six o'clock news. I doubted Edna and Donna would arrive much before 6.30, by the time they had said their goodbyes to Mary and Ray (and Warren and Jason) and loaded up the car with Donna's belongings. I wondered how her brothers were taking Donna's sudden departure. They had, after all, been together for all their lives, albeit not in very happy circumstances, so they would be pretty distressed, I thought.

Jill, my support social worker, was present whenever possible when a child was placed with me; however, I wasn't expecting her this evening. She had left a message on the answerphone while we'd been at the park, saying that she'd been called away to an emergency with new carers in a neighbouring county, and that if anything untoward arose and I needed her advice, to phone her mobile. I didn't think I would need to phone, as the placement of Donna with me would be quite straightforward; Edna was very experienced and would bring all the forms that were needed with her.

Five minutes later the doorbell rang and my heart gave a funny little lurch. I immediately stood and switched off the television. Welcoming a new child (or children) and settling them in is always an anxious time, and not only for the child. I must have done it over thirty times before but there was still a surge of worry, accompanied by anxious anticipation, as I wanted to do my best to make the child feel at home as quickly as possible. Adrian and Paula had heard the doorbell too; Adrian stayed where he was, intent on his Gameboy, while Paula came in.

'Is that Donna?' Paula asked.

'I think so.'

Paula came with me down the hall, and I opened the front door. I could tell straight away that parting hadn't been easy: Donna was clearly upset. She had a tissue in her hand and had obviously been crying; she looked sadder than ever and my heart went out to her. Edna looked glum too, and absolutely exhausted.

'Come in,' I said, standing aside to let them pass.

'Thank you, Cathy,' Edna said, placing her hand on Donna's arm to encourage her forward. 'We'll sit down for a while, and then I'll unpack the car.'

'Go on through to the lounge,' I said as they stepped passed me into the hall, and I closed the door. Paula walked beside Donna and tried to take her hand, but Donna pulled it away. I mouthed to Paula not to say anything because Donna was upset.

'You go with Adrian for now,' I said to Paula as we entered the lounge. She returned to sit beside him on the bench outside, where he was still engrossed in his Gameboy.

'It's one of those Mario games,' I said to Edna as she glanced out through the French windows at Adrian. Edna smiled and nodded. Donna had sat close beside Edna on the sofa and her chin was so far down that it nearly rested on her chest.

'Is everything all right?' I asked Edna.

She nodded again, but threw me a look that suggested they had had a rough time and that she would tell me more later, not in front of Donna. 'Mary and Ray gave Donna a goodbye present,' Edna said brightly, glancing at Donna.

'That's nice. Can I have a look?' I asked Donna. Children are usually given a leaving present by their foster carers, and also a little goodbye party, although I assumed that hadn't happened here. Donna was clutching a small bright red paper bag on her lap, together with the tissue she'd used to wipe her eyes. 'What did you get?' I tried again, but she shrugged and made no move to show me. 'Perhaps later,' I said. 'Would you like a drink, Donna? Or something to eat? I've saved you dinner if you want it.'

She gave that slight shake of the head, so I assumed she didn't want either now.

'I'll do the paperwork,' Edna said, 'and then I'll leave Donna to settle in. She's had a very busy day and I expect she'll want an early night.'

I nodded. 'What time do you usually go to bed, Donna?'

Edna glanced at her and then at me. 'I'm not sure, but she's ten, so I would think eight o'clock is late enough, wouldn't you?'

'Yes,' I agreed. 'That sounds about right. Adrian is the same age and usually goes up around eight and then reads for a bit.' I looked at Donna as I spoke, hoping I might elicit some response; it felt strange and uncomfortable talking about a girl of her age without her actually contributing.

Edna took an A4 folder from her large shoulder bag and, opening it, removed two sets of papers, each paper-clipped in one corner. 'I think I've already told you most of what is on the Essential Information Form,' she said, flipping through the pages and running her finger down the typing. 'I've only included the names and contact details of Donna's immediate family; there are aunts and uncles, but Donna sees them only occasionally. She had a medical when she first came into care and everything was fine. Also Mary and Ray took her to the dentist and optician, and that was all clear too.' It is usual for a child to have these check-ups when they first come into care.

'That's good,' I said, and I glanced at Donna, who still had her head down. She'd cupped the little red bag containing the present protectively in her hands as if it was her most treasured possession in the world.

Edna checked down the last pages of the Essential Information Form, and then leant forward and handed it to me. This would go into the file I would start on Donna, as I had to for all the children I looked after, together with the paperwork I would gradually accumulate while Donna stayed with me, and also the daily log which I had to keep and which Jill inspected regularly when she visited.

'The Placement Agreement forms are complete,' Edna said, flipping through the second set of forms. 'I checked them before we left the office.' She peeled off the top sheets and, taking a pen from her bag, signed at the foot of the last page. She did the same for the bottom set of forms, which was a duplicate of the top set, and then passed both sets of forms to me. I added my signature beneath hers on both copies and passed one set back. The Placement

Agreement gave me the legal right to foster Donna and I was signing to say I agreed to do this and to work to the required standard. One copy would be kept by the social services and my copy would go in my file.

'Nearly finished,' Edna said, turning to Donna.

I glanced through the open French windows at Paula and Adrian, sitting side by side on the bench. Adrian was still intent on his Gameboy and Paula was looking between the game and Donna, hoping Donna might look up and make eye contact.

'Here's Donna's medical card,' Edna said, passing a printed card to me. 'Will you register her at your doctor's, please? She's outside the catchment area of Mary and Ray's GP.'

'Yes, of course.'

'I think that's about it then,' Edna said, closing the folder and returning it to her bag. She placed her bag beside the sofa, glanced first at Donna and then looked at me. 'Do you have any plans for the weekend, Cathy?'

'Not especially. I thought we would have a relaxing weekend, and give Donna a chance to settle in. I will have to pop up to the supermarket tomorrow for a few things. Then on Sunday we could go to a park; the weather is supposed to be good.'

'That sounds nice,' Edna said. 'Donna is good at shopping. She likes to help, don't you, Donna?' We both looked at Donna and she managed to give that almost imperceptible nod. 'You will be able to tell Cathy what your favourite foods are when you go shopping,' Edna continued, trying to spark some interest. 'I am sure Cathy will let you have some of them.'

'Absolutely,' I agreed. 'You can help me choose, Donna.'

Edna's gaze lingered on Donna and I knew she was finding it difficult to make a move to leave. I wondered if Donna had been this quiet and withdrawn all afternoon, while she'd been with Edna at the office. Sitting forward, Edna said, 'OK, Cathy, could you give me a hand unpacking the car then, please?'

'Yes, of course.' I stood and went to the French windows. 'I'm just helping Edna unload the car,' I said to Adrian and Paula. 'You're all right there for now, aren't you?'

They nodded, Adrian without looking up from his game and Paula with her eyes going again to Donna.

'You can stay there, Donna,' Edna said, 'or you can go in the garden if you like with Paula and Adrian.'

Donna shrugged without looking up, and Edna left the sofa and began towards the lounge door. 'I'll come back in to say goodbye,' she said, pausing and turning to look at Donna. Donna shrugged again, almost with indifference, as though it didn't matter if Edna said goodbye or not; but I knew for certain that it did matter. The poor girl had spent the last hour saying goodbye – to Warren and Jason, to Mary and Ray, and now to Edna. I could only guess at what must be going through her mind as her social worker, to whom she was obviously very close, and with whom she had spent all day, was about to depart and leave her with strangers, albeit ones with good intentions.

I followed Edna down the hall and she stood aside to allow me to open the front door. She gave one of her little heartfelt sighs. 'I'm sure Donna will be fine by the end of the weekend,' she said. 'I'll phone on Monday and arrange to visit next week.'

'I'll look after her, Edna,' I reassured her. 'Don't worry. Has she been this quiet all afternoon?'

'She wasn't too bad until we went to say goodbye.' Edna lowered her voice and leant towards me in confidence. 'It was awful at Mary and Ray's. Donna was so upset to be leaving Warren and Jason, but the boys couldn't have cared less.'

'Really?' I said, shocked. 'Why?'

'I don't know. I had to make them say goodbye. They told Donna to her face that they were pleased she was going, and that they didn't want her to come back.'

'But that's dreadful!' I said, mortified.

'Yes, I know.' Edna shook her head sadly. 'I don't know what's been going on. Mary and Ray said Donna had being trying to dominate the boys and boss them around, but I'm sure it was only her way of caring for them; Donna has spent all her life trying to look after the boys as best she could. But Warren and Jason, only a year apart in age, are glued to each other and present a united front. As they are so much brighter than Donna I wouldn't be surprised if they have been bullying her. I've seen them play tricks on her and use their intelligence to poke fun at her. I've told them off for it before. All the same, Cathy, I have to say, I was shocked by their attitude tonight. Donna loves them dearly and would do anything for them. It's probably for the best that they are being separated, for Donna's sake. She's not fair game for the boys. She's got a big heart, and I know she's a bit slow, but you would have thought brotherly love might have counted for something.'

'Is Donna close to her older sister, Chelsea?' I asked.

'No. Chelsea and Mum are thick as thieves, and I'm beginning to think that Donna was out on a limb. You never really know what's going on in families behind closed doors. We brought the children into care because of severe physical neglect but emotional abuse is insidious and can be overlooked.' She paused. 'Anyway, Cathy, I'm sure Donna will be fine here. And when she does open up to you, I'd appreciate you telling me what she says.'

'Yes, of course I will.'

'Thanks. Let's get the car unpacked, and then I must get home to my hubby. He'll be thinking I've deserted him.'

Edna was truly a lovely lady and I could imagine her and her 'hubby' discussing their respective days in the comfort of their sitting room in the evening.

We made a number of journeys to and from the car, offloading a large suitcase, some cardboard boxes and a few carrier bags. Once we had stacked them in the hall, Edna said, 'Right, Cathy, I'll say a quick goodbye to Donna then go.'

We returned to the lounge, where Donna was as we had left her on the sofa, head down and with the red paper bag containing her present clasped before her.

'I'm off now,' Edna said positively to Donna. 'You have a good weekend and I'll phone Cathy on Monday; then I'll visit next week. If you need or want anything, ask Cathy and she will help you. And I think Paula is dying to make friends with you, so that will be nice.'

Edna stood just in front of Donna as she spoke but Donna didn't look up. 'Come on,' Edna encouraged kindly. 'Stand up and give me a hug before I go.'

There was a moment's hesitation; then, with a small dismissive shrug, Donna stood and let Edna give her a hug, although I noticed she didn't return it. As soon as Edna let go, Donna sat down again. 'Bye then, Donna,'

Edna said; then leaning out of the French windows, 'Bye Adrian, Paula, have a good weekend.'

They both looked up and smiled. 'Thank you.'

Edna collected her bag from where she'd left it beside the sofa and with a final glance at Donna – who was once more sitting head down with the present in her hands, and I thought trying hard to minimise Edna's departure – walked swiftly from the room.

'Take care and good luck,' Edna said to me as I saw her to the front door. 'I'll phone first thing on Monday. And thanks, Cathy.'

'You're welcome. Don't worry. She'll be fine,' I reassured her again.

'Yes,' Edna said, and with a quick glance over her shoulder towards the lounge, went out of the door and down the path towards her car.

I closed the front door and returned to the lounge. 'All right, love?' I asked Donna as I entered.

She slightly, almost imperceptibly, shook her head and then I saw a large tear escape and roll down her cheek.

'Oh love, don't cry,' I said, going over and sitting next to her. 'It won't seem so bad in the morning, I promise you, sweet.'

Another tear ran down her cheek and dripped on to the red paper bag in her lap, and then another. I put my arm around her and drew her to me. She resisted slightly, then relaxed against me. I held her close as tear after tear ran down her cheeks in silent and abject misery.

'Here, love, wipe your eyes,' I said softly, guiding her hand containing the tissue towards her face. She drew it across her eyes, then slowly lowered her head towards me, where it finally rested on my shoulder. I held her tight, and felt her head against my cheek as she continued to cry. 'It's all right,' I soothed quietly. 'It will be all right, I promise you, love. Things will get better.'

Paula came in from the patio and, seeing Donna crying, immediately burst into tears. I took hold of her arm with my free hand and drew her to sit beside me on the sofa. I encircled her with my right arm while my left arm stayed around Donna.

'Why's Donna crying?' Paula asked between sobs.

'Because a lot has happened today that has made her sad,' I said, stroking Paula's cheek.

'I don't like seeing people cry,' Paula said. 'It makes me cry.'

'I know, love, and me. But sometimes it's good to have a cry: it helps let out the sad feelings. I think Donna will feel a bit better in a while.' I remained where I was on the sofa with an arm around each of the girls, Paula sobbing her heart out on my right, Donna on my left, crying in silent misery, and me in the middle trying hard not to join in – for, like Paula, I can't stand seeing anyone upset, particularly a child.

Chapter Four

Silence

Adrian was not impressed. The phone had started ringing and, feeling unable to simply stand and desert the girls, I hadn't immediately answered it.

'The phone's ringing,' he said helpfully, coming in from the patio, with his Gameboy in his hand. He stopped as he saw the three of us and pulled a face, suggesting he didn't fully approve of this collective display of female emotion.

'I'll answer it now,' I said, throwing him a smile. 'Everyone will be OK soon.' This reassurance was enough for Adrian and he smartly nipped off into the garden, grateful he didn't have to be party to what must have appeared to a boy of his age to be blubbering nonsense.

I eased my arms from the girls and went to answer the phone on the corner unit. It was Jill.

'You took a long time to answer. Is everything all right, Cathy?'

'Yes. Donna is here.' I glanced over to the sofa as Paula took up the gap I had left and snuggled into Donna's side. Donna lifted her arm and put it around Paula. 'Yes, everything is fine,' I said.

'Cathy, I won't keep you now, as it's getting late. I just wanted to make sure Donna had arrived and there weren't any problems.'

'No, no problems,' I confirmed. 'Edna only left ten minutes ago. She's going to phone you, and me, on Monday. She brought all the forms.'

'Good. Well, enjoy your weekend. If you do need to speak to someone, Mike is back, and on call over the weekend; dial the emergency number.'

'OK, Jill, thanks.'

'And I'll phone on Monday, and visit as soon as I can next week.'

'Fine,' I said. We said goodbye and I hung up.

I glanced at the carriage clock on the mantelpiece. It was 7.40 p.m., after Paula's bedtime and getting close to Adrian and Donna's. I crossed over to the girls; they had both stopped crying now and Donna still had her arm around Paula. Both were sitting very still, as though appreciating the moment, although Paula was the only one to look at me.

'Girls,' I said gently, drawing up the footstool and squatting on it so that I was at their level. 'Are you feeling a bit better now?'

Paula nodded and, with her head still resting against Donna, looked up at her. Donna had her head down and rubbed away the last of the tears from her cheeks with the tissue. I put a hand on each of their arms. 'I think we will all feel better after a good night's sleep, and it is getting late,' I said. Paula looked up again at Donna for her reaction, but there wasn't one: Donna remained impassive, head lowered, with the little red paper bag in her hand. 'Donna, love, would you like something to eat?' I asked again. 'I have saved you dinner.' She gave her head a little shake.

'What about a drink before bed then?'

The same small shake of the head.

I hesitated, not really sure how to proceed. In many ways it was easier dealing with a child who was angry and shouting abuse: at least the pathway of communication at some level was open and could be channelled and modified. With so little coming back from Donna – she hadn't said a word yet – it was difficult to assess or interpret her needs. I hadn't thought to ask Edna if Donna had eaten, but even if the answer had been no, I could hardly force her to have dinner. 'Are you sure you don't want anything to eat?' I tried again. 'Not even a snack?'

The same shake of the head, so I had to assume she wasn't hungry, and if she hadn't eaten she could make up for it at breakfast. 'I'd love to see your present,' I said, looking at the little bag. 'So would Paula. Will you show us?'

Paula raised her head from Donna's side for a better view and Donna withdrew her arm. 'What did Mary and Ray buy you?' I asked. 'I bet it's something nice.'

Very slowly and not raising her head, and with absolutely no enthusiasm, Donna moved her fingers and began to open the top of the paper bag. Paula and I watched as she dipped in her fingers and gradually drew out a bracelet made from small multi-coloured beads.

'Oh, isn't that lovely,' I said. 'What a nice present.'

Donna cupped the bracelet in the palm of her hand, and I continued to enthuse, grateful for this small cooperation, which I viewed as progress. 'Can you put it on your wrist and show us?'

Donna carefully slipped the bracelet over the fingers on her right hand and drew it down so that it settled around her wrist. As she did, I thought of Warren and Jason's

parting shot, when they had told Donna not only that
were they pleased she was going but not to go back. I felt
so sorry for her.

'That's beautiful,' I said. I could tell that Donna was
proud; she supported the wrist with the bracelet with her
other hand, as though displaying it to its best advantage.
It wasn't an expensive bracelet; it was the type of 'infill'
present that one child gave another at a birthday party.
The beads were painted plastic, strung together on elastic
so that the bracelet fitted most-sized wrists. But if Paula
thought the gift wasn't as precious as Donna did, she
certainly didn't say so.

'That is pretty,' Paula said, touching it. 'I like the red
and blue ones.' And I thought if anything typified the
gaping chasm between children who had and those who
did not, it was the bracelet. In our wealthy society with its
abundance of acquirable material possessions, the gap
between children from poor homes and those who enjoy all
its advantages was widening. Paula had a couple of these
bracelets, possibly three, and also a bedroom packed full of
similar treasures which she'd received for Christmas and
birthday presents, and treats from grandparents; but I
knew from the way Donna cradled the bracelet that she
certainly did not.

'We will have to find a safe place for it in your bedroom,'
I said. Donna nodded.

I glanced at the clock again; I really had to start getting
all three children upstairs and into bed. There was no way
I was going to attempt Donna's unpacking now; it was too
late, and we would have plenty of time the following day.
'Now, love,' I said, placing my hand on Donna's arm again.
'We're going to take just what we need for tonight from

your bags and sort out the rest in the morning, all right? Once you've had a good night's sleep everything will seem a lot better. I'd like you to come with me into the hall and tell me which bag has your nightwear and washing things.' Then it occurred to me that Donna probably didn't know what each bag contained, as Edna had said Mary had done the packing that afternoon while Donna had been with Edna. 'Do you know what's in each bag?' I asked her.

Donna shrugged. 'Wait there with Paula a minute,' I said, 'and I'll take a look, unless you want to come and help me?'

She shook her head, and I left her sitting with Paula, who was still, bless her, admiring the bracelet, while I went down the hall, hoping I wouldn't have to unpack every bag and case to find her night things. I peered in the various carrier bags and found that Mary had put everything Donna needed for the night in one plastic bag, presumably guessing it would be too late for us to unpack properly. Picking up this carrier bag, I returned to the lounge.

The girls were still together and Donna was slipping the bracelet from her wrist and returning it to the paper bag. 'I've found what you need for tonight,' I said. I went over and, opening the bag, showed her inside. 'Nightdress, wash bag and teddy. Is there anything else you need, love?'

She shook her head.

The French windows were still open and Adrian was outside, now at the end of the garden having a last swing before he had to come in. It was nearly 8.30 p.m. and the air temperature was just starting to drop. 'Adrian,' I called from the step. 'Five minutes, and then I want you to come in and get changed.' He didn't say anything, but I knew he had heard me, for this scenario had been repeated most nights since school had broken up – I had left him playing in the garden, sometimes with the neighbour's children, while I got Paula ready for bed.

'OK, girls,' I said. 'Let's go up and get you settled. Are you sure you wouldn't like a drink before you go, Donna?'

She shook her head.

With a different child on their first night I would probably have put Paula to bed and spent some time talking to the child and getting to know them before settling them for the night. However, because Donna was not communicating I felt, as Edna had done, that she was exhausted. I was now dearly hoping that I would have Donna's cooperation in going to bed, but I was starting to feel a bit uneasy. If Donna didn't move and ignored my requests, or answered them with a shrug or shake of the head, what was I supposed to do? She was far too big for me to carry upstairs as I might have done with a little one, and if she didn't respond to my cajoling and persuading there was virtually nothing I could do. It crossed my mind that maybe that was how Mary had received the bruise to her arm – perhaps Donna had refused to cooperate despite all their efforts, and Mary and Ray had resorted to physically moving her; but I quickly let that thought go, for if that was so, then I was in big trouble, as I had no 'Ray' to help me.

'Right,' I said, using an assertive tone. 'I have got all you need for tonight, Donna. The three of us will go upstairs together. Donna, while I help Paula, you can get changed, ready for bed.' I had said it as though I meant it, as a request not open to debate. Paula immediately stood and came to my side, aware she was going to bed later than usual and not wishing to overstep the mark. Donna remained where she was on the sofa, impassive, head down and once more clutching the little bag with her present. 'OK, Donna, are you ready?' I said, and I felt another twinge of anxiety. She still didn't move and I saw Paula look at me questioningly, also worried by Donna not doing as I'd asked.

'Come on, Donna,' Paula said in her little voice. I looked at Paula and shook my head to indicate to her not to continue. Her request had sounded like a plea and I needed Donna to do as I had asked as a matter of course; I wasn't going to plead with her.

I took Paula's hand and gave it a reassuring squeeze, and with Donna's carrier bag in my other hand, I turned away from the sofa, ready to leave the room. There was a limit to how many times I could politely say that I wanted her to go upstairs before I started to look ineffectual and lose my credibility and authority. 'Right, we're going up now, Donna,' I said and, still holding Paula's hand, I began slowly and steadily towards the lounge door. As I went I was frantically searching for plan B if she didn't follow me, which vaguely centred around taking Paula up and coming down and trying again. But I knew that was likely to be even less successful than the first time, and I couldn't have Donna sitting down here all night. As a last resort I would have to phone the fostering agency and ask for help, although practically I wasn't sure what they could do either.

To my great and utter relief, as Paula and I stepped from the lounge and into the hall, Donna stood and began to follow us. I waited for her to catch up and then contin-ued down the hall. I didn't praise her, for I had to give the impression that I expected her to follow my instructions and requests. Although I felt dreadfully sorry for Donna, and my heart went out to her, she was only ten and like all children she had to do as she was told.

Paula and I went up the stairs first with Donna a step or two behind. At the top of the stairs I said to Paula, 'You go into the bathroom and do your teeth while I show Donna to her bedroom.' I wasn't sure what was going to happen next with Donna, and I didn't want Paula being party to any sudden outburst. Donna was so quiet and withdrawn it was unhealthy, and I had the feeling, as I had done when she'd first visited and gone down the garden with Paula, that she was like a tinder box waiting to ignite and go up in flames – you can only suppress so much emotion before something gives. While Edna had reassured me that Donna was 'a good girl', social workers, no matter how efficient they are, don't see the child on a daily basis as Mary and Ray had done, and they'd had problems with Donna.

Paula did as I asked and went to the bathroom while I continued round the landing to Donna's bedroom, with Donna following me in silence.

'All right, love,' I said, kindly but firmly. 'Here is your nightdress, teddy bear and wash bag.' I took the items from the carrier bag and set them on the bed. 'I'll leave you to get changed, and then I'll show you into the bathroom. We won't worry about a bath tonight. If you want the toilet, it is right next to your bedroom.' I pointed out towards the landing. 'I'll be back shortly.'

Without looking at her, and thereby not giving her room for refusal, I came out and closed the bedroom door; whether she did as I asked or not remained to be seen. I went round the landing and into the bathroom, where Paula was cleaning her teeth. I waited until she had finished and then went with her to the toilet, where I waited, as I did every evening at bedtime, outside the toilet door. The toilet, at the other end of the landing to the bathroom, was the room next to Donna's, and as I waited for Paula I listened, but I couldn't hear any movement. I prayed Donna was doing as I had asked and getting changed.

When Paula came out of the toilet I went with her into her bedroom and drew the curtains. Once she was in bed I took a book from her bookshelf and propped myself on the bed beside her with my feet up, as I did every evening, as part of our bedtime routine. 'I'm only reading one story tonight, love,' I said, 'as I need to get Donna settled.'

I had chosen a short story, but a favourite of Paula's – *The Very Hungry Caterpillar*, which I had been reading to her since she was a toddler. Paula knew it by heart and could also read most of the words. She joined in as I read, poking her finger through the hole in each page where the caterpillar was supposed to have eaten. At the end, where the caterpillar changes into a beautiful butterfly, I said, as I always said when I read this book, 'You are my beautiful butterfly.' Paula grinned and snuggled her head into her pillow, and I kissed her goodnight. 'Thanks for helping to look after Donna,' I said. 'I'm sure she'll be better tomorrow.'

Paula looked concerned. 'Mum?' she asked. 'Does Donna talk?'

I smiled. 'Yes, love, but she's finding it difficult at present because of everything that has happened to her. I am sure she will start talking to us soon.'

'Good. Because I don't like her being so quiet. It's a bit scary.'

'I know, love, but don't you worry.' I got off the bed and kissed her goodnight again. 'Everything will be all right. Now, it's late and I want you to go straight off to sleep.'

'Is Adrian coming in soon?' Paula asked.

'Yes, just as soon as I've got Donna settled.'

'Will she go to bed at the same time as me every night?'

I smiled. 'No, she's older than you, and it's well past your normal bedtime.'

'I know.' Paula giggled and buried her head under the sheets.

'Night, love,' I said again. 'Sleep tight.' Coming out, I blew her one last kiss and drew the door to but left it slightly ajar as she liked it. I went round the landing and knocked on Donna's door. There was no reply, so I knocked again, then slowly opened the door and put my head round. Donna had changed into her nightdress and I inwardly breathed a sigh of relief. She was sitting on the bed with the red paper bag in her hand. 'Do you want to put your present in this drawer for now?' I said, going in and opening one of the drawers in the wardrobe. 'It will be quite safe in there.'

She shook her head and clutched the bag tighter.

'OK, but you will have to put it down when you have your wash or else it will get wet.' I picked up her wash bag containing the flannel and toothbrush, and in my firm but kindly tone said, 'This way to the bathroom, love.' I turned and left the room decisively as though I expected her to follow, which she did.

In the bathroom I put her flannel on the towel rail with ours and her toothbrush in the mug with ours. 'The toothpaste is there,' I said. 'That tap is the hot water and that one is the cold.' Obvious to us, but less obvious to a newcomer because the red and blue marks on the taps had worn away with use. 'This is your towel,' I said, pointing again to the towel rail. 'Do you need anything else?' Donna shook her head. 'OK, when you have finished, go to the toilet and then I will come and say goodnight.'

I came out, and went downstairs and into the lounge. The light was fading now at nearly 9.00 p.m. and there was a nip in the air. I stood at the French windows and called Adrian in, and unusually he came with the first calling.

'Good boy,' I said. 'Now straight upstairs and change into your pyjamas. Donna will be finished in the bathroom by the time you are ready to go in. You can leave your shower until the morning as we're late.'

'Cool,' he said, which was his favourite expression, used to denote most things that met with his approval.

'And not too much noise when you go up: Paula is going off to sleep.'

'I'll have a drink first,' he said, and he went through to the kitchen, while I closed and locked the French windows.

Leaving Adrian to pour himself a glass of milk, I returned upstairs, taking a couple of Donna's carrier bags with me, which I placed in her bedroom. The water had stopped running in the bathroom and I went round and knocked on the bathroom door, which she had left ajar. 'All right?' I asked, going in. She nodded. 'Have you had your wash and done your teeth?' I noticed she was once more clutching the red paper bag. She nodded again.

'Good girl. Straight into bed then. It's after nine o'clock.'

She followed me silently round the landing and into her bedroom. I pulled back the sheet – there was no need for a duvet, as it was too hot – and I stood aside and waited for her to get into bed. 'Do you have your teddy bear in bed with you?' I asked, picking up the clearly much-loved threadbare soft toy.

She nodded.

'Has he or she got a name?'

She shrugged and laid her head on the pillow. I tucked the teddy in beside her and then draped the sheet over her. I drew the bedroom curtains and returned to stand beside the bed. 'We'll unpack all your things tomorrow,' I said, leaning slightly forward. 'Have a good sleep and you can have a lie-in if you wish: there's no rush tomorrow. If you need me in the night, you know where my bedroom is. Just knock on the door. I'm a light sleeper, so I will hear you.' I hesitated and looked at her. She was on her side, facing out into the room. She was staring straight ahead and had one arm around the teddy. There wasn't much else I could say or do that night, although I felt there was plenty I should be saying and doing to help her. 'Sleep tight, love, and see you in the morning. Would you like a goodnight kiss?' I always ask the fostered child this when they first arrive; it's an intrusion in their personal space to just assume they want a kiss.

She nodded slightly and I leant further forward and kissed her forehead. 'Night, love, sleep tight. We'll have a good day tomorrow. We'll unpack first – it's nice to have all your things around you. I'm so pleased you have come to stay with us.'

I hesitated again, hoping, wishing, she would say something, some verbal acknowledgement that she was all right and not in need of anything. But there was absolutely nothing.

'Night, love,' I said again. 'Would you like your bedroom door open or closed?' She gave a small shrug. 'OK, I'll close it a little.'

With a final glance at her I came out and pulled the door to without shutting it fully. Adrian was in the bathroom, having changed into his pyjamas, and was now finishing his washing and teeth brushing. I waited on the landing until he came out, and then I saw him into bed. 'If you're reading tonight, it's only for a short while,' I said. Although we didn't have to be up early for school in the morning, if Adrian didn't have enough sleep, he was not at his best, to put it mildly. Kissing him goodnight, I left him reading by the light of his lamp and came out and shut his bedroom door right to, as he liked it. I looked in on Paula, who was fast asleep; then I listened outside Donna's door. There was no sound, but I didn't go in in case I disturbed her. I would check on her later on my way to bed.

I went downstairs, locked the back door, and then flopped on to the sofa in the lounge and put my feet on the footstool. I was absolutely exhausted, and it seemed incredible that only ten hours had passed since I had received Jill's call about Donna. It wasn't only anxious anticipation of Donna's arrival, and welcoming her, that had drained me, but the relentless effort to get any form of acknowledgement from her, and the worry about what was really going on inside her head. As I sat on the sofa and slowly, gradually, began to relax, I realised that even environment, and it is important they are kept until the child feels comfortable about letting them go; which was why Mary had packed them and sent them with Donna.

There were two pairs of plastic trainers with the toes out and the laces missing, which I placed at the bottom of the wardrobe, leaving the new trainers and sandals beside her bed. There were a few pieces of very old school uniform – a bobbled sweatshirt and a torn T-shirt, both with the school's logo, and a badly stained skirt. Donna had come into care right at the end of the summer term, so Mary and Ray hadn't replaced her school uniform; I would do so at the start of the next term. There were half a dozen pairs of new pants and socks, and a few pairs of white faded grey, which I packed at the bottom of the wardrobe. There was a badly stained and ripped anorak, which I assumed had been Donna's coat before coming into care, and also a new lightweight summer jacket, which I hung in the wardrobe. As I worked, separating and sorting the clothes, Donna continued to stand a little way from me, either shaking her head or nodding if I asked her something that required a yes or no answer, or shrugging if my question needed a choice.

I talked as I worked, and continually sought her opinion and advice on where things should go, in the hope of getting her to join in. 'Shall we put this in here? This is a pretty top – where did you get it from? We'll make this the drawer for your underwear,' and so on, but there was absolutely no response. Once the suitcase was empty, I heaved it on to the top of the wardrobe out of the way and asked Donna to bring in the last of the bags and boxes from the landing, which she did. These appeared to

though I had fostered over thirty children, Donna was the first to have spent an entire evening in the house and gone to bed without uttering a single word. I wondered just how long she could keep it up.

Chapter Five

Cath-ie

Donna maintained her vow of silence, if that is what it was, for the whole of the weekend. Not having slept well on Friday night, I rose early on Saturday morning, and went downstairs for a coffee. At 8.00 I heard movement coming from Donna's bedroom and I went up, knocked on her door and entered.

She was in her nightdress, sitting on the edge of the bed and staring at the carpet. I asked her if she had slept well and if she needed anything, and was met with the same shake of the head. I left her to get dressed, and she finally came down at nearly 10.00, by which time Paula and Adrian had long since eaten their breakfasts and were playing in the garden. I asked Donna what she would like for breakfast and gave her the options – a choice of cereal, toast or egg and bacon. But there was no response other than a shrug, so, unable to decipher her preferred menu, I gave her the safe bet of cornflakes, followed by toast and honey, with a drink of juice, which she ate slowly and in silence, alone at the table. I had taken my coffee to the table as I gave her the breakfast, but she seemed so uncomfortable with my presence that eventually I busied myself in the kitchen and left her to eat alone. When she had finished, I told her to go and brush her teeth and have a

wash, which she did without comment, while I clear[ed] away her breakfast things.

If I had thought it was hard work the previous evening, it got steadily worse during the day, and not wishing to be unkind, it was like having a zombie in the house. Her downcast face, her stooped shoulders, her slowly lumbering gait would have suggested depression had she been an adult, and I thought that if she didn't improve over the weekend I would phone Jill and Edna first thing on Monday and suggest I take her to the doctor.

After Donna had finished in the bathroom I told her we would unpack her things. I had already carried up all the bags and boxes and stacked them on the landing. I now pulled the large suitcase into her bedroom and, setting it on the bed, opened it. 'We'll hang up these clothes in the wardrobe,' I said, and I began unfolding her jeans and joggers and draping them on to the hangers. Then I took the jumpers and T-shirts and laid them in neat piles in th[e] drawers of the wardrobe. Donna stood by in silence, h[er] head slightly lowered and her arms loosely folded in fro[nt] of her, watching me but not helping, although I encou[r]aged her often.

It was obvious which clothes Mary and Ray had bou[ght] – they were new – and which had come with her f[rom] home – a selection of worn and faded joggers and T-sh[irts] which not even a jumble sale would have taken. I sta[cked] the old clothes at the bottom of the wardrobe, alth[ough] clearly she would be wearing the new ones, and th[ose] bought for her. There is a great temptation for [foster] carers to throw out all the rough stuff children brin[g] with them when they come into care, but these are fa[miliar] things for the child in an otherwise unfamiliar and s[trange] contain her personal things – two worn books, a torn magazine, a bare and grubby doll, a new story CD, and a crayoning book with felt-tip pens. I told Donna I would leave her to put those things away, and I opened the empty drawers, and also pulled out a store-away box from under the bed.

One of the carrier bags which I had looked in and put to one side seemed to contain an assortment of what looked like old rags. I now picked it up, and I felt Donna watching me from under her lowered eyes as I pulled it open for a closer look. There were a couple of very old vests and pieces of what looked like torn-up sheets. I wondered if these were comforters – I'd had children of Donna's age and older arrive with chewed and torn security rags and blankets which they obviously needed to keep with them until they were no longer needed. But these were very dirty and I thought that Mary would have washed them if Donna had to have them close to her, and one smelled distinctly of disinfectant.

'What are these for?' I asked lightly. But there was no reply, not even a shrug. 'Shall I get rid of them?' Donna shook her head rigorously, with more enthusiasm than she'd shown in response to any of my previous questions. 'I'll put the bag in the wardrobe then,' I said. I slid open the door at the bottom of the wardrobe, which was a separate compartment, and placed the bag inside. I had a feeling that Donna was still watching me intently, although for the life of me I couldn't imagine why this bag of old and dirty rags was of any importance to her.

'I'll leave you to unpack that last box,' I said, 'then come down, and we'll have a drink and a snack before we go to the shops.'

I went downstairs, where I made up some fresh lemonade, dropped in some ice cubes and prepared a plate of cheese on crackers, which I placed on a tray. I called Donna, who came down straight away, and I carried the tray into the garden, where Adrian and Paula joined us at the table on the patio. As they gathered round the table I poured the lemonade and placed the cheese and biscuits in the centre for everyone to help themselves. Adrian and Paula delved in and then watched as Donna finally, slowly and laboriously took one. I saw Adrian and Paula surreptitiously watch her, and whereas Paula had been all over Donna the day before she was now slightly guarded and kept a small distance between them. If I was finding Donna's unremitting silence daunting and unnerving, how much worse must it have been for a child of Paula's age? Paula was used to trusting and reaching out to people, and usually made friends easily with the children who stayed with us, even those who were noisy and rude. This was something completely new to her, as it was to Adrian and me.

The day was heating up quickly and I wanted to get what I needed from the shops before the car became uncomfortably hot. The quick trip to the supermarket that I had mentioned to Edna the day before, which had seemed very positive when Edna had told me that Donna liked shopping and liked to help, now loomed as something else to overcome with one-sided conversation and a large measure of patience. Once we had finished the snack I bundled everyone into the car, showing Donna where to sit and checking her seatbelt was on. At their ages, all three children had to be on booster seats by law and in the rear of the car, and there wasn't an awful lot of room.

Paula, the smallest, was in the middle, with Donna and Adrian either side. There was the usual elbowing between Adrian and Paula when they first got in and fastened their seatbelts. Once they were settled, I started the car, fed in the sing-along cassette and began the ten-minute journey to the supermarket. Normally Paula would have joined in the catchy rhymes but she sat, as did Adrian, in unnatural silence, further intimidated, I thought, by Donna's withdrawn and now close presence.

At the supermarket I took a small trolley and went up and down the aisles, dropping in what we needed. Adrian and Paula, as usual, chose a couple of 'treats' each, which was their reward (or bribe) for enduring another shopping trip. Donna, despite Edna's assurance of her liking shopping, walked beside the trolley, head down and taking no interest whatsoever. I repeatedly asked her if she liked this or that, lingering at the displays of unhealthy but tempting biscuits and crisps, but there was nothing beyond a shrug, or on one occasion a brief nod. Even at the ice-cream cabinet she barely raised her eyes, and certainly didn't express a preference. Over the years I've taken many children to the supermarket and I have experienced many different reactions – from a child stealing when I wasn't looking to a full-scale tantrum (often) when I wouldn't buy all the sweets that had been demanded – but never before had I experienced complete and utter silence and indifference.

Arriving home, I gave everyone a carrier bag and we made one journey into the house and took them through to the kitchen. Adrian and Paula went straight out into the garden, while Donna hovered, arms loosely folded in front of her and head hung down. I asked her if she would like to help me unpack. She shrugged without looking up and continued to stand, a haunted silhouette in the doorway of the kitchen.

'Donna, love,' I said at last, 'you can do what you like, play in the garden, help me, or look at a book, but find something to do until lunchtime, pet.' She moved away and, head down, shuffled off. Presently I saw her appear in the garden and sit on the bench on the patio, watching Adrian and Paula playing in the sandpit. I viewed the fact that she had actually gone outside as a positive sign, and I watched her for a few moments longer; then I stopped unpacking the bags and went to offer some encouragement.

'Donna, would you like to play in the sandpit too?'

She shook her head.

'What about the swings?'

The same shake of the head.

'Do you want a bat or ball, or a bicycle out of the shed?'

Nothing, so I returned inside and finished the unpacking.

I made sandwiches for lunch and, with a packet of crisps for each of us, carried the tray outside to the table. We ate under the sunshade and in silence. Adrian and Paula were even quieter now – the unhealthy and oppressive silence was contagious, and like a smog it seemed to hang in the air.

'I thought we would spend the rest of the day in the garden,' I said. 'Then tomorrow shall we have a day out somewhere?'

'Sure,' said Adrian, without his usual enthusiasm and suggestions of where we could go.

Paula looked up at Donna for her input and predictably was met with nothing. Paula continued eating her egg sandwich and crisps in silence, and as soon as she and Adrian had finished they scuttled off; I remained where I was at the table, opposite Donna. I looked at her. Here we were in the garden on an idyllic summer's day, surrounded by flowers in all their colourful glory, with a gentle breeze faintly stirring the trees, and Adrian and Paula without a care in the world, and Donna was in abject and withdrawn misery. I reached out and touched her hand.

'Donna, love,' I said gently. 'You are going to have to start talking to me some time. It's too lonely for you otherwise.' She withdrew her hand from mine and shrugged. 'I know it's difficult for you, sweet, but you can trust me. I want to help you, but I need you to start talking to me. Adrian and Paula were looking forward to you coming to live with us, and they want to be friends with you.'

She shrugged again and, leaving the rest of her sandwich, got up from the bench and went to sit in the lounge. I sighed. My prognosis of a good night's sleep making all the difference now seemed laughable. And if I was honest, part of me was becoming irritated by her continual rejection of my best efforts, for I was sure she had some control over this unrelenting front she was hiding behind. I knew she was suffering, but she must have been talking at Mary and Ray's; otherwise they would have raised the alarm and Edna would have certainly told me. I could only assume that it was as a result of being separated from her brothers, and having to move, but how on earth I dealt with it was another matter. I decided the best course of action was to carry on as much as was possible with normal family life and include Donna, but not expect her to participate, in the hope that eventually she would feel comfortable enough to drop the barriers and join in. If nothing had changed by Monday morning, I would phone Jill and Edna and ask for help.

I took Paula and Adrian to one side and tried to explain the position to them, because I couldn't just ignore Donna's persistent silence: it was like ignoring the elephant in the room. 'Carry on as normal,' I said. 'Talk to Donna but don't expect her to reply or join in.' They said they would try, but clearly it was difficult for them. Later Paula made a few brave attempts to include Donna in her play but with no success.

That evening I ran a bath for Donna while she stood by me in silence, and then I left her to wash and change into her nightdress. I said goodnight and told her that the following day we would go out somewhere. I kissed her goodnight, said sleep tight, came out and pulled the door to. I consoled myself that while Donna wasn't engaging with me at any outward level at least she was cooperating and doing what I was asking. The day before I had been worried that she might stubbornly refuse to do anything, which would have been even more difficult, if not impossible to deal with.

Sunday evening approached. We had spent the day at a small adventure park, where Donna had sat and watched Paula and Adrian enjoying themselves with all the other children but not joined in once. I knew I would have to phone Jill and Edna first thing in the morning. I would ask them how to handle the situation because clearly my strategies were not working. I began the bedtime routine, and I left Donna to change into her nightdress and have her wash and do her teeth while I went downstairs and wrote up my log notes. Paula was already asleep and Adrian was getting changed into his pyjamas in his bedroom.

When I heard the bathroom door open and Donna return to her bedroom, I went upstairs to say goodnight. She was in bed with her arm around the teddy and had closed the bedroom curtains. I was half inclined to say a brisk goodnight and come out, for I was finding it difficult not to take her refusal to speak to me personally. I felt very frustrated and not a little hurt that she was making no attempt to communicate at all. But something stopped me from taking this line, and instead I went to her bed and knelt beside it.

I stroked her forehead and she didn't pull away. 'Donna, love,' I said, 'I know you are hurting but you must start talking to me. I can't help you if you don't.' I paused and continued to stroke her head. I really didn't know what else to say. 'I'm here to help you, and we all want to see you happy. Can you tell me what the matter is?'

She shook her head.

I hesitated, stopped stroking her head, and stood. 'OK, love, you get off to sleep.' I moved away, but as I went to the door I heard her voice, so faint I could have missed it.

'Cath-ie,' she said, pronouncing the two syllables separately. At last! I thought, and I could have jumped for joy.

I immediately returned to the bed. 'Yes, love? What is it?'

'I'm sorry, Cath-ie,' she said in a small voice.

I knelt down again and stroked her forehead. 'There is no need to be sorry, pet. All I want is for you to be happy. Will you try to talk to me tomorrow?'

She nodded.

'And to Paula and Adrian? They would like that.'

She nodded again.

'Is there anything you want to tell me now?' She looked at me for the first time since arriving, her big brown eyes doleful and full of pain. She was an attractive girl, her light brown skin soft and flawless, but her pleasant features were dulled by her inner turmoil. 'Yes?' I encouraged.

'It's my fault,' she said quietly.

'What is, sweet?'

'It's my fault my brothers and me came into care.'

'No, it's not, love,' I said, gently but firmly. 'Not at all. And being in care is not a punishment. It's to help your mum and give her a rest.'

'Mum says it's my fault. She said I should have tried harder.'

'Harder at what?'

'Looking after the house, and Warren and Jason. I did my best, but it wasn't good enough. And Mary and Ray didn't want my help.'

I continued to stroke her forehead. 'Donna, at your age, love, you should not be responsible for looking after the house or your younger brothers. That is the adult's responsibility. It was nice of you to help, but it was your mother's job to look after you, just as Mary and Ray are looking after your brothers now, and I will look after you. Do you understand?'

She nodded.

I paused. 'Is that what's bothering you, or is there something else?'

She gave a slight shake of her head.

'All right, love, we'll talk about this more tomorrow, but I'm very pleased you felt you could tell me.' I smiled and she looked directly at me again and, although she didn't return my smile, I thought I saw a slight lifting of the dreadful melancholy that had frozen her expression into sadness.

'Night then, love.' I kissed her forehead.

'Night, Cath-ie,' she said, again separating the second syllable.

I came out and with huge relief went into Adrian's room to say goodnight.

'Donna's talking,' I said.

'Cool. Now she can play with Paula.' I wasn't sure if this was a comment on Donna's progress or that Paula had been taking up rather a lot of his time recently.

I said goodnight to Adrian and, with my usual warning about not reading until too late, came out and went downstairs. I went into the lounge, where I wrote up my log notes with considerable relief and some small satisfaction that I had got there in the end and Donna was finally talking.

That night I slept very well, after sleeping badly the previous two, and when I went downstairs it was just after 7.00 a.m. At the end of the hall, I was surprised to find the door to the kitchen slightly open – I usually made sure all the downstairs doors were shut before I went to bed. I tentatively pushed the door wider open and went in. As I did, I started and did a double take. I couldn't believe what I was seeing. Donna was on her hands and knees, scrubbing the kitchen floor for all she was worth. She was using the rags that had been in the carrier bag in her bedroom.

Chapter Six

Amateur Psychology

'Whatever are you doing?' I asked, amazed. Donna was in her nightdress, and the floor was awash with puddles of water and the sopping wet rags, which were dotted around her.

She didn't answer, but continued rubbing one of the rags back and forth across the floor.

'Donna?' I said again. I began walking across the wet and now slippery tiled floor, with my bare feet squishing on the tiles. 'Donna?' I went right up to her. She must have heard me, and seen me out of the corner of her eye, but she kept on scrubbing furiously. Both of her hands clutched the rag in front of her and she rubbed it backwards and forwards as though her very life depended on it. In different circumstances I might have seen the funny side of it – a child frantically mopping up a spillage before I could see it, with their well-meant intentions making it a lot worse. But not now. This was no spillage – there was too much water and Donna's work was all-consuming and frantic.

'Donna?' I said again, more firmly; then I placed my hand on her shoulder, hoping to break the motion. My hand jerked back and forth in time with her frenzied cleaning. 'Donna, stop now,' I said loudly. 'You don't have to do this.'

'I do,' she said, and she continued, now pushing the cloth round and round. The water sprayed against my ankles. I thought she must have tipped the washing-up bowl full of water over the floor, for there was far too much water for it to have come from the wet rags alone. She must have left her bedroom and come downstairs very quietly, for normally I heard a child out of bed and on the landing.

'Donna, I want you to stop. Now!' I said, and again I touched her shoulder.

'No! I must clean,' she said, her voice rising in panic. 'I must! I must! I have to clean the kitchen floor.'

'No,' I said, raising my voice above hers. 'You don't have to. Stop it, now! And you are not supposed to be in the kitchen. It isn't allowed.' Which was true: it was a house rule that I didn't have young children in the kitchen, for safety reasons, but I hadn't yet explained the house rules to Donna.

Gradually the frantic scrubbing grew less frenzied, and then came to a halt. Her hands on the rag became still, but she remained on all fours, bent over the rags. 'Don't hit me,' she said. 'I've done my best.'

I stared at her, horrified. 'Of course I'm not going to hit you. I don't hit anyone, and certainly not a child.' I continued to look at her, as I tried to understand what was happening. Keeping my voice even, I said, 'Donna, I want you to stand up, and dry yourself. We need to talk.' My firmness masked my anxiety, as I continued to search for a reason that could have brought Donna down here in the early hours to do this.

I took the hand towel from the rail by the sink and held it out. 'Now please, Donna, stand up and dry your hands and legs. You're soaking.' The front of her nightdress was sopping wet where it had trailed in the water; it dripped as she stood. I passed her the towel and she slowly wiped her hands, then bent down and wiped her knees. I watched her: the frenzied movements of her scrubbing had vanished and she had once more resumed her slow lethargic manner. She finished wiping off the excess water from her legs and handed back the towel. Although her legs and hands were dry, her nightdress was still dripping. 'I think we had better get you changed first before we talk,' I said.

She shrugged.

I reached out and took her hand, and she allowed me to lead her from the wet and slippery floor of the kitchen, across the carpet of the annexe and into the hall. I let go of her hand as I led the way upstairs. Adrian and Paula were still asleep – it was just before 7.30 a.m. I went into Donna's bedroom, took a set of clean clothes and underwear from her wardrobe and laid them on the bed. 'Get dressed, please,' I said. 'I'll be back in a minute. Leave your nightdress in the laundry basket on the landing.'

Donna didn't say anything but made a move towards the clothes. I came out, pulling the door to behind me. I went to my bedroom, where I quickly dressed and ran a brush through my hair. My morning routine having been disrupted, I would have to shower later, after I had spoken to Donna. What had been going through her head to make her rise at the crack of dawn and creep downstairs with her bag of rags and start the ritualised cleaning, I couldn't begin to guess. It hadn't been proper cleaning, as if she had wanted to make a difference; nor had it been a small task, as Adrian and Paula sometimes performed, which I would have to admire with great delight – 'Look, Mum! We've tidied the toy box!' No, Donna's work had been a frenzied attack, almost as if she was acting out something, which hadn't been aimed so much at accomplishing a task as releasing something in her. Edna's almost throwaway comment came back to me – 'Mary thinks she might have OCD.' I knew very little about OCD, other than that it was an obsessive need to do something over and over again; was this how it manifested itself?

I went round the landing and knocked lightly on Donna's door. 'Are you dressed?' I asked quietly, not wanting to wake Adrian and Paula.

Donna's small voice came back. 'Yes, Cath-ie.'

I went in. She was sitting on the bed, hunched forward, arms folded into her waist and head down. The colourful beads from her bracelet were now strewn across the floor.

'Oh dear, have you broken your bracelet?' I asked, wondering if this had anything to do with what had just happened in the kitchen.

She shook her head, and in that movement I saw a small guilt. I was almost certain that the two incidents were somehow connected, and that she had possibly broken the bracelet on purpose.

'Donna,' I said, sitting next to her on the bed, 'can you please try to tell me what's going through your mind?' It was at times like this that I really wished I was a psychiatrist, with a better understanding of what made children tick, rather than a mother and carer who had to rely on intuition, some training, and experience from looking after children.

Donna shrugged again.

'When we were in the kitchen, why did you think I was going to hit you?' I asked gently, taking her hand in mine.

She didn't resist, and I stroked the back of her hand and waited.

She shrugged again.

'Come on, love. I want so much to understand and help you. But I can't unless you try to tell me. Why were you cleaning? You didn't accidentally spill something, did you?'

She shook her head.

'So why did you think I was going to hit you? That worries me.'

Her mouth opened and closed before she spoke; then eventually she said quietly, 'My mum did. If I didn't clean well.'

'Your mum hit you for not cleaning properly?' I asked.

She nodded.

Good grief! I thought, but I kept my voice steady as I asked, 'How often did that happen, Donna?'

She shrugged again, then after a moment said, 'Lots. It was my job to clean the house for when Edna came. Mum said if I didn't keep the house clean Edna would take us away.'

'I see,' I said. 'Thank you for telling me.' The logic of trying to clean the house before the social worker made her visit had a dismal ring of truth about it. Edna had said she thought Donna had felt responsible for them being taken into care, and Donna had admitted to me the night before that she blamed herself, but I doubted Edna knew the extent of Donna's sense of responsibility, or that her mother had made her clean, and had hit her for not doing the job properly. I would have to remember as much as possible of what Donna was telling me so that I could write it in my log notes, then tell Edna when I spoke to her. 'Donna, when you say your mother hit you "lots", what do you mean? Every month? Every week?'

'Every day,' she said in a small voice. 'With a coat hanger.'

'A coat hanger?' I asked, horrified.

'A wire one. She unbended it so it was long. It hurt.'

I inwardly cringed and gently rubbed the back of her hand. 'I'm sure it did hurt, sweet. That was very, very wrong of your mother. No adult should ever hit a child. A mother shouldn't, and I certainly won't.' Obvious, but not necessarily to Donna, who – from what she was telling me – had been beaten on a daily basis.

'The boys used a skipping rope,' she added matter-of-factly.

I stopped rubbing her hand. 'Your brothers hit you too?'

She nodded. 'With the skipping rope. It had a wooden end on it.'

I stared at her, aghast. 'Why did they hit you?'

'When I didn't do the cleaning as good as I should. Mum said they could. And they liked it.' I felt such a surge of anger towards Warren and Jason at that moment that had they been in the room I would have given them a good telling-off, although in reality they were probably as much victims as Donna was, having learned their behaviour in a household that appeared to survive on perverted discipline.

'Donna, love,' I said, 'that was so very wrong of them. People don't hit each other, and certainly not members of the same family. Brothers and sisters, mums and dads should take care of each other, not bully them and cause them pain. I will never hit you,' I said, reinforcing what I had said before. 'Neither will Adrian or Paula.' The notion of which seemed slightly ludicrous, given that Adrian and Paula were much smaller than Donna, but then Warren and Jason were only six and seven.

Donna gave a faint nod, and I continued to look at her downcast profile. 'What about Chelsea and your dad? Did they hit you?'

'Chelsea did, but not Dad. I looked after him when he wasn't well. I tried to get him to take his tablets, so that he would be well. He was kind to me.'

Well, at least that was something, I thought. Donna had one ally in a house of abusers, as long as she reminded her schizophrenic father to take his medication. What a horrendous way to live! 'Did your mother hit your brothers and Chelsea?' I asked. All the information I gathered would help Edna, and ultimately the judge to decide the long-term care plans for the boys and Donna.

'Sometimes Mum hit my brothers,' Donna said softly. 'But not often. Only when the boys were really getting on her nerves. Sometimes Chelsea and Mum had an argument and they hit each other.'

'The boys didn't get hit for not doing things like cleaning?' I asked.

Donna shook her head. 'Mum only hit them when she had been drinking and they got on her nerves. She loves them.'

'I'm sure your mum loves you too, sweet,' I said, finding not for the first time since I'd been fostering that I had to separate parental love and the way the parent behaved, and also wanting to offer Donna something positive. 'Mum has got a lot of problems and I don't suppose the drink helped.'

'She always hit me more after drinking,' Donna confirmed.

I nodded, and looked from Donna to the floor and all the little coloured beads from the bracelet, which were spread around her feet and into the far corners of the carpet. 'Why did you break your bracelet?' I asked gently. 'I thought you liked it very much?'

She shrugged. I noticed a small muscle twitch nervously at the corner of her eye. 'They wouldn't let me clean.'

I hesitated, trying desperately to piece together the few words she was offering and make sense of her actions. 'You broke the bracelet because you remembered you weren't allowed to clean? What, at Mary and Ray's house?'

She nodded.

'Did that make you angry?'

She nodded again.

'What? Angry with Mary and Ray?'

Another nod.

'You must have been up very early this morning. You were asleep when I looked in last night, and the bracelet wasn't broken then.'

'I have to get up early to clean the house.'

'Not here you don't,' I said firmly. 'I see to the cleaning here. You don't have to do it.' I then realised I was taking the same route that Mary and Ray had probably taken in not letting her help at all. 'Donna, you don't have to worry about the cleaning here, but you can help me. I am the adult, and housework is my responsibility, but I can certainly find you some jobs to do.' I didn't know if I was handling this right, or simply repeating what Mary and Ray had said and thereby going down the same path and getting it wrong. 'Is that what Mary said?' I asked.

Donna nodded. 'Well, she was right, in that respect. You don't have to clean now, and you certainly won't get hit for not doing it.'

'I do,' she suddenly blurted. 'I do have to clean. I do!' And again I thought of Edna's mention of OCD, for it seemed Donna was admitting to some form of obsession, though whether it was OCD or not I hadn't a clue.

'OK, Donna,' I said slowly. 'If I understand you, you feel you need to clean, probably because of all the cleaning you had to do at home. I think this morning you needed to let something inside you come out. Some anger? And I think you broke the bracelet because you remembered that Mary wouldn't let you help, and you took your anger out on the bracelet. Is that right?'

Donna nodded, and then, unbelievably, she smiled, her whole face lighting up. 'Can I help you clean here, Cathy?' she asked.

'Yes, of course you can. But I will find you some jobs to do. I don't want you getting up early and flooding the kitchen again.' I smiled, and she actually managed a small laugh. I gave myself a mental pat on the back. I might not have been a psychiatrist, but I had managed to get it right this time.

'And I can help you look after Adrian and Paula?' she asked, still smiling.

'Yes, of course you can, Donna. But remember you don't have to, and it wasn't your fault you and your brothers came into care.'

She leant towards me and planted a little kiss on my cheek. 'Thank you for letting me help, Cathy. You're nice.'

I smiled again, and drawing her to me gave her a big hug. 'So are you, love.'

What I didn't know was that my simplistic solution of agreeing to let Donna help had unleashed something which would quickly gather momentum and have far-reaching effects. It would be outside anything I had experience of, or knew how to deal with.

Chapter Seven

Runt of the Litter

I was feeling pretty pleased with myself when Jill phoned at ten o'clock on Monday morning.

'Yes, we are doing OK,' I confirmed. 'Donna was very quiet and withdrawn to begin with, but she is now talking and starting to join in.' I told Jill about the beating Donna had received at the hands of her family for not cleaning properly, and also about her frenzied floor scrubbing at our house, and the bag of rags she had brought with her, presumably for this purpose.

'The poor kid,' Jill said with a heartfelt sigh. 'It's just as well she has been separated from her brothers, if they have been bullying her to that extent.'

'Yes,' I agreed, and I explained how I was going to give her little jobs to do, so that she could join in and have some responsibility.

'That's how I would handle it, Cathy. And you're obviously keeping detailed log notes? It sounds as though Edna wasn't aware of some of this.'

'Yes, my notes are up to date,' I confirmed, and then I updated Jill. 'Donna has contact tonight; I think she is seeing her whole family. And school begins again a week on Wednesday.'

'Thanks. I'll speak to Edna today, and I'll visit you later in the week. If you need me in the meantime, phone.'

'Will do.' I paused. 'Jill, do you think Donna is suffering from this Obsessive Compulsive Disorder? I really don't know much about it.'

'Neither do I. But I shouldn't think so. There aren't any other symptoms, are there?'

'Such as?'

'From what I know of OCD the person repeatedly performs a task in a ritualised pattern. Like insisting a chair or book is in a particular position before they can leave the room. It has to be exactly right to within millimetres; otherwise the person becomes very anxious. The person can move an object dozens and dozens of times before they are satisfied. We all do it to some extent, for example when we return and double check the back door is locked before we go out, although we know it is. But people suffering from OCD take it to obsessive lengths, and it governs their lives.'

'No, there hasn't been anything like that,' I said. 'Just this one incident of cleaning the floor. And what Mary told Edna.'

'I'm sure it's not OCD. Donna will be fine. You've dealt with it, and she's been able to open up to you and start talking. Well done.'

'Thanks,' I said, grateful for the praise.

When Edna phoned an hour later I updated her as I had done Jill. When I had finished Edna was very quiet.

'Dear me,' she said at last. 'I knew those boys got the better of Donna sometimes but I had no idea they were actually whipping her – with a skipping rope?'

'That's what she said.'

'No wonder the poor kid didn't settle at Mary and Ray's.' She paused again. 'Cathy, as you know we brought Donna and the boys into care because of severe neglect. There was a suspicion of physical abuse but I'd no idea they were all beating Donna, and I have been working closely with that family for over three years now.' She stopped again and I knew Edna was blaming herself for not spotting the depth of the abuse. 'Donna had some bruises on her back and legs when she first came into care and had her medical. She told the doctor she had fallen in the garden at home. I expect she was too scared to say anything else.'

'Yes,' I agreed.

'Dear me,' Edna said again. 'I'm going to talk to her mother, Rita, and also to Mary and Ray, and those boys. I shall also be keeping a close eye on the family at contact tonight. Donna is such a sweet thing. She wouldn't hurt a fly.'

'I know, she's lovely,' I said. 'Edna, this bag of rags she's brought with her – did it come from home or Mary's?'

'I really don't know. Why?'

'It seems a strange thing for a child to bring with her. I mean the rags aren't security blankets or comforters. They're cleaning rags.'

Edna paused. 'Look, Cathy, I've got a lot of questions I need to put to Mary and Ray, and the boys, after what you have told me. I also need to visit Rita and Chelsea as a matter of urgency. Can I phone you back later?'

'Yes, of course.'

'I've given you the details for the contact tonight, haven't I?'

'Yes, thanks.'

There was another pause. 'What is Donna doing now, Cathy?'

'She's in the garden with Adrian and Paula.'

'Good. We'll speak later. Thanks, Cathy. And thank goodness I moved her!'

I hung up and went down the hall and into the lounge, where I looked out of the French windows to check on the three children. They were grouped around the basketball post, taking turns at aiming and throwing. Donna appeared to be in charge and was organising the game, running to retrieve the ball from where it landed and handing it to Adrian or Paula for their turn to take a shot.

I watched for a few moments, and then called, 'Donna, you make sure you have a turn as well.' She smiled sheepishly, almost embarrassed, and then passed the ball to Adrian for his turn. Oh well, I thought, if she was happier organising the game rather than joining in, I'd leave them to it, and Adrian and Paula certainly weren't complaining.

Having had a full day out the day before, we were spending today around the house and in the garden. Entrance fees for children's amusement parks are horrendous now, and yesterday's excursion had cost me over £70 – £10 each to get in and then there had been lunch and drinks. Like many parents, I couldn't afford to provide non-stop entertainment throughout the summer holiday; and nor did the children need it – Adrian and Paula were just as happy amusing themselves in the garden on a fine day.

I made a sandwich lunch, and Donna appeared and asked if she could carry the tray outside. I placed the tray containing the sandwiches and crisps in her outstretched hands, and I followed with a jug of orange squash.

'I'll fetch Adrian and Paula,' Donna said helpfully, setting the tray on the table on the patio.

'Thanks, love.'

I watched her stroll down to the bottom of the garden. She was talking more now she had a role, and it was like having a little mother's helper. 'Adrian and Paula,' I heard her call from a distance, as I sometimes did. 'Come on now, your lunch is ready.'

They both stopped what they were doing and began to run up the garden towards me. I smiled: they had come a good deal quicker than when I called them.

'Are your hands clean?' Donna asked as they sat on the benches either side of the table ready for lunch.

Adrian and Paula turned over their hands to show their palms, as too did Donna. 'I suppose we should really give them a wipe,' I said, 'as you are having sandwiches.'

'Shall I fetch a cloth from the kitchen?' Donna asked.

I was about to say yes please when I realised that I ought to start implementing my policy of not having children in the kitchen. 'No, don't worry. I'll fetch it.'

I went into the kitchen, where I took the carton of Wet Ones from the cupboard and tore off three strips. I handed one to each of them and waited until they'd finished wiping their hands and passed the used tissues back to me.

'Let's have a look?' Donna said, and Adrian and Paula offered their hands for inspection. I smiled again. Donna was certainly more conscientious than I was, and with far better results, particularly from Adrian, who as a young

boy did not believe that cleanliness was next to godliness –
just the opposite in fact!

A few clouds rolled in that afternoon, but the air was
still warm, and with the French windows wide open we
spent a lazy afternoon in and out of the garden, pleas-
ing ourselves. Donna organised some running races
between Adrian and Paula, and then my neighbour's
boy, Billy, who had heard all the excitement, climbed up
the tree to see over and asked if he could come round
and join in. I told him he could but that he had to ask
his mother first. Sue came out of her house and said it
was fine, but only for a couple of hours as they were
going out later. She helped him clamber over the fence
and I introduced him to Donna. Billy joined in the
hopping race that Donna was organising while I chatted
over the fence to Sue.

'She looks like she's going to be a big help,' Sue said,
nodding to Donna.

'Yes, although I would like to see her playing more –
you know, joining in and having fun. She has been organising the games all day. She always puts herself last.' I obviously couldn't say anything more to Sue (or any of my
other friends and neighbours for that matter) about
Donna's situation or background, as these were highly
confidential, and Sue appreciated that. She knew I fostered
and was used to seeing children suddenly appear and then
disappear from my back garden.

During the afternoon I regularly brought out drinks for
the children and also offered ice creams from the freezer.
Donna didn't want an ice cream to begin with. 'No, let
them have them,' she said, nodding to Adrian, Paula and

Billy, as if there weren't enough for everyone and they should have first call.

'Donna, love,' I said, 'there is plenty for everyone. I'm sure you would like an ice cream. There's choc ice, raspberry ripple or an ice lolly.' I offered her the open cartons.

'Oh all right then, if you insist,' she said, and I smiled at the quaint adult term she had used. She quickly dipped her hand into the box of choc ices and took one, as though at any moment the offer might be withdrawn or she was doing something prohibited.

I returned the rest of the ice creams to the freezer and then stood for a moment at the kitchen window, watching her. Adrian, Paula and Billy were sitting on the grass in a small circle, eating their ice creams, but Donna was on the bench on the patio a short distance away, almost as if she was overseeing them. I continued to watch her slow measured movements as she gradually peeled down the wrapper of the choc ice and took small bites, savouring each mouthful as if it was the first and last. It was almost as if an ice cream was a forbidden pleasure for her, and she ate as though it was the first time she had ever tasted one – a precious treat that was not likely to be repeated. By the time she had finished, the last of it had melted away and she came into the kitchen to rinse her fingers.

'Did you enjoy that?' I asked lightly, as she turned on the tap.

She nodded.

'I always have ice cream in the freezer in summer,' I said.

'Do you?' She turned to look at me, her expression one of amazement and surprise.

I passed her the hand towel. 'Yes. And next time we go shopping you can tell me which ice creams you prefer, and choose some food you like.'

'I like anything, really, Cathy. But not coleslaw.'

'Coleslaw?' It was my turn to look surprised, for I would not have associated coleslaw with a child's preference. 'No, I don't think Adrian and Paula do either,' I said. 'I buy it sometimes for myself.'

Donna finished wiping her hands and folded the towel neatly on to the towel rail. She was very methodical and precise when it came to folding items like her clothes or the towel. 'I always had to eat coleslaw at home,' she continued. 'So I'm not too keen on it now.' I smiled again at the adult phrase 'not too keen'. She often used such phrases, which sounded quaint on a child's lips.

'I expect your mum thought coleslaw was good for you,' I suggested.

She nodded. 'We had to buy it because it was on the list. But no one liked it, so I had to have it.'

'Oh, I see,' I said, not really seeing at all. 'What, with salad?'

'No, by itself. I had it for my dinner and tea.'

I looked at her. 'I'm not understanding you, Donna. You can't just have eaten a tub of coleslaw for your dinner and tea?'

She nodded quite matter-of-factly as if I should have known. 'When Mum's giro came through she gave me some money to go shopping. There was a list I had to use each week. I took Warren and Jason with me. There was coleslaw on the list because Edna had told Mum it was good for us. But no one liked it, so when we got home with the shopping everyone took what they wanted from the bags, and there was just the coleslaw left. Warren and Jason are smarter than me, so they got what they wanted from the bags first. Warren always had the custard cream biscuits and Jason had the loaf of bread. Chelsea had the ham and I was left with the coleslaw. Mum didn't eat much. She had beer instead.'

I stared at her, dumbfounded. 'And that was your dinner or tea?'

'Both,' she said.

'What about on the other days, when you didn't have the giro? What did you eat then?'

'What was left. Sometimes the tub of coleslaw lasted two days, and the bread did. Warren always ate all the custard creams on the first day, although I told him not to.'

'Then what?'

'The neighbours fed us. And sometimes we walked to my aunt's. And when we were at school we had breakfast there, and school dinner.'

'And no tea?'

'Not until it was giro day again.'

Bloody hell, I thought. No wonder she liked her food, and ate everything I put in front of her. 'Well, at least the coleslaw was better for you than Warren's choice of biscuits.'

'So you know I don't like coleslaw?' she confirmed.

'Yes, I know, Donna.'

'But I like sitting at the table to eat. Do all foster carers have tables and chairs?'

'Yes, I think so.' Donna certainly wasn't the first child I'd fostered whose family home had never had a dining table and chairs.

'You know, Donna,' I said, 'that wasn't a good diet. It's a wonder you weren't all ill.'

'Chelsea said it gave her spots.'

'She could be right. And Donna?'

'Yes?'

'Have you ever had an ice cream before?'

'Oh yes, of course! Edna bought me one when we came to you for the visit on Friday. It was lovely. I really enjoyed it, and the one you gave me today. That was nice too.'

'So that was your second ice cream just now?'

She nodded. 'I've tried lots of new things since I've been in care.' I smiled sadly. 'I think I might like being in care, Cathy. People are so nice to me.'

Edna phoned again at 4.00 p.m., having visited Warren and Jason at Mary and Ray's. She asked if she could be overheard and I said no: Donna was with Adrian and Paula, watching children's television in the lounge. She said Warren and Jason had admitted to hitting Donna, and when Edna had questioned them further they'd confirmed that they'd used an old skipping rope. Edna had asked them why they'd been so cruel to their sister and they had said it was because Donna hadn't done what Mum had told her to – clean the house properly. The boys also confirmed that their mother had told them to beat Donna, and when Edna had asked where all this had taken place, they'd said usually in the kitchen when Donna was on her hands and knees trying to clear up the cat shit. My thoughts flipped to the morning when I had found Donna on all fours in the kitchen and she'd pleaded, 'Don't hit me. I've done my best.' Edna said that the boys had told her that their mother and Chelsea also regularly hit Donna, and that they wouldn't let her have any new clothes. Edna was obviously appalled and horrified, particularly as Warren and Jason could see absolutely nothing wrong in what they had done and showed no remorse.

'Cathy,' Edna said, 'I asked the boys separately if they hadn't thought what they were doing was wrong, and that it hurt Donna, and do you know what they said? That because Donna was so stupid she wouldn't feel it!'

'She's not stupid,' I erupted. 'And she certainly felt it, although she probably didn't ever say so. And Edna, do you know what the poor girl had to eat when there was money for food? The stuff no one else wanted!' I told her about the coleslaw and the shopping, although I didn't point out that the coleslaw had been at Edna's suggestion. 'I persuaded her to have an ice cream today,' I said. 'It was only the second one she'd ever had in her life. The first one you bought her when you visited us. She's ten years old and living in an affluent society, for goodness sake! And I know not having ice cream doesn't amount to child abuse, but it is indicative of the miserable, deprived existence she led. I expect the boys enjoyed an ice cream when there was the money for treats!'

Edna was silent for some moments. 'I know, Cathy. I remember when I bought her that ice cream she was so grateful. What I didn't know was the level of deprivation and also about the abuse that had been aimed at Donna. Warren called her the runt of the family. Now where on earth did a boy his age learn a term like that?'

'I haven't a clue, but from what I'm picking up on here it sums up how they treated her — like the runt of the litter.'

We were both quiet. I knew I shouldn't have exploded: it sounded as though I was blaming Edna, who, bless her, undoubtedly had done her best, but apparently she hadn't been able to see through the united front presented by the rest of this dysfunctional travesty of a family.

'I'm going to see Rita and Chelsea tomorrow,' Edna said after a while. 'They weren't in today when I called. I pushed a note through their letterbox saying I would call back tomorrow. How has Donna been this afternoon?'

'She has been organising games for Adrian and Paula,' I said. 'And also the boy from next door, who came to play.'

'Good. I'll see you later briefly when you bring Donna to contact.'

'Yes,' I said, and, still subdued from what I'd heard, I replaced the receiver. I then checked in the lounge, where the three children were watching cartoons.

I left them for another fifteen minutes, then told Donna to have a quick wash and change into some clean clothes, ready for contact. At 4.45 p.m. I bundled everyone into the car — with some protest from Adrian, whose programme I had interrupted — and drove to the social services office in Brampton Road. It wasn't the social services' main office but a large Victorian detached house that was used as overspill, and housed the Children and Families team. I pulled onto the driveway and left Adrian and Paula in the car while I took Donna into the small reception area that had once been the hall. I gave our names to the receptionist and she phoned through to Edna, who appeared almost immediately through the security-locked inner door.

'Hello, Cathy, Donna,' she said with her warm encouraging smile. 'I hear you've had a lovely time in the garden today, Donna. And also that you went out for the day yesterday?'

Donna nodded shyly.

'Your mum and brothers are already here,' she continued to Donna. 'Dad won't be coming today, as he's not feeling so well.' I thought I heard Donna give a little sigh and so too, it seemed, had Edna, for she threw me a pointed glance. 'I shall be supervising contact as usual, Donna, so there is nothing for you to worry about.' Then, looking at me, Edna said, 'I'll see you at six thirty. Thank you for bringing Donna.'

'You're welcome. See you later, Donna.' I left the building and drove home, where Adrian managed to finish watching his programme before it was time to return for the end of contact.

Donna didn't say much in the car coming home and I knew Edna would tell me if anything had emerged at contact that I should know about. Once home, I began the bath and bedtime routine – Paula first, then Donna and Adrian.

As I said goodnight to Adrian, and was about to leave him reading, he said, 'Mum, I need to ask you something.'

'Yes, love.' I returned to beside his bed. 'What is it?'

'Is Donna in charge of us?'

I looked at him carefully. 'What do you mean exactly?'

'Well, in the garden today she kept bossing us around and telling us to do things like she was our mother, only not like you do,' he added quickly. 'It was all right to begin with, when she was organising a game, but then she wouldn't let up. She kept telling us and Billy what to do. Paula said she was in charge.'

'No, of course Donna isn't "in charge". I'll have to explain to Paula.'

'And will you tell Donna? I don't want her to keep telling me what to do the whole time,' Adrian added.

'Yes, I understand. I'm sorry. You should have said something to me sooner.'

'It was difficult with her being there the whole time.'

'I'll keep an eye on it tomorrow and if necessary I'll speak to her, OK?'

'Yes.'

I kissed him goodnight again and came out feeling that perhaps he was overreacting, being a bit sensitive to having a child living with us who was the same age, physically bigger and in some respects more mature. But I would watch more closely tomorrow. I had already noticed that Donna could be a little forceful in her desire to organise. When she had been helping me with some chores in the house I had found that more than once she'd tried to take over and tell me how it should be done. And whereas, as an adult, I could laugh it off and subtly direct her to doing something as I wished, at his age Adrian obviously didn't have such resources and had taken it personally. Well, that was how I saw it – until the following morning.

Chapter Eight

Dirty

It was raining in the morning and I suggested we went to the cinema for the eleven o'clock show to see the new Walt Disney film. Adrian, Paula and Donna were upstairs, taking turns in the bathroom to brush their teeth and have a wash while I cleared away the breakfast things. Suddenly there was a cry from Paula, and Adrian came flying down the stairs.

'Mum! Come quick! Donna's hit Paula!'

I dropped the tea towel and flew out of the kitchen, along the hall and upstairs. Paula was in the bathroom, standing beside the basin with her toothbrush in her hand and tears streaming down her face. Donna was standing beside her.

'Whatever's happened?' I asked, taking Paula and cradling her in my arms.

'She hit her!' Adrian said, coming in behind me.

I looked at Donna, who was standing expressionless in front of me. 'Did you hit her?' I asked sternly.

'She did!' Adrian yelled from behind me.

'All right, Adrian. I want to hear it from Donna or Paula.'

Donna said nothing and I looked at Paula. 'Did Donna hit you?'

She nodded, tears still running down her face.

'Where?'

Paula stretched out her left hand and I saw a large red mark on the back of it. 'Did you do this, Donna?' I demanded.

She nodded slowly, not at all abashed. She looked sad, but then Donna always looked sad, even when she was playing, apart from the couple of times she'd smiled yesterday. 'Paula wouldn't do as I told her,' Donna said at last. 'I told her to do her teeth properly and she didn't.'

'That's no reason to hit her!' I said. 'No one in this house hits anyone, ever. I'm surprised at you, Donna! You know how much hitting hurts! Now go to your room while I see to Paula, and then I want to talk to you.'

She hesitated, and in that hesitation I saw the first sign of resistance, an insolence, a 'take-me-on-if-you-dare' look, and I thought of the bruise Mary had received to her arm – from a similar incident, perhaps? 'Now! Donna!' I said, and I held her gaze.

There was another second's hesitation, and my heart pounded as I felt a cold shudder of fear. She was nearly as tall as me and sturdy. I knew that if she'd wanted to she could have done real damage – to people and property. Gone was the downtrodden-victim look and in its place I saw insolence and determination. Then she stamped her foot and pushed past me, knocking into me as she went. She stomped round the landing and then slammed her bedroom door shut. Paula was holding on to me tightly and Adrian was very still and pale.

'It's all right,' I reassured them both. It was one of the few times I'd actually felt threatened by a foster child, and clearly Adrian and Paula had felt so too. I had looked after children before who had kicked and screamed and tried to thump me when they'd been very upset, but they'd been smaller and more easily contained. Again, my thoughts went to Mary and Ray, and the two of them having to struggle with Donna to remove her from their bathroom, after she had done what? I needed to find out. Was this a new development, or a repetition of something that had happened at Mary and Ray's?

I continued to hug Paula, then I put my arm round Adrian and drew him to my side. 'It's OK,' I reassured them once more. 'I'll speak to Donna and make sure it doesn't happen again.' Although in truth I wasn't at all sure how I was going to do this. I didn't know what I was dealing with; Donna had suddenly turned on Paula and for no apparent reason.

'All right, love?' I asked Paula gently, easing her from me and looking at her. She had stopped crying, but her hand was still red. 'That was very naughty of Donna. I'm going to tell her off,' I said, reinforcing the point. I didn't want Paula or Adrian believing that hitting was in any way acceptable. I'd known foster carers whose own children's behaviour had deteriorated in line with a foster child's, rather than the foster child following the example of the carer's 'well brought up' children.

I gave Paula and Adrian another hug, and Adrian said, 'I'm fine now, Mum.'

'Good boy. Will you look after Paula for a bit while I speak to Donna?'

He took her hand. 'Come on, Paula, you can play on my Gameboy.' Which was a real treat for Paula – to be allowed access to the much-coveted 'Super Mario' leaping over obstacles. Pacified, Paula trotted round the landing with Adrian and into his bedroom.

I took a moment, and then went round to Donna's room. I was feeling far from composed. I was going to speak to Donna, and then I wanted to talk to Mary and Ray and try to find out more. If I had a child in my house who could threaten my children, I needed to know exactly what I was dealing with. Edna had dismissed Mary and Ray's failure to look after Donna, as I had done, as it being too much for them to look after three children, with the inherent suggestion that Mary and Ray could have handled it better. Now I had big doubts and I was wondering if I had done them something of a disservice.

Donna's door was shut right to from her having slammed it. I drew myself up, took a deep breath and, knocking briefly on the door, opened it and went straight in. She was sitting on the bed, looking morose, with her arms folded across her chest and rocking back and forth.

'Donna,' I said firmly, ignoring the pang of pity I now felt for her at seeing her so dejected. 'I need to talk to you.' I didn't sit next to her but stood a little way in front. I wanted to keep the height and distance between us, just in case she went for me. 'Donna, you need to understand that in this family, as in most other families, we don't hit each other. I don't hit you or Adrian or Paula or anyone. And children do not hit each other. Do you understand?'

She didn't say anything. Her eyes were trained on the ground and she continued to rock back and forth. In a different situation I would have immediately gone and comforted her, for she looked so lonely and unloved, but now I needed to make sure that she understood her behaviour was totally unacceptable. Although Paula had recovered, and the injury was relatively minor, it had nevertheless been an assault, which would have hurt Paula emotionally, and reduced her trust not only in Donna but in other children. And with Donna twice the size of Paula, who was to say that another attack wouldn't be a lot worse? I needed to keep everyone safe.

'Donna, this is a safe house,' I said in the same firm manner. 'Paula feels safe here, Adrian feels safe here and you are safe here. No one purposely hurts anyone else. I need to hear you tell me that you understand, and that you won't do it again.' I waited. Donna continued looking down and rocking. I waited some more. I wasn't sure how to proceed now. 'Look, Donna,' I said in a less authoritative tone, 'I know lots of bad things have happened to you, but you must try to leave them behind. We all look out for each other here, and you will find if you look after Adrian and Paula they will be just as keen to look after you.'

I paused again, but there was no response; Donna hadn't looked up or stopped rocking. I decided she could do with a few minutes to reflect on what I'd said, before I hugged her and we put the incident behind us. 'OK, Donna,' I said, 'I want you to think about what I've said. Then when you feel able, come down and tell me that it won't happen again. And I also think you need to say sorry to Paula.'

Still nothing. I turned and slowly left the room, drawing the door to behind me, but not closing it. I went downstairs, and to the phone on the hall table, and dialled Edna's number.

'Edna,' I said as soon as she answered. 'It's Cathy, Donna's carer.'

'Hello, Cathy?' I could tell by her tone she guessed something was wrong.

'We've had a bit of a problem here,' I said. 'And I would like some more information.' I explained what had just happened and finished by saying that I thought it would be useful if I could speak to Mary and Ray and find out exactly what had happened there.

I could hear the relief in Edna's voice, for doubtless she had thought that with Donna hitting Paula I would be calling an end to the placement and asking for Donna to be moved. 'Yes, of course, Cathy,' she said. 'I have their telephone number here. I'm so sorry you've had to deal with this. I don't understand what has got into Donna. I've never seen that side of her.'

I waited for her to read out the telephone number, which I wrote on the pad I kept beside the phone in the hall and repeated back to her. 'I'm going to phone them now,' I said.

'Yes, Cathy. I'll speak to them myself later as well. I'm so very sorry.'

I severed the line and keyed in the numbers to Mary and Ray. It was all quiet upstairs – Adrian and Paula were still ensconced in his bedroom with the Gameboy, and I assumed Donna was contemplating, and I hoped taking on board, what I had said, ready to offer an apology to Paula. I listened to Mary and Ray's phone ringing; then a female voice answered.

'Is that Mary?' I asked.

'Speaking.'

'This is Cathy Glass, Donna's carer.'

'Oh, hello.'

'I hope you don't mind my phoning. Edna gave me your number. We've had a bit of an incident here this morning and I felt I needed to speak to you to try to learn more.'

I thought there was a small hesitation before she said, 'Sure, go ahead.' I also heard boys' voices in the background and I assumed they were those of Warren and Jason, playing.

I began positively, and said that Donna was settling in well, but that out of the blue she'd smacked my daughter this morning, and I was wondering if Mary had had any similar incident when Donna had been living with her. I didn't say that I knew Mary had received a bruise, or add any more; I wanted to hear what she had to say. What Mary told me didn't in any way lighten my concern.

'Donna was fine when she first arrived,' Mary began. 'A bit quiet and too compliant, but otherwise OK. She was used to looking after her younger brothers, although they often teased and bullied her. She was more like their mother or carer than an older sister, and I thought I should take some of the responsibility from her. So many of these children come into care having never had a childhood because of all the responsibility they've had at home.' I agreed and knew from what Mary was saying that she was a sensible, level-headed and experienced foster carer, and that what she was giving me was an objective and rational account. 'The problems began when I tried to discourage Donna from continually fussing around the boys. She fussed around them so much that they really resented it. She also tried to discipline them, which they resented, and I stopped it. It was unhealthy; she wouldn't let them be, and she couldn't see that they were making fun of her. They are a bright pair and can easily get the better of her. I was very shocked when they admitted to Edna that they'd beaten her with a skipping rope. You know Edna came here and spoke to them?'

'Yes,' I said.

'The situation quickly deteriorated and really, Cathy, there was no way the three of them could stay together. Donna was trying to control not only the boys' lives but ours as well. My husband is a full-time carer and stood by me. But Donna even tried to order him around and resented either of us doing anything for the boys. She actually started to physically push us away if we went near Warren and Jason. We asked for her to be moved after a particularly ugly scene in the bathroom. Ray and I were trying to get the boys ready for bed. They were a bit hyper but no more so than usual. Donna wasn't having any of it. She came storming in and demanded to know what we were doing. She grabbed my arm and bent it back – I thought she was going to break it. Ray had to drag her off. I've still got the bruise.' Mary stopped as my worst fears were confirmed.

'Thank you, Mary,' I said slowly. 'I'm going to have to think carefully how to handle this.'

'How old are your children?' she asked.

'Six and ten.'

'I only have my seventeen-year-old son living with me now. I'd be very careful if I were you, Cathy. Donna's a big girl and could really hurt someone smaller.' She paused. 'Will she stay with you?'

'I hope so. I don't want her to feel rejected, but I'll have to see how it goes. Donna has obviously come from a highly abusive family, and I know it's not her fault, but I can't have my children placed in permanent danger.'

'No. Quite,' Mary said. 'Ray felt I had been placed in danger.'

I paused. 'Mary, one last thing. Edna mentioned the term OCD. I think you had suggested it?'

'Yes. Donna displayed some strange habits here. She kept washing her hands in a really agitated way, over and over again. I had seen a programme on television about OCD, and it looked very similar to what Donna was doing. Has she done that with you?'

'Not to my knowledge.'

'To be honest, it's the least of her problems. I think Donna is like a firework waiting to go off. Goodness knows what has gone on in that family, but I think Donna bore the brunt of it. I was sorry to see her go, but Ray and I couldn't have looked after her and the boys: it was impossible.'

'Yes, I understand. I'm going to have to make sure she doesn't try to replicate the situation here with my children, which is possible. Thanks for your time, Mary.'

'You're welcome. Please say hello to Donna for me. I've got my fingers crossed for you. I hope it works out. We'll probably bump into each other at school when the term starts.'

'Yes. Thanks,' I said again, and I slowly put down the phone.

As I did, I heard Donna's bedroom door open and she appeared on the landing. Very slowly she came downstairs. Her head was down and her shoulders were hunched forward; her whole stance was dejected, as it had been when she'd first arrived. She came to a halt just in front of me and slowly raised her head. Her large brown eyes were so full of sorrow my heart went out to her.

'I'm sorry, Cath-ie,' she said, pronouncing the two syllables separately. 'I'm sorry I hit Paula. Shall I say sorry to her?'

'In a minute, Donna. First I need to talk to you. Come with me into the lounge, please.'

Compliant and subdued, she followed me down the hall, and we sat together on the sofa. Outside the French windows the rain was sheeting down; today was set for a mixture of sunshine and showers.

I turned to her. 'Now listen, love. It's important you understand why you are saying sorry to Paula.'

'Because I hit Paula,' she said quietly.

'Yes, I know, but do you understand why it was wrong to hit Paula?'

Donna shrugged.

'Hitting hurts, obviously, you know that, but it also it makes that person afraid of you. You felt like that when your mother and Chelsea and your brothers hit you, didn't you?' Donna gave an almost imperceptible nod. 'It's an assault on the whole person and makes that person wary of you. You don't want Paula being afraid of you, do you? You want to play with her like a sister, and Adrian like a brother.'

Donna didn't say anything, so I continued with the second part of what I needed to say. 'Now, love, it's nice that you want to help me look after Adrian and Paula, but that's my job. I would like you to help in the house, but I will tell you what to do. We don't want Adrian and Paula feeling that you are bossing them around, do we? Because it's not nice to be bossed around and made to do things, is it? I'm sure you know that.' I hoped I was making sense.

Donna gave a short nod. 'Shall I say sorry to Paula now?' she asked.

'Yes, that would be nice. I'll call her down. But first let me give you a big hug. I want you to be happy here, just as I do Adrian and Paula, OK?'

Donna let me put my arms around her and I gave her a hug, although she didn't actually hug me back. Then, leaving her in the lounge, I went upstairs to fetch Paula. Whether I was getting through to Donna and could succeed where Mary and Ray hadn't remained to be seen. It appeared that Donna had come from a family that was highly abusive, where they had shown each other absolutely no respect, or kindness. It was a case of trying to undo all that and start over again – the process of socialisation that is begun in healthy families with the child is a toddler and continues through to adulthood.

Upstairs, Paula and Adrian were still engrossed in the Gameboy, the upset apparently receding with each new point scored on the game.

'Donna would like to say she is sorry,' I said. 'I have spoken to her and she understands it must never happen again. And, Adrian, I have also said she mustn't tell you or Paula what to do, and that I'm in charge. I shall be watching her carefully, all right?' I smiled and they smiled back; then Paula scampered off the bed and took my hand, and we went downstairs and into the lounge, where Donna was as I'd left her, on the sofa.

'I'm sorry, Paula,' Donna said as soon as we walked in.

'I forgive you,' Paula said, and she went over and planted a big kiss on Donna's cheek.

'Good girls,' I said.

Donna didn't say any more, so I left it at that and hoped that we could move on and put the incident behind us.

We didn't make the 11.00 a.m. showing of *The Lion King*, but went instead to the next showing of the film at 1.45 p.m. I bought popcorn and sat with Donna on one side of me and Adrian and Paula on the other. I was being careful, and had started the vigilance which I would keep up for as long as was necessary. I hoped that at some point in the future I would be able to relax my guard and the children would be able to play or be together again without me being present. But for the time being if they went anywhere together then I would be close by. I was grateful there was only a week until the start of the new school term, for it was going to be hard work having to be continually aware of where Donna was in the house or garden.

When we returned home after the film it was just gone 4.00 p.m. The sun had come out and the last of the rain had evaporated. The grass was dry enough to play on, and the children went outside, while I watched from the kitchen window as I prepared the vegetables and meat for the evening meal. Donna kept her distance, and once more sat on the bench on the patio while Adrian and Paula played. I hadn't stopped her playing with Adrian and Paula – indeed it would have been nice if she had joined in. But I would make sure she didn't keep organising Adrian and Paula, for then it was only a short step to dominating them, and possibly replicating what had happened at Mary and Ray's, with Donna trying to take over – using force if necessary.

We ate at 6.00 p.m., and then at 7.30 I began the bedtime routine. Leaving Donna in the lounge doing a jigsaw, I took Paula up first. Adrian had popped next door to play with Billy for a while, and when I called him back at 8.30, Donna had already taken her turn in the bathroom. Once Adrian had finished his shower I went in to say goodnight to him, and as I did I heard Donna's door open as she went out and into the toilet. When I'd finished saying goodnight to Adrian, and had also had a look at the illustrations in the book he was reading – *The Magician's Nephew* by C.S. Lewis – I came out and saw that the toilet door was still shut. Donna had been in there for over twenty minutes!

'Are you OK?' I called lightly, not wanting to wake Paula but wondering if Donna was feeling unwell.

There was no reply.

'Donna?' I said again, 'are you all right?'

There was still no reply, but I could hear the tap running. I knocked lightly on the door. Nothing. The locks on the toilet and bathroom doors (as in most foster carers' homes) were out of reach of the children as part of the safer caring policy so that children couldn't lock themselves in, either accidentally or in a fit of pique. 'Donna?' I said again, easing the door open and ready to close it again quickly if she was on the toilet.

But she wasn't on the toilet. She was standing beside the small hand basin, washing her hands. The plug wasn't in, and the hot water tap was on full. She stood with the nailbrush in one hand, roughly scrubbing the back of the other hand.

'Donna?' I asked.

There was no answer, but she kept scrubbing; then, turning her hand over, she continued on the palm and fingers. It wasn't normal washing: it was the same frenzied scrubbing I'd witnessed in the kitchen, only now it was directed at her hands and not the kitchen floor. As I watched, and she appeared oblivious to my presence, she swapped the nailbrush over and began on the other hand, scrubbing her skin with fierce determination and her face set hard.

My first reaction was to close the door and move away – it was as though I had looked in, and stumbled on, some private ritual. I felt I was a voyeuristic intruder, seeing something I shouldn't be party to. But as I looked, I saw that the light brown skin on her hands was now red and angry with scratches from the nailbrush. I knew that what she was doing wasn't healthy and she needed to stop.

'Donna,' I said firmly, 'stop that now.' I didn't want to go too close in case she lashed out at me, as she had done with Mary. 'Donna, don't do that,' I said again. 'You are making your hands very sore.'

She continued. I went closer, and then, risking a thump, I placed my hand on her arm. 'Please stop. Your hands are clean now. You are making them sore.'

'They're not clean,' she suddenly blurted while still scrubbing. 'They're dirty. Mum says I have to get the dirt off.'

'Donna, your hands are clean,' I said, keeping my voice even. 'Please stop it now.' I reached over and switched off the tap, half expecting her to push me, or grab my hand, or hit me. She didn't, nor did she try to turn on the tap again, but she carried on scrubbing her hands with the nailbrush, over and over again. I could see the scratch marks the nylon bristles were making and the angry red weals. 'That's enough,' I said. Then I slowly took the nailbrush from her hands, and reaching for the towel, folded her hands in it. 'Let's dry them,' I said, lightly patting the towel. 'You've made your hands so sore.' I carefully dried her hands, and she didn't resist. Then I returned the towel to the rail and looked at her hands. Both sides of both hands were an angry red; had she gone on scrubbing for much longer I was sure she would have drawn blood. 'Come on, love,' I said. 'Let's get you into bed. It's been a bit of a rough day for you.'

I led Donna into her bedroom and turned back the sheet. She slowly, compliantly, climbed into bed. I sat on the edge of the bed, and she put her head on the pillow and seemed to relax a little. I stroked her forehead. 'What's the matter, love?' I asked gently. 'Can you tell me?'

A tear escaped and ran down her cheek, then another. 'Mum says I have to wash all the dirt off, but it won't come off. I keep trying.'

'Darling, your hands are spotlessly clean,' I said. 'I expect they are even cleaner than mine.' I was trying to put the incident into perspective, lighten her mood, and possibly even diffuse her obsession and raise a smile. I placed my own hands palms upwards on the pillow to show her. 'Look, no one's hands are spotless all the time.' She drew her left hand from beneath the sheet and placed it, palm upwards, next to mine. 'It's not so bad on this side,' she said, referring to her palm, 'but it's the other side. Mine is dirty, not like yours.'

I frowned, puzzled; her hands were perfectly clean, although red from the scrubbing. Mary's suggestion of OCD hung in the air. Donna turned her hand over so that it was palm down and I did the same with mine. Her hand was of course clean, although her skin was a little darker than mine because she was of dual heritage. I looked at our hands side by side on the pillow and was about to reassure her again that her hands were clean when, with a stab of horror, I realised what she meant.

Chapter Nine

Outcast

'And Donna's mother has convinced her that's she's dirty, and has to scrub it off! It's her natural colour, and the poor girl has been trying to get rid of it! It's nothing to do with OCD. Donna is trying to wash away her skin colour!'

I was on the phone to Edna at 9.30 the following morning, so incensed that I was nearly shouting down the phone.

'I've been up half the night trying to convince her it's natural, and something to be proud of. Do you know her mother even gave her wire wool in the bath, and told her to keep scrubbing until she was as white as her! What the hell is wrong with that woman? She wants locking up! And what about the boys? They're dual heritage too, aren't they? Have they been told to scrub off their skin colour?' I could feel my heart pounding and my cheeks flushing.

'No,' Edna said evenly, 'the boys don't do that. Mary would have said.'

'Well? Does Chelsea do it? Has Rita told her she's dirty too?'

'No,' said Edna subdued. 'I don't think so.'

'Edna, Donna has been victimised by that family at every conceivable level – whipped for not doing the housework, made to feel responsible for them coming into care and told she is dirty because her grandmother is black! I assume Rita didn't think Donna's father was dirty when she slept with him! It's just as well I don't have to meet Donna's mother at contact! She has a lot to answer for.' I stopped and wondered if I had gone too far, but I was seething, on Donna's behalf. I took a breath. 'Donna is completely messed up. She has spent her whole life being vilified, and being told she is rubbish. I think you had better get her some therapy fast before it's too late, because I don't know how to deal with this. Someone needs to try to undo some of the damage that has been done to her, and I'm no psychologist!'

Edna hesitated. 'I'll raise the possibility of therapy with my manager,' she said quietly, 'but as you know, Cathy, they don't usually like to put children into therapy until they are settled. After the final court hearing, when we know where Donna will be living, would be the usual time. Donna is on an Interim Care Order and Rita has the right to object to anything we do. If I suggest therapy I'll lose what little cooperation I have from her.'

I seethed some more, but I knew from experience that Edna was right on both counts. While Donna was on an ICO her parents maintained certain rights to her and could raise all sorts of objections. Rita could make life very difficult for all concerned, not least for Donna, who would still be seeing her mother at contact. I also knew that therapists were reluctant to begin therapy until the court had made a decision about the child's future, and the child was settled wherever the judge decided they would be living. It was generally held that to begin therapy before then would be like lifting the lid on Pandora's box and could actually make the child more disturbed.

'I assume Donna won't be returning to Rita's care after all this?' I said.

'At this point we don't know. But it's looking increasingly doubtful.' Which was as much as Edna could say at present, until all the reports had been compiled and put before the judge at the final court hearing.

'Has the date for the final hearing been set yet?' I asked, calming my tone and looking at the practical issues.

'It's provisionally booked for next May,' Edna said, still subdued. 'Can I come to visit you and Donna tomorrow?'

'Yes, please. Jill is coming in the morning. Could you make it after one o'clock so that we can have some lunch?'

'Would two o'clock be all right?'

'Fine. I'll put it in the diary.'

'And I will speak to my manager about the therapy,' Edna finished by saying. 'But in the meantime if there is anything I can do, please let me know. And obviously I'll talk to Donna when I see her and reinforce what you have said.'

'OK, Edna.' There was nothing else I could say, other than asking if Donna could start her life over again in different circumstances, which unfortunately Edna couldn't make happen.

'Thank you, Cathy. See you tomorrow, and say hello to Donna for me.'

'I will do.'

I continued to watch Donna like a hawk, for her benefit as much as for Adrian's and Paula's. I knew where she was at any given moment and also what she was doing. Gone was any thought of simply letting the three of them amuse themselves, so I arranged games which we all played together, although Donna had difficulty 'playing' as such, presumably because she had never played as a small child. But at least she joined in, and went through the motions, and I hoped that by doing so one day she would find real enjoyment in playing. I organised rounders, bat and ball, basketball and, when it rained, Monopoly and jigsaw puzzles. It was obviously important that the children played as naturally as possible, but I hoped my being in charge would help reinforce in Donna's eyes the difference between my adult role and hers as a child.

I would have played with the children anyway, for some of the time, but having to do it continuously was pretty exhausting and meant that I had to catch up on the house-work in the evening when they were in bed. However, some of the chores, like preparing the vegetables, dusting and tidying, became a group activity: I gathered everyone together and gave them a task each, while watching that Donna didn't dominate.

I removed the nailbrush from the wash basin in the toilet, and also the pumice stone from the bathroom, which could have done great damage if Donna had set about using it to try to remove her skin colour. When Donna went upstairs to go to the toilet, or when she had a bath, I found an excuse to hover on the landing, and I listened for any sounds that might have suggested she was trying to scrub off her skin. I reinforced to Donna that children weren't allowed in the kitchen when I wasn't there, again separating our roles, and at every opportunity I praised her, and particularly her appearance. We went shopping, and I bought her a new skirt and blouse and told her how pretty she looked, which Paula reinforced. I told Donna I would buy her new school uniform on the first day of the term because, as with most junior schools now, the logoed uniform could only be bought from the school office, to help raise school funds.

How much of my positive encouragement to raise Donna's self-image was getting through to her was difficult to say. Donna met any praise or encouragement with a bashful, very doubtful shrug – hardly surprising considering I was trying to undo ten years of abuse. Her self-esteem and confidence were zero, and if I asked her to do anything her first reaction was 'I can't' or 'I don't know how.'

Jill and Edna came as arranged and by the end of the day I felt we had all been over 'social workered'. It was a relief when Edna finally left at 4.15 p.m., having spent over two hours with us, an hour of it alone with Donna in the lounge. It is usual for the social worker to spend time alone with the looked-after child in case the child wants to raise any issues that they would feel uncomfortable about raising with the carer present. I knew Edna would be talking to Donna about what had happened recently, and also continuing my efforts to improve Donna's self-image.

'You look lovely,' Edna said to Donna, not for the first time, as we finally saw Edna to the door. But Edna's compliment was met with the same self-deprecating shrug that met all my attempts to raise Donna's self-esteem.

Jill had also praised Donna when she'd visited that morning. Jill's primary responsibilities were to check that the placement was progressing as it should and that I had all I needed to care for Donna, and to offer me support and advice where necessary. As I had kept Jill and Edna

updated on a daily basis, when Jill checked my log notes
there were no surprises. She signed and dated my record,
and I returned the file to the locked drawer of my desk in
the front room. Jill had also been in regular phone contact
with Edna, so both were fully abreast of what was going
on.

I had raised the matter of the forthcoming school run
with Edna because I had realised that the logistics of dropping Adrian and Paula off at their school, which was in the
opposite direction to Donna's and had the same start time
of 8.50 a.m., were going to cause me a problem. Foster
carers normally take their foster children to school, as they
would their own children, but sometimes that was physically impossible, as it would be in this case, without Donna
or Adrian and Paula arriving very late. In situations like
this approved escorts are used to take the foster child to
school, although this is avoided wherever possible: not
only is it a heavy call on the social services' budget –
approved escorts are very expensive – but it is clearly
preferable for the looked-after child to have their carer (*in
loco parentis*) standing in the playground with the other
mothers rather than being collected by a taxi.

Fortunately my problem was solved when Edna said
that Donna enjoyed helping at the breakfast club at her
school and would like to continue to do this. The breakfast
club started at 8.15 a.m., so I could drop Donna off first
and then take Adrian and Paula to their school for 8.50.
This arrangement wouldn't be necessary on the first day,
however, as Donna's school went back a day before Adrian
and Paula's. I asked my neighbour, Sue, if Adrian and Paula
could stay with her for an hour while I took Donna to
school on that first morning. Sue was happy to oblige: we

helped each other out from time to time, although I could never have left a looked-after child with Sue because she wasn't an approved carer.

Donna had contact on Friday, as she had done on Wednesday, and following the same routine I took her in and left her with Edna in reception. As before, Donna was quiet in the car on the way home and I was particularly vigilant for the remainder of the evening. I was aware that, despite Edna supervising the contact, Donna had just seen her family, which could have easily reinforced all her feelings of worthlessness. I felt it wouldn't be long before Donna started to make comparisons between the life she had led at home and the one she led now. When she saw the hurt and injustice that had been inflicted on her I was expecting an explosion of unprecedented anger, for as Mary had said Donna was like a firework waiting to go off.

It was with some relief that I would no longer have to be ever vigilant, and also with some regret that the lazy unstructured days of the summer holidays had come to an end, that on the following Wednesday morning I had everyone up, dressed, washed and breakfasted by 8.00. I took Adrian and Paula next door to be looked after by Sue at 8.20. Donna's school's breakfast club didn't begin until the second day of term, so we left a bit later on that first day. I drove the fifteen-minute journey to Belfont School and arrived at 8.35. I had plenty of time to buy the uniform and introduce myself to the head before the day started at 8.50. I parked in a side road a short distance from the school as a few children in their uniforms strolled past with their mothers.

'OK, love?' I asked Donna, silencing the engine and glancing at her in the rear-view mirror. 'I'm looking forward to meeting your headmistress again. I wonder if she will remember me?'

'Do you know Mrs Bristow?' Donna asked.

'I used to. I looked after a boy a few years ago who went to your school. He won't still be there now, though: he's fourteen and at secondary school.'

'Mrs Bristow is nice.'

'Yes, very,' I agreed. 'It's a good school. I know you are going to do really well this term.'

Donna gave her usual self-deprecating shrug, which she gave at any suggestion she might actually be good at something. I got out of the car and then went round and opened her door, which had the child lock on. She stood beside me on the pavement and looked at the other children heading towards the school. 'Let me know when you see your friend, Emily,' I said, 'and I'll say hello.' Donna nodded.

We went to the end of the road then turned the corner that would take us towards the main gates. As we did, Donna let out a small cry and her face suddenly lit up.

'There's Mum!' she cried. 'And Warren and Jason! And Aunt May, and Granny Bajan!'

I looked, and saw the group standing directly in front of the school gates. Oh dear, I thought, and on our first morning! Foster carers do run into looked-after children's natural families, and in some instances it doesn't matter. Indeed, in the past I had worked closely with children's natural parents, and it was always preferable for the child to see everyone cooperating. But this appeared to be a welcoming party of unprecedented proportions – at least I hoped it was welcoming. To deal with it I would have to put aside my own feelings towards Rita for Donna's sake. I would also have to make Edna aware of this meeting; Donna's contact was carefully supervised and this unscheduled contact clearly would not be.

Donna had quickened her pace and nearly ran the last few steps towards the chatting, laughing throng. As I approached, I searched the gathering of six adults, a teenager and two boys, trying to identify who was who among the adults. Granny Bajan from Barbados, Donna's gran on her father's side, stood on the edge of the group. She was a plump, kindly-looking woman, in her late fifties and very dignified; she greeted Donna with a big hug and then looked at me.

'Hello, I'm Cathy, Donna's carer,' I said.

Mrs Bajan smiled. 'Nice to meet you, Cathy.' Her Caribbean accent caused her words to rise and fall like music. 'But this is so sad,' she added, and I assumed she meant the children being in care.

A smartly dressed middle-aged white couple on my right introduced themselves as Mary and Ray and we shook hands.

'Quite a welcoming committee,' Ray said quietly and I smiled. I looked at Jason and Warren, aged six and seven; with their big brown eyes and sweet open faces, it was very difficult to imagine how they had perpetrated the abuse they had on Donna. But then, at their ages, in a dysfunctional family where morality, respect and kindness were in short supply they had doubtless simply followed the example of their mother and done as she had bade. Removed from that situation and now living with Mary and Ray, and being shown the correct and loving way to

behave, they would hopefully eventually change their ways
– they were young enough to relearn how good families
worked. I felt no anger towards them.

Jason and Warren were all over the person I now took
to be their mother, Rita, and she was all over them.

'Is that mum?' I asked Mary and Ray quietly.

They nodded. 'And that woman next to her is Rita's
neighbour,' Mary said. 'Not sure yet who the other woman
is. We got here just before you.'

I looked at Rita. I knew from the Essential Information
Forms that she was in her early thirties, but she could have
easily been fifteen years older. She was a short dumpy
woman, badly overweight, and with long unkempt thin fair
hair straggling around her shoulders. She was wearing a
faded cotton T-shirt and a short skirt, both of which were
stretched tightly across her stomach and hips. The T-shirt
had risen up to reveal a pierced belly button and stretch
marks. She had an arm around each of the boys and could-
n't get enough of them. I noticed she had completely
ignored Donna's arrival. Donna, having received a hug
from Granny Bajan, now stood watching her mother and
the boys, perhaps waiting for her turn to be hugged,
although she didn't seem to be expecting it.

'Hello, Rita,' I said, taking a step forward. 'I'm Cathy,
Donna's carer.' Rita ignored me and continued hugging
and tickling the boys. I thought they were going to be well
hyped up by the time they got into school, and I wondered
what the other parents and children who were passing on
their way in were making of this noisy gathering.

Beside Rita stood a teenage girl, also badly overweight,
and with her stomach showing and revealing a similar
piercing. She was chewing gum and staring into space, and

I could see the likeness Edna had spoken of. Without doubt it was Chelsea, and she looked like Donna, more than Donna looked like her brothers, although Donna, Warren and Jason were supposed to have the same father.

'You must be Chelsea?' I said, smiling. She glared at me and continued chewing; I guessed she had assumed her mother's hostility towards me. Apart from the neighbour that Ray had pointed out, another white woman stood on the edge of the group. I took her to be in her forties; she had blonde hair and a walking stick. I looked at her and she made eye contact.

'I'm May, Donna's aunt,' she said. I smiled and nodded, and remembered that Donna had said she went to her aunt's sometimes for her meals; I wondered if this was the same aunt. I didn't know if May and Rita were sisters; I couldn't see any family likeness.

I looked again at Donna, who still hadn't been acknowledged by her mother but was clearly hoping that at some point Rita would leave the boys and at least look at her. I saw Mary and Ray looking at Donna too. I felt dreadfully sorry for her as she stood like an outcast on the edge of the group, while her two brothers competed for, and enjoyed, their mother's attention.

'How are you, Donna?' Mary asked. 'You're looking great.'

Donna gave a shy half nod.

'She is doing very well,' I said, loud enough for Rita to hear. 'I am so pleased with her progress.'

'That's excellent,' Ray and Mary both said. Rita said nothing and didn't even glance up.

It was nearly 8.45 a.m. and I was becoming mindful of the time. I wanted to go into reception before the bell rang to buy Donna's uniform and make sure the school had my contact details, and also hopefully say hello to the head, Mrs Bristow. Donna would see her brothers later in the playground and also at lunchtime, and given that Rita was ignoring her, and no one else seemed in any rush to speak to her now that her gran had given her a hug and Mary and Ray had said hello, I thought there didn't appear to be much point in hanging around. Indeed there was every reason why we shouldn't: with each passing minute, as Donna stood on the edge of the group and was ignored, her rejection seemed more pronounced and pathetic. She looked so sad and I felt the indignation of her exclusion even if she didn't.

'Donna,' I said, 'I think we should go into school now so that I can buy your uniform.' She glanced at me and then looked anxiously at her mother, clearly hoping that her mother would seize this last opportunity to at least say hello, if not hug her, as she was still doing with the boys. Despite the appalling treatment Donna had received at the hands of Rita, Rita was still her mother, and there was doubtless a bond there. Time and time again I had looked after children who had been dreadfully neglected and abused but had still maintained a bond with their parents, and still sought their approval, affection and attention. Only in the absolute worse cases of horrendous (often sexual) abuse did children sever the bond as soon as they could and reject the parents. What I had seen happen, though (and what I thought might happen in Donna's case), was that as time went by and the child started to make comparisons, and judgements on the way they had been treated, they reduced their dependency on their parents and the bond weakened, disappearing altogether if the child was adopted or placed with long-term carers. But for now Donna craved the attention of her mother, and it was pathetic to watch her being ostracised.

'Donna,' I said again, moving closer to her. 'We really need to go now.'

'Yes, and we should be going in too,' Mary said.

It was always difficult ending these impromptu meetings; in contact the start and end times of the session were clearly stated to everyone, and strictly adhered to. 'Come on, Donna,' I said again.

It wasn't Donna who spoke next, but Rita. 'Come on, boys,' she said, 'give me one last hug.' She drew them to her and at the same time, looked over their heads to Donna. 'And you can piss off, you cunt,' she sneered, and then she spat.

I gasped. Ray and Mary looked at each other, horrified, and Granny Bajan said, 'May the Lord forgive you, Rita.' The neighbour remained impassive, as though it was a run-of-the-mill comment that she'd heard before. And Aunt May said, 'Rita,' in a cautionary tone. Chelsea grinned maliciously while Donna simply stood there, as though half-expecting this or something similar.

I touched Donna's arm. 'Come on, love,' I said quietly. 'Let's go in now.'

With a final glance at her mother, who was still cuddling the boys, Donna came with me, and I quickly led the way up the short path to the main entrance. The door opened as we approached and Mrs Bristow appeared.

'I was just coming out,' she said, looking worried. 'Are you all right?'

I nodded. Although Mrs Bristow couldn't have heard Rita's comment, being a very experienced head she would have been aware that the meeting was not advisable at any level, and undoubtedly had had to deal with similar situations with looked-after children before. 'Perhaps I could have a word with you once I've got Donna settled,' I said.

Mrs Bristow nodded, but she was still anxiously watching Ray and Mary through the window in reception. They were trying to persuade the boys away from Rita. After another few moments the boys broke away and ran down the path and round the side of the building towards the playground, followed by Ray and Mary. Rita and her gathering slowly turned and wandered off.

Mrs Bristow let out a quiet sigh of relief and returned her attention to us. 'It's lovely to see you, Donna, and to see you again, Cathy.' We shook hands, and she gave Donna a hug. 'Edna has given me your contact details,' she said to me. 'And I understand you want to buy Donna a new uniform.' She smiled at Donna. 'That will be nice, won't it?'

'Yes,' I said and I smiled too, hoping that an entire new school uniform might in some small way be recompense for her mother's atrocious rejection and comment. I was still appalled and shaken by what I had just seen and heard; I would obviously be logging the details and my observations in my notes when I returned home, and also making Edna aware of it.

Mrs Bristow took us through to the office. Kay, the school secretary, remembered me; we exchanged greetings and she too gave Donna a big hug. 'Good to see you again, Donna,' she said, 'and looking so well.' Kay was lovely, warm and welcoming, exactly what a school secretary should be. I guessed she had a soft spot for Donna and her brothers, as she had done for the last child I'd looked after who had gone to the school. Edna had said that Donna liked school very much; clearly school had been her lifeline. For so many children who have appalling home lives, school is often the one place that can be relied upon to be constant, safe and secure.

Mrs Bristow left us and said she would be back later when I had sorted out the uniform. Kay took us through to the stock room, where I bought two school sweatshirts, three T-shirts to go underneath, two skirts, PE kit and a bag to put the kit in, together with another bag for Donna's reading book and homework; all of it was navy, with the school's logo in red.

Donna changed into the uniform, and Kay and I said how smart she looked; Donna dismissed the compliment with her usual self-effacing shrug. Kay gave me a carrier bag for the clothes Donna had changed out of, and we returned with Kay to the office, where I wrote a cheque for the uniform and accessories. Foster carers receive a grant to cover most of the cost of a new uniform. The bell had rung and Kay suggested Donna now went straight through to join her class. I gave Donna a hug, told her again how smart she looked and said I would be waiting in the playground for her at the end of school. I watched her disappear through the door that would take her to the classroom.

'Poor kid,' Kay said once Donna had left us.

'Yes,' I agreed. 'And do you know what her mother said to her?' I was fuming, at last able to give vent to my fury. 'I can't believe it!'

'I can guess,' Kay said dryly.

'I won't repeat it, but it was foul.'

Kay nodded, and by her expression I could see that she had probably had similar dealings with Rita. 'It's the drink,' she said.

I said nothing; drink or not, it was a dreadful expression to use, especially to a child. I considered it the worst of all swear words, and for a mother to use it to her daughter was abominable.

Kay sorted out and gave me various printed sheets – a list of term dates for the year, forthcoming school events and PTA activities, and a copy of the school's new prospectus. Mrs Bristow reappeared and suggested we went into her office for a quick chat. Her office was as I remembered it from five years before: carpeted in bright red, the walls adorned with children's work, and with an area with toys for young children to play while their parents talked to her.

'I'm still reeling from the way Rita spoke to Donna,' I said as we sat down in the armchairs (I couldn't remember Mrs Bristow ever sitting behind her desk – she was far too 'user-friendly'). 'You will never believe what she called Donna! And she didn't even say hello, let alone hug her.'

Mrs Bristow looked at me, sombre and concerned. 'Donna has been so badly treated by that family,' she said. 'I raised my fears about her and the boys when they first joined the school. I can't tell you how relieved I am that the children have finally been taken into care. Why did Donna have to leave Mary and Ray's?'

'There were some problems between her and the boys,' I said. 'I don't know all the details.' And I left it at that. If Edna hadn't seen the need to give Mrs Bristow all the details, it wasn't incumbent on me to do so. Although Mrs Bristow was a caring and highly professional head, I didn't want Donna's reputation in any way sullied at school by my describing her aggressive behaviour at her previous foster home. Donna had moved on from that and I was dealing with her aggression and other issues at my home. At school Donna could just be Donna, a ten-year-old who would improve and make the most of her education. I felt sure that if there were any issues at school in respect of Donna's behaviour then Mrs Bristow would tell me. I doubted there were, though, because, as with many children like Donna, she had been operating a double standard – between acceptable behaviour at school and what went on at home.

'I want to help Donna all I can with her school work,' I said. 'I understand she is in the year below the group for her age?'

'Yes,' Mrs Bristow confirmed. 'Donna has mild learning difficulties, but to be honest I think a lot of her poor learning ability has been a result of her home life. Now she's settled with you I'm sure she'll make huge progress.' Which was exactly my feeling. Then Mrs Bristow spent some time telling me about Donna's strengths and weaknesses in her school work, and said that she would give me a copy of Donna's PEP (Personal Education Plan), which all looked-after children have. It would help me to work alongside the school and reinforce the work her teacher was concentrating on.

'Do you think Rita will be outside the school again?' Mrs Bristow finished by asking.

'I've no idea,' I said. 'I hope not. Donna and her brothers have supervised contact on Mondays, Wednesdays and Fridays. We can do without that every morning.'

'I'm thinking it might be better if you and Mary and Ray used the staff entrance to enter and leave by. It's at the rear of the school and is security locked. I could give you the pass number. Rita has already been warned by Edna that she is not allowed on the school premises or else I will call the police, which is presumably why she waited outside this morning and not in the playground.'

'I would appreciate that,' I said. 'It was very unpleasant for Donna. I understand Donna helps out at breakfast club, so we will be coming early in future.'

'Yes, at eight fifteen. I'll update the class teacher, Beth Adams. She's hoping to meet you briefly at the end of school.'

Mrs Bristow wrote down the security code for the staff entrance on a piece of paper; we said goodbye and I left the building. Outside there was no sign of Rita, but then she had come to see the boys, not Donna and me.

I drove home, now even more aware of the dreadful injustice that had been inflicted on Donna by her mother, and telling myself it was little wonder Donna behaved as she did sometimes. I collected Adrian and Paula from my neighbour, and then the three of us spent a leisurely afternoon in and around the house and garden. And it would be dishonest of me not to admit that it was a lot easier to have just Adrian and Paula, and not have to be continually vigilant. However, I remained hopeful that, given time, Donna would improve to the point where I could trust her again with Adrian and Paula.

When I returned to collect Donna at the end of school, I took Adrian and Paula with me; they were keen to see Donna's school and also I didn't feel I could ask my neighbour to look after them again. They were most impressed when I drove into the staff car park, and even more so when I keyed in the security number and let us in through the staff gate. We waited in the playground with the other parents for Donna's class to come out, and when Donna appeared and saw the three of us I thought she looked just a little bit proud. She came over and said 'Hi,' to Adrian and Paula, as other children were greeting their younger siblings.

Beth Adams, Donna's class teacher, followed Donna out and came over and introduced herself. She was in her twenties and very pleasant; she told me she was from New Zealand, and was here on a year's contract with her husband. I said again that I wanted to help Donna with her school work, and she said she would put extra work sheets in Donna's reading folder, and also that there would be set homework, and Donna was expected to read her book every night. I thanked her for all she was doing for Donna, and the four of us then left the school by the staff entrance, with the children feeling somewhat aloof at their new elevated status.

That evening over dinner I casually asked Donna if Aunt May, whom I had met that morning, was the same aunt she had sometimes visited for her meals.

Donna nodded. 'She uses a walking stick because she's got a plastic foot. Warren used to run off with the foot and hide it.'

I smiled at this childish, if not a little unkind, prank.

Adrian giggled. 'Why has she got a plastic foot?' he asked, while Paula sat there looking nonplussed, having no idea what a plastic foot was.

"Cos her other one got burnt off when she was a baby,' Donna said. 'Her mum hung her over the fire and it got burnt off.'

We stopped eating. 'No! Surely not?' I said. 'That sounds to me like the story of Pinocchio, who sat too close to the fire.' Adrian nodded, Donna shrugged and the subject was left at that.

Later Paula asked me what a plastic foot was and I explained about prostheses and how some people didn't have limbs, without going into too much detail, which could have been upsetting for a child of six. The following day when I spoke to Edna and told her, among other things, about the 'welcoming party' at school, she confirmed Donna's account of how Aunt May had lost her foot. As a baby it had been so badly burned when her mother (who was also Rita's mother) had held May over a coal fire that it had had to be amputated. The family had a history of abuse that went back three generations.

Chapter Ten

Tablets

The routine of our school week began in earnest the following day when I woke Adrian, Paula and Donna at 7.00 a.m., and had them dressed, washed and breakfasted and in the car by 7.50. I saw Donna into her school to help with the breakfast club at 8.15; then I drove back to Adrian and Paula's school to arrive at 8.40, which gave us ten minutes to mingle in the playground before the bell went at 8.50. In the afternoon I did the reverse, and first collected Adrian and Paula, who came out at 3.10 p.m., and then made a dash to Donna's school for her dismissal time of 3.30. This arrangement relied on Adrian and Paula coming out exactly on time, and I mentioned to Beth Adams that I might occasionally be a few minutes late, if the traffic was heavy or Adrian and Paula weren't dismissed at exactly 3.10. As it turned out, though, Donna was usually five or ten minutes late leaving the classroom, as she was always the one who volunteered to help clear up if the room was in a mess.

'Donna likes to help so much, doesn't she?' Beth Adams commented to me after school one day. 'She'll even give up her lunchtime if something needs doing; she's always asking me for jobs to do.' I agreed, although I felt that Donna's eagerness to clean and tidy wasn't altogether healthy, and was probably a legacy of her role at her mother's when cleaning had been her responsibility. I would rather have seen her stream out with the other children, not caring a damn about the state of the classroom and happy to leave it to someone else.

After a few days Donna pointed out her friend Emily to me and I introduced myself to her and her mother; they were both aware Donna was in foster care. Emily's mother, Mandy, was very friendly and told me about Emily's learning difficulties, and how she really appreciated Emily having Donna as her friend – someone her own age in the same class. I said it was important we kept their friendship going, and that I would like it very much if Emily could come to tea. Mandy agreed, but said that Emily was a little shy and asked if we could leave it until later in the term when Emily had resettled into the school routine. They were Polish and had spent the entire summer holidays in Poland, and Emily had found the transition back not an easy one. We always chatted briefly when we saw each other in the playground at the end of the school day.

On Mondays, Wednesdays and Fridays I had to do a quick turnaround after school because of Donna's contact. As soon as we arrived home at 4.00 p.m. Donna washed and changed, and then had her evening meal, ready to leave the house again at 4.40 for contact at 5.00. I had started giving Donna her evening meal before contact, as Edna had said that Donna was 'pigging out' on the biscuits at contact because she was hungry, and then feeling sick. Indeed, on more than one occasion when I'd collected her we'd had to drive home with the car window open as she had felt so rough, and then she hadn't wanted her dinner. On these evenings Paula, Adrian and I ate when we returned from taking Donna to contact and before we had to get back into the car to collect her. It was a rush, but Adrian and Paula had grown up being herded in and out of the car for contact, as do other children of foster carers. Contact always takes priority, even to the extent of rearranging and sometimes cancelling one's own appointments.

Our routine of school continued and accelerated towards the half-term holiday in October. The evenings vanished, for apart from the contact, which dominated three of the evenings, there was homework to be done, the evening meal to be cooked and eaten, baths to be had and the children's favourite television programmes to be watched, before we began the bedtime routine. I maintained my vigilance with Donna whenever she was with Adrian, and particularly when she was with Paula, for while we hadn't had another incident of Donna actually hitting Paula, Donna would still try to dominate and chastise Paula and tell her what to do, often repeating my instructions with a lot more authority than I had given them. So if I said to Paula, 'Come on, it's time to do your reading,' Donna would echo, 'Your mother told you to do your reading. Now!' To which I would gently reply, 'It's OK, Donna, I'll tell Paula. You don't have to, love.' I suppose Donna felt chastisement was part of the role of looking after younger siblings, which it had been when she'd been living at home. I hoped that this behaviour, like others, would diminish over time.

I continued to monitor Donna's washing: when she had a bath or went to the toilet I stood on the landing, listening for any sound that might have suggested she was washing with more vigour than she should – trying to rub her skin colour off again; although having removed the nailbrushes and pumice stone I felt there was less chance of her doing real damage to herself with the sponge and flannels that were left. I also remained concerned about Donna's poor self-image – not only in respect of her dual heritage but also with her self-esteem in general, which was non-existent. Mrs Bristow assured me that she was already seeing positive changes in Donna and felt that she was gaining confidence. Her teachers and I praised Donna at every opportunity. I continued to give Donna little jobs to do in the house so that she felt she was helping, but I was gradually reducing these, hoping to wean her off her need for drudgery and subservience. When she performed a task her manner was so servile it was uncomfortable to watch. However, Donna wasn't ready to let go of this role yet, and in order to exorcise her compulsion she discovered a new behaviour which was quite bizarre.

I went up to her bedroom one day to find the whole room littered with hundreds of tiny bits of paper torn from old magazines, which she had bought with her pocket money.

'That's a right mess,' I said, not best pleased. 'And I've only just vacuumed.' The tiny bits of paper were everywhere – all over the floor, the bed, the bookshelves and every available surface.

'I'm going to clean it up,' she said laboriously, and immediately dropped onto all fours and began steadily picking up the tiny scraps of paper. Half an hour later the room was spotless again.

After that it became a regular pursuit: Donna spending thirty minutes tearing up the paper and then another thirty minutes clearing it up. When she had exhausted her own supply of magazines or drawing paper, she asked me if she could have the old newspapers, which I reluctantly gave her. I wasn't at all sure I should be encouraging this, for it seemed it could be reinforcing exactly the behaviour I was trying to persuade her out of – cleaning. I talked to Edna and Jill about it and they both thought that it was a pretty harmless way of her acting out her role from the past, and as long as it didn't escalate, to let her continue. They said that it should slowly disappear over time, but that if it didn't then it could be addressed at therapy when it was started after the final court hearing in May. I asked them if I should let her do more in the house, as it seemed to me that I might have caused this new development by stopping a lot of her 'housework', but they said no, it would be a retrogressive step, and I was handling it correctly. I told Adrian and Paula not to say anything or laugh if Donna's bedroom door was open and they saw her tearing up or picking up the paper for this was her way of dealing with her past.

'She can clean my room,' Adrian said to me with a cheeky grin.

'Absolutely not,' I said. 'That's your job.' But I knew Donna would have done it if he'd asked.

Apart from the times when Donna tried to tell Paula what to do or chastise her, she remained very quiet and compliant – too much so, I thought. Her voice was always flat and expressionless, even when there was a treat to be enjoyed, as though she didn't dare express any excitement or pleasure. I was sure, as Mary had been, that Donna was internalising a lot of her pain, frustration and anger, and that at some point it would explode.

* * *

I was right, and it happened in October, during the week's half-term holiday from school.

Donna's contact continued during half term, so I had to make sure that when we went out for the day on Monday, Wednesday and Friday we were back home relatively early. On Tuesday, when we weren't constrained by contact times, I took the opportunity of having a full day out, and we visited a theme park, which was about an hour's drive away. It was an excellent day, and I knew that Donna had enjoyed it as much as she could enjoy anything, although she hadn't said much and had needed a lot of persuasion to go on the rides.

On the way home Donna reminded me that she had contact the following day. 'I know, love,' I said. 'Don't worry, I won't forget.' She then said that her dad would be going and that he had been there on Monday. Her father had made intermittent appearances at contact, about every fourth one. I had never met Mr Bajan, but I knew he was the only one in the immediate family who hadn't abused Donna, and that his illness – paranoid schizophrenia – prevented him from taking a more prominent role in her life.

'He hasn't been taking his medication,' Donna said reflectively a short while later. 'I told him on Monday to take it. Otherwise Edna will have him locked up.' Donna was referring to her father being sectioned under the Mental Health Act, which seemed to happen a couple of times a year when he stopped taking his medication and began behaving irrationally and sometimes violently.

I glanced at Donna in the rear-view mirror. 'Edna doesn't have him locked up,' I said. 'When your dad doesn't take his tablets he can't cope, so he is taken into hospital. The doctors make sure he has his medicine and then he is well enough to go home again. Don't you worry: I'm sure Edna or your mum will tell him.'

Donna didn't say anything more in the car, but having been responsible for making sure her dad took his medication when she had been at home, she had clearly recognised the signs of him not having taken it, and this was proved the following day.

On Wednesday I took Donna to contact at 5.00 p.m., and I had just returned home when I got a phone call from Edna saying she was terminating contact immediately, and could I collect Donna straight away? Edna spoke quickly and anxiously – a sharp contrast to her usual calm and reassuring manner. She said she'd called the police and an ambulance for Mr Bajan, and that I should wait in the car outside the social services offices and Donna would be brought out to me. I told Adrian and Paula that Donna's father had been taken ill at contact, and we were going to collect her early, and to put on their shoes, which they had only just taken off. With mounting anxiety and no idea what to expect, I drove back to the offices in Belfont Road. As I turned into the road I saw two police cars and an ambulance parked on the forecourt at the front of the building. I pulled into the kerb a little way back and turned off the engine.

'Why are the police here?' Adrian asked.

'I think it's in case the ambulance crew need help,' I said, leaving it at that. I knew that sometimes schizophrenics could suffer from delusional hallucinations and become violent, but to talk about that to the children would have been frightening.

We sat in the car for about ten minutes, and I was expecting to see Donna appear at any minute with Edna.

Instead, after another few minutes the front door of the building suddenly burst open and, as we looked, two uniformed police officers came out, followed by another two, with a man I took to be Donna's father struggling between them. They were holding an arm each. He was a large man and appeared to be very strong. He was shouting and struggling, and trying to fight off the demons that clearly plagued him. 'Fuck off! Fuck off! I've told you! I'll have you crucified like him!' he yelled. He pulled and wrenched from side to side, and it was clear that it was all the officers either side of him could do to restrain him and stop him from breaking free. The officers were talking to him quietly, perhaps trying to reassure him, but I doubted he could hear over the noise of his shouting and wailing.

Behind them came the ambulance crew: two paramedics, one male and one female. There was no sign of Edna, Donna, Rita, Chelsea or the boys, all of whom had attended contact. Adrian, Paula and I watched, mesmerised and horrified by the scene. The female paramedic opened the ambulance doors and lowered the steps.

'Oh no! On no! Oh no!' Mr Bajan wailed. It was truly pitiful and frightening to watch. He struggled and cried out, pulling back from the steps of the ambulance. I thought that when he was well he would have the same dignity as his mother, for despite his illness he seemed a proud man and was smartly dressed in grey trousers and an open-neck shirt.

Adrian was at his side window, enthralled and appalled by what he was witnessing. Paula had slunk low in her seat with her hands pressed over her ears. 'He'll be all right. Don't worry,' I said, trying to reassure them, although I could feel my own heart racing; it was very upsetting. A young couple walking along the street hesitated, and then ran past the end of the forecourt.

Mr Bajan continued shouting as the two police officers guided him to the foot of the ambulance steps, ready to climb up, and then he set up the most dreadful wail. I could see his face contorted with pain and anger as he tried to fight off his internal tormentors. His skin ran with sweat and his eyes bulged. No wonder in bygone days it was thought the mentally ill were possessed. The poor man looked as though he was at the mercy of some unseen evil spirit that was hell-bent on destroying him and would stop at nothing to achieve it.

The other two officers helped, and it took all four of them to slowly manoeuvre Mr Bajan up the two steps and into the ambulance. The paramedics followed them in and closed the rear doors. I don't know what happened then; I assumed he was sedated, because a few minutes later the rear doors of the ambulance opened and all four police officers came out, together with the female paramedic, and it was quiet inside. She closed the ambulance doors and said something to the police officers; then she went to the driver's door of the ambulance and got in. Two of the officers got in one of the police cars, while the other two returned inside the building. The ambulance and police car pulled away from the forecourt and left with their blue lights flashing and sirens wailing.

'Cor,' Adrian said, impressed by the ambulance, as any boy his age would be.

I turned again to Paula in the back. 'It's OK, love. You can take your hands down now.'

She slowly lowered her hands from her ears. 'I don't like shouting,' she said in a small voice.

'No, I know. It's all right now. Mr Bajan was very upset and they are taking him to the hospital. The doctors will make him better.'

We sat in subdued silence for another ten minutes; then Edna appeared with Donna. She saw my car and, as she came over, I got out and stood on the pavement. I could see that Edna was maintaining a calm façade for Donna's sake, but her anxiety showed in her face. She was talking quietly to Donna as they approached, and Donna looked deathly pale.

'I'll phone you later,' Edna said to me, 'when I've finished here. Donna's very upset and I think she just needs to get home now.' She touched Donna's arm, and I opened the rear door of the car and waited while she got in. 'I'll speak to you later, Cathy,' Edna said again anxiously. 'I've still got the boys, Rita and Chelsea inside.'

'All right, Edna. Don't worry.'

She returned into the building as I got into the car.

'Are you all right?' I asked Donna gently.

She shrugged. Paula and Adrian were looking at her with sympathy and concern.

'Let's get home,' I said, and I started the engine.

Donna didn't say anything during the twenty-minute journey home. She sat beside Paula, with her head down and hands clasped tightly together in her lap. When we arrived home and I opened the front door, she went straight up to her bedroom. A minute later I heard a loud bang come from her room, quickly followed by another and another. Telling Adrian to stay with Paula in the lounge, I shot upstairs. Donna was screaming now at the top of her voice; giving a brief knock on her door, I opened it.

She was darting around her bedroom, screaming, and picking up anything and everything that came within reach and hurling it against the walls. 'Donna!' I said loudly. 'Stop that.' She glanced at me but continued screaming and throwing everything that came to hand – the portable CD player, her crayons, books and games, her teddy and the china ornaments she'd started collecting with her pocket money. I stayed by the door, not daring to go further in, in case her anger turned on me. She pulled the sheet off the bed and ripped it, her teeth gritted, her face set hard. 'Donna!' I said again. 'Stop! Donna, now!' She went to the curtains and yanked one down with such force that the rail came out of the wall in a shower of plaster. 'Donna! Stop it! Do you hear me!' My heart was pounding and my mouth was dry.

Suddenly she froze, the screaming stopped, and she dropped to her knees and began sobbing uncontrollably. She was bent forward, clutching her head in her hands and rocking back and forth.

I slowly went in and towards her as her sobbing grew. I knelt beside her, and then tentatively placed my hand on her shoulder. Her head was down and she was rocking and crying. I began lightly rubbing her back. 'It's OK, love,' I soothed. 'I understand. It'll be all right now.' She continued to rock and cry, and I slowly slid my arm around her shoulders. Gradually the sobbing eased. 'Donna, look at me, love,' I said gently and, placing my hands on hers, I slowly lowered them from her face. Her eyes were red and swollen and her breath was coming fast and shallow. 'Everything is all right now.' I drew her to me and she allowed her head to rest on my shoulder.

'I told Dad to take his tablets,' she said between sobs. 'I told him on Monday. Mum doesn't tell him. She's useless. She only thinks about the boys. He needs to take his tablets. It's my fault.' Her body stiffened and she was digging her nails into the palms of her hands.

'Donna, love, I know you told him, but it's not your fault. Your daddy is a grown man. Somehow he will have to find a way to remember to take his tablets. The doctors will help him work it out.'

She gave a dismissive shrug and I felt pretty impotent. I knew from what Edna has said that periods of Mr Bajan not taking his medication had been a pattern of their lives, and with no one at home now to remind him to take them, it was a pattern that was likely to continue. Schizophrenia is a controllable disease, thanks to modern medicine, and it was so sad that Mr Bajan's life and the lives of his children continued to be blighted by something as simple as remembering to swallow some tablets.

'Will I get it, and be like him when I'm older?' Donna said suddenly. She had stopped rocking and turned to look at me.

'No, love. Absolutely not.'

'Mum says it's in his family, and I'll end up as loony as him. She says I already am, and sometimes I think she's right. I think and do weird things.'

'No,' I said firmly again. 'You won't. There's nothing wrong with you, Donna, and there won't be.'

'Mum says I'm a nutter already,' Donna said. 'She says I should be locked up like him.'

I stopped myself from vilifying her mother. 'Donna, that was a very unkind thing for her to say, and it certainly isn't true. Trust me, you are doing fine, and once your dad starts taking his tablets again he will be fine too.'

She seemed to accept this, and I thought that the next time I spoke to Edna I would ask her to reinforce to Donna what I had said. For it is often the case with a medical condition that if you believe you are suffering from it, you can start to imagine the symptoms developing.

'Has that been worrying you?' I asked gently. 'That you might develop the illness your dad has?'

She nodded. 'Mum says I have it, and that's why I'm so odd.'

'And does she say that about Warren and Jason too?'

'No.'

Which I thought was interesting, considering they were supposed to have the same father and therefore the same possible genetic susceptibility.

'Donna, it was a very unkind thing to say, and it certainly isn't true. You are one of the healthiest people I know, and Edna says so too. You have been through so much at home and now you are doing really well.'

'You know Mum didn't want me, Cathy?' she said. 'I was an accident. She tried to get rid of me by poking a knitting needle inside her, but it didn't work.'

I inwardly recoiled, and I wondered if Donna knew exactly what she was saying, but I wasn't about to explain abortion to a ten-year-old. 'That was a cruel thing to say,' I said. 'And I'm pleased it didn't work because otherwise I wouldn't have you here now. I like looking after you and I'm very glad you are living with us.'

She looked at me again, her eyes round and imploring. 'Are you? Are you really?' She was surprised.

'Yes, darling, I am. You are a lovely person and I know you are going to do very well.' I was pleased Donna was finding it easier to talk to me, and I hoped that by talking about her worries and what had happened she would start to find some release. I glanced around at the debris of her trashed bedroom.

'Mum had a hot bath and drank a bottle of gin as well,' Donna added, 'when the knitting needle didn't work. Why did she do that, Cathy?'

I hesitated. Donna clearly knew more than the average ten-year-old, but even so I didn't want to go into the gory details of abortion. 'She was trying to have what's called a termination,' I said. 'But I would like to leave telling you more about that until you are older. It would be easier then. Is that OK?'

She nodded, and then let out a little laugh.

'What is it?' I asked, surprised that anything could be funny in what she had just told me.

'Mum said it didn't work because there wasn't enough hot water. Chelsea had taken it all, so I guess I have to thank her for saving me. And Chelsea doesn't even like me!'

I marvelled at Donna's adult ironic humour. 'Well done Chelsea, I say! Donna, you are a lovely person and what-ever happened in the past is gone. Things will be much easier for you now, and that will help you get better at everything.' I put my arms around her and hugged her. She didn't return the hug, but neither did she immediately move away. We sat quietly for some time until she finally eased away.

'I'm tired, Cathy,' she said. 'Can I go to bed? I'll clear up in the morning.'

'Yes, love. Have an early night. And Donna, next time you feel really angry we'll find another way of letting it out. Like hitting a cushion hard, or running round and round the garden. It does help.'

She nodded. 'I'm sorry. I liked my bedroom.'

'OK, love. Now take your nightdress into the bathroom and get washed and changed while I find you a new sheet. The curtains will have to stay as they are for tonight. I'll see if I can fix the rail back on the wall tomorrow.'

'Sorry,' she said again, and taking her nightdress from under her pillow she went through to the bathroom.

I took a clean sheet from the airing cupboard and replaced the old one, which having been ripped in half would be consigned to the rag bag. I collected together all the broken pieces of ornaments and dropped them in the waste-paper basket, which I then put out on the landing ready to take downstairs. I didn't think Donna would use the broken china to self-harm, but I wasn't taking any chances. Although some of her anger had come out I knew there was still a long way to go before she was free of all the hurt, anger and rejection that must still be boiling inside her. I checked there was nothing sharp left in the room, looking under the bed, on the shelves and in the drawers. The portable CD player was miraculously still working, and the crayons and other things could be cleared up tomorrow. I left the curtain hanging off the rail; I'd have to fetch the stepladder from the shed in the morning and see if I could fix the bracket onto the wall with filler.

When Donna returned from the bathroom I tucked her into bed and kissed her goodnight. 'All right now, love?' I asked before I left.

She nodded. 'Night, Cathy. Will you say goodnight to Adrian and Paula for me?'

'Will do, love. Sleep tight.' I came out and closed the door.

I carried the waste-paper basket with the broken china downstairs and tipped the contents into the kitchen bin. I then went into the lounge, where I spent some time talking to, and reassuring, Adrian and Paula that Donna was all right, and so too would her father be now that he was in hospital.

At 8.00 p.m., just as I'd returned downstairs from seeing Adrian and Paula into bed, the phone rang. It was Edna, still at the office in Belfont Road. 'How is she?' she asked, sounding exhausted. I told her about Donna venting her anger on her room, and what she had said about her worries of mental illness, and her mother telling her about terminating the pregnancy. Edna listened in silence, occasionally tutting and sighing in dismay.

'Rita tried to blame Donna tonight for Mr Bajan's behaviour,' Edna said. 'Rita said, "Look what you've done now. It's your fault, you silly cow." I stopped her before she said anything else. I knew Mr Bajan hadn't been taking his medication as soon as he walked into contact. He was speaking on a toy mobile phone – you know, the ones that play ringing noises when you press the buttons. He said he was talking to God, only I don't think God could have got a word in edgeways over his continuous babble. Warren and Jason carried on playing; they're used to their father's behaviour. Rita and Chelsea told him he was a nutter and silly old fool and laughed at him. Donna was the one who tried to talk to him and look after him. I stopped the contact immediately.'

'How long will he be in hospital?' I asked.

'It's usually about three months before he is stabilised, but he might be discharged sooner.'

'Is there no way he can be reminded to take his medication?'

'Not while he is living with Rita. I am going to see if I can find him a place in sheltered accommodation, because this has been going on for too long now and he's having too many relapses. He lived with his mother for a while and she made sure he took his tablets, but she's away for most of the winter, and Mr Bajan keeps gravitating back to Rita. She doesn't remind him about his pills; she's got her own problems with the drink and drugs. The only one who helped him was Donna, and it's hardly the responsibility of a girl her age.'

'No. That's what I told her.'

Edna sighed. 'Anyway, I'm going home now, Cathy. I haven't had anything to eat all day and I've a report to write for another case which is due in court next week. I've been up until midnight writing reports every night for a week. Was there anything else, Cathy?'

'No. I'll tell Donna I've spoken to you.'

'Thanks. Goodnight, Cathy.'

I said goodnight, and as I went upstairs to check that Donna was asleep I thought how conscientious and hard-working Edna was. It was indicative of the huge workload social workers carried that in order to do her job properly Edna spent her days tending to the needs of her clients and her evenings catching up on the paperwork.

Chapter Eleven
A small Achievement

'Why don't you hit people?' Donna asked on Monday morning in the car on the way to school.

'Because it is an assault on the person; it hurts and makes them afraid of you. Talking is a better way of working out disagreements. It's wrong to hit another person, and certainly very wrong for an adult to hit a child.' I had said similar things to Donna when she'd first arrived and had viewed corporal punishment and physical violence as the norm, but often during car journeys Donna reflected on things and suddenly asked a question unrelated to anything immediate. Adrian and Paula did it too; I think the soporific motion of the car encourages reflection, and indeed my thoughts sometimes wander while I'm driving.

'But what if a child doesn't do as they're told?' Donna said. 'Shouldn't you hit them then?' Again, I had covered this previously, but clearly something was now gelling in Donna's mind.

'No, never. As a parent you have to be very patient and sometimes explain something over and over again. If a child still won't do as they are told, or they are being very naughty, then I find stopping a treat usually works wonders.' I glanced at Adrian in the rear-view mirror: he was sitting so quietly and angelically that he could almost have sprouted wings and a halo. He had recently been on the receiving end of my philosophy, and had lost thirty minutes of television time for continually kicking his football into the flowerbed when I'd asked him to use the goalposts at the bottom of the garden, which were away from the plants.

'My mum hit me,' Donna said, a short while later.

'Yes, I know, love.'

'So did Chelsea, Warren and Jason.'

'Yes, you told me, and it was very wrong of them.'

'Mum didn't hit Warren and Jason much – only when they got on her nerves when she'd been drinking. And when they wouldn't go into her bed.'

I glanced in the rear-view mirror again, this time at Donna. She was sitting back in her seat and gazing through the side window. 'What do you mean, she hit them when they wouldn't go into her bed?'

'Mum liked them to go into her bed sometimes when Dad wasn't there, but they didn't want to.'

'What? To give them a cuddle, you mean?'

I saw Donna shrug. 'She didn't hit them much but she made them go into her bed when they were naughty.' I wasn't sure what Donna was saying. Many children go into their parents' bed for a cuddle but this sounded as if it had been a punishment for the boys.

'I don't understand, Donna. Can you explain?' She shrugged again. I had stopped at a set of traffic lights and I briefly turned to look at her. 'Why did they have to go into her bed when they had been naughty? Didn't they like having a cuddle in bed?'

'I don't know,' she said. 'I was never allowed in. But if they were naughty Mum said, "You'll go into my bed for that." And when they came out sometimes they were crying.'

'Did she hit them?'

'I don't know. I had to stay downstairs.'

I put the car into gear as the lights changed and I pulled away. 'And Warren and Jason didn't tell you what had happened in your mother's bedroom?'

'Mum told them not to tell anyone. She said if they did it would be all the worse for them next time.'

I tried to concentrate on the traffic, at the same time listening to what Donna was telling me. I didn't like what I was hearing, and I was feeling decidedly uneasy. Whatever had gone on when Rita had summoned Warren and Jason to her bedroom certainly didn't sound like a family cuddle. I needed to try to find out more so that I could inform Edna; I would also have to write all this in my log when I got home.

'I see,' I said, thoughtfully. 'How often were the boys made to go into your mother's bedroom?'

'When Dad wasn't there,' Donna said. 'I guess about once a week.' Adrian and Paula were gazing out of the windows, blissfully unaware of any sinister undertones in what Donna was saying. 'They had to go to the toilet when they came out,' she added. 'Sometimes Jason had wet himself.' From what, I wondered? Fear?

'And your brothers didn't ever say what had happened?'

'No. Warren said it was better to be hit with a coat hanger like Mum did to me than go into Mum's bed.'

I braked as the car in front slowed. Good grief, I thought, that's definitely not a cuddle. 'And he never told you why?'

'No. Mum said they mustn't or else.'

'OK, love, thank you for telling me. I'll tell Edna. It doesn't sound very nice to me.'

'No, you can't tell Edna!' Donna said, her usual flat and emotionless voice rising. 'Mum will be angry, and we'll all be in for it. I'll get another beating.'

'No you won't,' I said firmly. 'You are not at home now, and neither are your brothers. And it's important that Edna knows that Warren and Jason were upset because she can make sure it doesn't happen again.'

'Oh yes,' Donna said, and I could hear the relief in her voice. 'I'd forgotten that. She can't be angry with me at contact because Edna stops her.'

'That's right, love. You see, I told you life would get better.' And as I glanced in the rear-view mirror I saw a brief smile of relief and contentment flicker across her face.

Having seen Donna into school, I took Adrian and Paula to their school, and as soon as I arrived home I wrote up my log notes, including what Donna had said, as near verbatim as possible. At this stage it was impossible to know the significance of what she had told me, or its relevance in the light of what might come out in the future. The detailed log notes foster carers have to keep are sometimes requested by the judge for the final court hearing, if he feels their content is pertinent to the case. Although Donna hadn't witnessed first hand what had happened in her mother's bedroom, and the boys hadn't told her, because of Rita's threats, Donna had said enough to leave me with a heavy feeling of unease. Clearly she was starting to reflect on the life she had led with her mother and the one she now led with me – that is, in a normal family – and she was beginning to draw conclusions and recognise the things that hadn't been right at home. Donna, like many children who come into care for similar reasons, had assumed the neglect and abuse she'd suffered were the norm. It was taking time for her to realise that the life she'd led wasn't normal and some things were clearly bad. It never ceases to amaze me what some children believe is acceptable simply because they have grown up with it, and have never known anything different. One girl of five I looked after thought it was perfectly normal to be tied by the legs and arms to the bed and left for a day and night without food or water as a punishment for bad behaviour.

Although I would be seeing Edna briefly before and after contact the following day, I didn't want to discuss what Donna had told me in front of her, so once I'd finished writing up my notes I telephoned Edna. She wasn't in the office; her colleague said she was on a home visit, and I left a message with her asking if Edna could phone me when she returned. What Donna had said played on my mind as I tidied up the living room, vacuumed the carpets and then went outside to do a spot of gardening. It was a fresh autumn day, and as I pruned the bushes, which had become unruly during the summer, I had a growing feeling of disquiet. I thought of Adrian and Paula, who had climbed into my bed at the weekend for a cuddle when they were younger; Paula still did if she woke early. I remembered my brother and me clambering into my parents' bed, and I thought how far removed that was from what Donna had told me about Warren and Jason, who had been made to go to their mother's bed as a punishment and had come out crying and in need of the toilet. In most families the parents' bed is a safe and inviting place for a young child to spend a leisurely hour on a

Sunday morning, but it sounded far from a safe place to be at Donna's house.

I had just come in from the garden at 11.30 a.m. when the phone rang, and it was Edna, returning my call.

'Hello, Cathy. Is everything all right?' she asked as she always did if I phoned her.

'Donna is fine,' I reassured her. 'And this may be something or nothing, but I think you should know what she told me this morning. If you could just hang on a moment I'll fetch my notes so that I can tell you exactly what she said.'

'Yes of course, Cathy. Go ahead.'

I left the phone in the lounge and went through to the front room, where I took my log notes from the drawer of my desk. I returned to the phone, and having explained to Edna that we had been in the car going to school when the conversation took place, I read out my notes. Edna was silent as I finished; then she said, 'I shall speak to the boys after school today, Cathy. I'll phone Mary and Ray and tell them I'm coming. The boys obviously haven't said anything to Mary and Ray, but they wouldn't if they'd been scared into secrecy. I don't like what I'm hearing, Cathy. I know Rita only had eyes for the boys, but if Donna is telling the truth it sounds as if there might be more to it. I've never known Donna lie before, but do you think she is telling the truth? Or could she be trying to get Warren and Jason and Rita into trouble – getting her own back?'

'I don't think Donna is capable of that type of manipulation,' I said. 'But obviously I can't know for sure.'

'No. OK, Cathy. Thanks. I'll speak to the boys later. If Donna says anything else, will you let me know, please, and also could you print out a copy of your notes and let me have them tomorrow at contact. I hope Donna is making this up.'

'Yes,' I agreed. 'So do I.'

Edna phoned that evening from the office at 7.00 p.m., after she had seen Warren and Jason. 'They have been sworn to secrecy,' she said. 'I knew from their faces there was something they weren't telling me. Jason was about to say something but Warren elbowed him in the ribs to make him be quiet. Mary and Ray are going to talk to the boys separately, and see if they can find out anything. I shall also be having a word with Chelsea to see if she can throw any light on this, although I'll have to get her away from Rita first; they're as thick as thieves at present. I take it Donna hasn't said any more?'

'No. If she does know anything further it will come out in her own time.'

'All right. Thanks, Cathy. I'm off home now.'

Every evening after school, Donna, Adrian and Paula did their homework before watching children's television. Paula's homework was usually reading; Adrian had work sheets to complete and sometimes needed help; Donna had reading and work sheets and required more help. She was on a reading scheme designed for the average seven-year-old and starting to make some progress. In addition to the reading and work sheets, she had been asked to start learning her times tables, ready for a test on Friday. The whole class was being tested on the two times table, and I knew that when Beth Adams had told me of this new target she hadn't held out much hope for Donna being able to learn and fluently recite the table. I was determined we would prove her wrong. Donna had mild learning difficulties but it didn't mean she couldn't learn.

Armed with a whiteboard and black marker pen, I took Donna into the lounge after dinner, and we sat on the floor. I slowly recited the two times table as she wrote down the numbers. Beth Adams had given each of the class a printed sheet with the table on it, but what I had in mind would be more visually stimulating, and therefore more likely to be remembered. It would also be more fun than a typed piece of paper. Donna wrote very slowly and meticulously as I repeated the table, rubbing out a number if she wasn't completely satisfied. Her writing was a stark contrast to Adrian's: the same age, he wrote in a flurry, covering pages with writing as his thoughts spilled out. It was quarter of an hour before Donna was satisfied with the columns of figures she had produced, and we then sat either side of the whiteboard and I pointed to each line and we read it together: 0 X 2 = 0, 1 X 2 = 2, 2 X 2 = 4, and so on until the end. We went through it a second time, and then a third time to familiarise Donna with the pattern and rhythm of the table.

'OK, Donna,' I said, 'now we are going to learn it in groups of three. That's easier than trying to learn the whole table to the end.' I covered up the lower nine lines of the table with a sheet of paper, leaving only the top three lines visible, and we read them together: '0 X 2 = 0, 1 X 2 = 2, 2 X 2 = 4.' Then I told Donna to read these first three lines by herself out loud, which she did with some hesitancy. Then a second and third time.

'Good,' I said. 'Now I want you to look away. Look at the wall and see how many of these first three lines you can remember.' This would have been ridiculously easy for the average child of ten, and indeed for a much younger child, but Donna had learning difficulties and I knew she would need more reinforcement and time to learn.

'I can't,' she said flatly, glancing between the wall and the three exposed lines of figures.

'Yes you can,' I said positively. I felt, as Mrs Bristow had, that some of Donna's learning difficulties could well be due to lack of confidence.

'I don't know them,' Donna said, not even willing to try.

'Yes you do. I'll help you to get started. We'll read the first three lines together again, and then I want you to look away and see if you can remember any of them.'

'0 X 2 = 0, 1 X 2 = 2, 2 X 2 = 4,' we chanted together.

'OK, Donna, look away and have a go. 0 X 2 = ' I said, leaving the answer blank.

'0,' Donna said.

'1 X 2 = ' I said.

'2,' Donna supplied, then unaided she said, '2 X 2 = 4.'

'Excellent!' I said. 'Now again from the beginning. 0 X 2 = '

'0. 1 X 2 = 2, 2 X 2 = 4,' she said.

'Well done!' I clapped. 'And again, this time a bit faster.'

'0 X 2 = 0, 1 X 2 = 2, 2 X 2 = 4.' She was smiling now, almost grinning, and surprised at her ability to achieve something she hadn't thought was possible.

'Right,' I said, 'now we are going to look at the next three in the table.' I slid down the paper that covered the whiteboard to reveal the next set of three, and we read them together: '3 X 2 = 6, 4 X 2 = 8, 5 X 2 = 10.' We read them a second and third time, and then Donna read them alone. Then as before I got her to look away and, with less resistance this time, she recited them – to her utter amazement and my great relief and praise. Before we attempted the next set of three I wanted her to consolidate what she had learned so far and hear and see the rhythm of the first six lines. We read the lines together twice, then I got her to look away and she began to recite them from memory. She hesitated and needed prompting but we got there in the end.

So we continued for the next forty minutes, with me releasing three lines at a time and endless repeating and consolidating what she had learned, until we reached 12 X 2 = 24. When it came to putting them altogether and reciting the whole table, Donna's confidence faltered, and she said she couldn't remember any of it. I said we'd recite it together, which we did, with my voice mainly in the background as a prompt. Donna faltered with 6 X 2, 8 X 2 and 9 X 2, got 10 X 2, and then fell away again at the end. I told her how well she had done and she glowed from the praise. 'We're stopping now,' I said. 'That's enough for tonight. You must be tired out.'

The following morning in the car instead of having the radio on I began reciting the two times table. Adrian joined in, and on my second run through so did Donna, very quietly and only offering those she was sure of. I was concerned that Adrian, completely fluent in all his tables (as were most of his class), shouldn't emphasise Donna's learning difficulties by his prowess. After I had dropped Donna off at school I explained to Adrian (and Paula) that Donna could learn as well as anyone but it took her a little longer and perhaps they could curtail their enthusiasm, especially Adrian, when we practised the times tables in the car. Such a conversation was always difficult for me when we looked after a child with learning difficulties, for clearly I had to acknowledge and praise my own children for their achievements, without undermining that of the fostered child, who was finding learning more difficult. That afternoon when I collected Donna from school I set up the chant of the two times table in the car and all three children joined in, with Adrian and Paula, as I had asked them, giving Donna the louder voice.

I went through the two times table again with Donna that evening – just the two of us, seated in the lounge. She was fluent up to 5 X 2 but then stumbled on 6 X 2, 7 X 2, 8 X 2 and 9 X 2, picking up the rhythm again for the last three. And so we continued for the rest of the week, chanting the table in the car and at home at any opportunity. It had turned into something of a game, with Donna now asking if we could run through it just one more time, which I always did, although secretly I was sick of the sound of it, as I'm sure Adrian and Paula were. But I wasn't doing it solely so that Donna knew her table but also to prove to her that she could do it, which would raise her confidence and help her learning and self-esteem in general.

On Thursday evening, the day before she was going to be tested at school, she stumbled a few times on the first run-through, and then managed it word perfect. I praised her immensely and said, 'Donna, there is something I want to try now. Don't worry if you can't do it but just have a go. I'm going to ask you questions on the tables, jump around and see if you know the answers. You have done so well learning them, so let's see how well you can do these.' I began easily with 2 X 2 and she gave the correct answer of 4; then I asked 5 X 2 and she answered 10. I returned to 0 X 2, then 3 X 2 and so on, until I had covered the easy ones; then I began on those that had caused Donna problems.

'6 x 2?' I asked.

'12.'

'Excellent! 8 x 2?' She didn't know, and I saw her confidence immediately tumble. 'Don't worry,' I said. 'Go back to the last one you do know and say the table from there in your head. You know 5 x 2.'

'10,' she said.

'So in your head, go on from there.'

Half a minute later she had come up with the right answer of 16. I clapped and said, 'Great! Excellent!' I knew that in the test she might not have time to go through the whole table to supply the answer, and I hoped she wouldn't panic and forget the lot, so I said, 'If Miss Adams asks you one and you can't remember, don't worry, just leave a space and go on to the next one, which you will know.'

On Friday in the car going to school instead of reciting the table I dotted around with the questions: '3 x 2? 6 x 2? 11 x 2?' I had already primed Adrian and asked him not to answer, and as I glanced in the rear-view mirror I could see him sitting with his lips pursed tightly to stop the answers from spilling out. I smiled at him. Donna couldn't remember 7 x 2 or 9 x 2, and took some moments to go through the whole table in her head until she could supply the answer. With lots of praise and wishes of good luck, I saw her into school and returned to the car, with some relief that I wouldn't have to listen to the two times table again until Paula had to learn it in a year or so.

As I opened the door and got in Adrian and Paula were giggling.

'What's the matter with you two?' I asked with a smile.

'Listen to Paula,' Adrian said.

Paula laughed, and then in a bright clear voice she recited the two times table from beginning to end, word perfect. Without learning difficulties, and having listened to the tables in the car, her brain had automatically picked up and stored the information effortlessly. It highlighted the huge work Donna, or any child with learning difficulties, had to put in to achieve the same result.

'Well done,' I said to Paula. 'I expect it will be the three times next week!'

That evening when I met Donna from school the question that was burning on my tongue was answered as soon as I saw her. Her slow laborious way of walking was nowhere to be seen, and she bounded to my side.

'I got them all right!' she said, her face lighting up.

'You did? All of them!'

'Yes. And when Miss Adams jumbled up the questions I answered them!'

'That's absolutely fantastic!'

Beth Adams was just behind Donna and clearly wanted to speak to me. She stepped round the other children, who were filing out and meeting up with their parents in the playground. 'Donna has done amazingly well,' she said. 'She could write the table, recite it and answer all the questions. She has earned two house points for her team.'

We both praised Donna again, although Donna hardly needed our praise; having achieved something she had thought was impossible was praise enough.

I could tell that Beth Adams was pleased, and astounded. 'It's the three times table next week,' she said. 'I've put the work sheet in Donna's bag.'

'Thank you. We'll make a start on it over the weekend.'
I did some quick mental arithmetic myself and calculated
that if we had to learn one table a week, by the time we got
to twelve it would be past Christmas and into the New
Year!

We left, as usual, through the staff exit and crossed to
the car, where Adrian and Paula were waiting. As Donna
got in, without being asked, she said. 'I got them all right!'
Adrian and Paula were as pleased as she and I were.

Learning the two times table typified Donna's ability to
learn, and also mild learning difficulties in general. She
wanted to learn and could learn, but it just took her a bit
longer.

That evening when I took Donna to contact the first
thing she said when Edna met us in reception was, 'I've
learnt my two times table, and I was tested, and got them
all right! I got two team points.' Edna knew the significance of this and was truly and genuinely in awe of
Donna's achievement. She praised her immensely, and then
thanked me for all the hard work I had put in. I later
learnt that Beth Adams had asked Donna how she had
learned her tables so well, and Donna had told her what
we had done. Beth Adams had then phoned Edna and told
her of my input, and also that Donna was starting to learn
in other areas with a newfound confidence. I was so very
pleased.

However, I also learnt that when Donna had gone into
contact that evening, and had told her family of her
success, her mother and Chelsea had ignored her and
turned their backs. Edna had said, 'Rita, Donna's got
some good news. Listen to her.' Donna had repeated her
news, and Rita had shrugged, while Warren and Jason

said, 'Easy peasy,' and laughed. It was Edna who told me this, not Donna: she had just accepted yet another rejection.

Chapter Twelve

Working as a Family

By the first week in November I was beginning to feel that Donna was making some real progress, and things were going pretty well. Although she still found it almost impossible to play with Adrian and Paula, preferring to watch them or amuse herself, I was finding I could relax a little and be less vigilant when she was in a room with Paula. Donna didn't appear to be trying to dominate and chastise Paula as much as she had done in the past.

The first week in November was a busy one for 'official' visits: Jill and Edna both paid their six-weekly visit, in the evening after school, Jill on Tuesday and Edna on Thursday. I had been in regular contact with both of them since they had last visited – Jill by telephone, and Edna when I saw her briefly before and after contact. Their visits were therefore more perfunctory than they might have been otherwise – just to see Donna at home and make sure everything was going all right. When Edna visited she also took the opportunity of telling me that Warren and Jason still hadn't said anything to Mary and Ray about the 'punishment' (if that was what it was) that they had received in their mother's bed, although, like Edna, Mary and Ray were convinced that the boys were hiding something, and felt that it would take time before they trusted them sufficiently to confide in them. The boys might have been unwilling to betray their mother, as they had been her favourites and they appeared to have a stronger bond with her than Donna did, presumably because their treatment at her hands had been less severe, or their silence might have been based on fear – no one knew at this stage.

The Guardian Ad Litem phoned that week as well and made her first visit the following Tuesday. Her name was Cheryl Samson. She was appointed by the court for the duration of the case and her role was an important one. As the Guardian for the boys and Chelsea as well as Donna, she would visit all the parties involved in the case a number of times, then write a detailed report for the judge, stating her findings and what she believed to be in the long-term best interest for the children. Her final recommendation as to where the children would live permanently would be vital to the judge when he made his decision at the final court hearing in May the following year. Cheryl was an experienced Guardian and quite forthright in her manner. When she arrived she spent some time talking to Donna and me together, and then me alone. She had met all members of Donna's family and was also in regular contact with Edna.

'Donna has been completely rejected and victimised by Rita,' Cheryl said to me, 'to an extent I have never seen before. She has been a scapegoat, blamed for all the family's ills. Why, I don't know, but Rita can't even look at her when they are in the same room. I'm not sure how much good contact is doing Donna, and I shall be looking to reduce it as we approach the final court hearing.'

'For the boys as well?' I asked. If it was just Donna's contact that was reduced it could have appeared to her a further victimisation by singling her out again.

'Absolutely,' Cheryl agreed. 'I can't see there is any way they can return to live at home, so contact needs to be reduced for all the children. Rita can't get off the drink and drugs and she is refusing any help. Edna has put in so much support but there has been no improvement in the home. I do not want Donna and the boys to follow in Chelsea's footsteps. Chelsea is just fifteen and we've now found out she's pregnant!'

'Oh no! Really?'

Cheryl nodded. 'Rita announced it to Edna yesterday after contact, as though it was something to be proud of. Edna has been trying to persuade Chelsea to go into foster care for some time, and Rita told Edna she couldn't move her now she was pregnant. But she's wrong on that count. I want Chelsea moved into a mother and baby unit, assuming she is pregnant and it's not a ruse of Rita's making. Chelsea says she doesn't know who the father is; apparently there's a choice of three.'

I didn't comment; it wasn't for me to pass judgement on Chelsea's morals, although of course it was illegal to have sexual intercourse with a girl under sixteen. 'Will Chelsea keep the baby?' I asked. I remembered that when I had seen Chelsea outside the school gates on that first day of term she'd appeared grubby and uncared for, barely able to look after herself, let alone a baby.

'We'll give her a chance and monitor her closely, which is another reason why I want her in a mother and baby unit.'

I nodded. 'It's Donna's birthday on the sixteenth of November and she would like a bowling party,' I said, lightening the subject. 'We are going to ask her brothers to come, but what about Chelsea? Should we invite her?'

'It's a nice thought, but Chelsea is sure to turn up with Mum, so I think the answer is no. Edna will arrange a birthday tea for Donna at contact, so Chelsea will have the chance to celebrate Donna's birthday then, if she has a mind to.' I knew what Cheryl meant: judging from the reception Donna had been receiving from Chelsea and Rita at contact it was hardly likely they were going to put much effort into celebrating Donna's birthday. One of the reasons I had suggested we invited Chelsea was to try to forge a better relationship between her and her sister, but I would be guided by the Guardian. I couldn't risk Rita, with her bad attitude towards Donna, turning up at the party and possibly ruining it.

'All right,' I said. 'Is there anyone else in the wider family I should invite? Cousins?'

'No. I should keep it to your family, Donna and the boys. And there's her special friend Emily at school?'

'Yes, that's right. We shall be inviting Emily. Donna doesn't find it very easy to make friends, so there will just be the seven of us, including me.'

Cheryl smiled. 'She'll enjoy it. I doubt she will have had a party before, of any description. I don't think she even had presents on her birthday and Christmas last year.' Which unfortunately was true for many of the children I fostered.

On Sunday I helped Donna to write some colourful birthday invitations; on each one she had to fill in the name of the person invited, the time and the venue, and sign it. I had already booked the bowling alley for Sunday

15 November, the day before Donna's birthday. The package they offered included an organiser/entertainer, two
games of bowling for each child, a party tea and a 'goody
bag' to take home. I had asked Donna sometime before,
when I had first brought up the subject of her birthday,
what she had done for her last birthday, and she had
shrugged and said she didn't know, from which I had
guessed that it was nothing, or something so insignificant
as not to merit being treasured as a fond memory. Now as
we worked side by side on the table in the annexe, and I
watched her slide the invitations into the envelopes and
then address them with so much care and precision, I casually brought up the topic again.

'You are doing a really good job there, Donna,' I said.
'Have you ever written birthday invitations before?'

She shook her head. 'No.'

'Not all families have birthday parties, but we do,' I said.
'It's nice to have fun.' She didn't say anything but concen-
trated on meticulously sliding the next invitation, which
was to Warren, into the envelope. 'I think it helps you to
remember your birthday if you do something a bit special.
It is an important day, after all.'

'I can remember my last birthday,' Donna said stoically.
'Very well. I had to do the washing.'

I glanced sideways at her. 'Oh yes?'

'Mum said as it was my birthday everyone could have
clean clothes. Dad wasn't there, but Mum, Chelsea and the
boys all went and changed and brought me their dirty
washing. Then Mum went round the house and gathered
up all the clothes and rags that were lying around, and the
stuff from her wardrobe, and dumped it in the kitchen. I
spent all day washing. We didn't have a washing machine

like you do, and it took ages in the sink. Then I had to try and get it dry, 'cos no one had any more clean clothes, and we didn't have a washing line. Mum hit me with a wet towel when I couldn't get it dry, and then told Chelsea and the boys to hit me.'

I looked at her and swallowed hard. Donna had said it so matter-of-factly she could have been telling me how she'd poached an egg; she was now carefully filling in her name on the next invitation, making sure she didn't make a mistake. I couldn't speak for the lump in my throat and I waited for the moment to pass.

'How do you spell Adrian?' she asked glancing up at me.

I swallowed again, and spelt it out. 'Donna, love,' I said, placing my hand on her arm and trying to raise a smile, 'one thing I can guarantee is that you won't be doing any washing on your birthday this year, or at any time in my house.'

She smiled sadly.

When she'd finished writing the invitations I asked Donna again if there was anyone else in her class or the school whom she wanted to invite to her party, but there wasn't; she then gave me my invitation, and Adrian and Paula theirs. We smiled and thanked her. Donna would give out Emily's and her brothers' invitations at school the following day. I opened my invitation and said I would be happy to come to her party and she smiled.

However, at bedtime when I tucked Paula into bed she said in a subdued and embarrassed voice, 'Mum, I don't want to go to Donna's party. Do I have to?'

I looked at her, surprised — that wasn't like her. 'Why not?' I asked. 'What's the matter? There's only us and Warren, Jason and Emily going.'

'Nothing's the matter. I don't want to go,' she said quietly.

I sat on the bed. 'Paula, there is something the matter. You must have a good reason for not wanting to go to something as important as Donna's birthday party?'

'I don't like her,' she said and she looked at me, half-expecting to be told off. This was totally out of character for Paula, and I knew there must be something badly worrying her. I settled myself on the bed for a long chat. Paula wasn't easily fazed, but when something did trouble her it became ingrained and took a while to uncover.

'What made you say you didn't like Donna?' I asked gently. 'I know she doesn't play with you, but she hasn't hit you again, has she?'

Paula shook her head. 'She didn't hit me.'

'So what has made you feel like this?' There was a long pause. 'Come on, Paula, I need to know so that I can put it right. This is important for all of us. If something is going on you must tell me.'

There was another long pause before Paula eventually said, 'Adrian doesn't like her either.'

I was taken aback, and also a little annoyed that I wasn't getting any closer to the root cause of the problem. Clearly there had been a conversation between Adrian and Paula that I hadn't been party to. 'Why doesn't Adrian like Donna?' I asked.

'Same reason as me.'

'Which is?'

'She doesn't like us.'

I gave an inward sigh. I was going round in circles, and I was starting to wonder if it was just a childish falling out, although I couldn't remember an incident taking place that could have led to them 'falling out'; indeed Donna hardly interacted enough with Adrian and Paula for there to have been a tiff.

'What makes you think she doesn't like you, Paula?' I asked. 'I'm sure Donna does like you.'

'No she doesn't,' Paula said adamantly.

'Well, tell me why you think that and I'll try to put it right. I can't do anything unless you tell me. How long have you both felt like this? And why haven't you said anything before?'

'You are always too busy with Donna, and you like her. We didn't want to make you upset.' And I had a sinking feeling, not for the first time since I'd started fostering, that I really wasn't getting it right after all, and I hadn't seen what was going on under my own nose.

'Look, love,' I said, 'I am never too busy to listen to you and Adrian. I thought you knew that. I like Donna, and I feel very sorry for her because of her past, but that doesn't mean I love you less. I had no idea that Adrian and you felt this way, and you should have said something sooner – at bedtime. We always have a chat at bedtime. Now, love, can you please tell me why you think Donna doesn't like you, so that I can do something about it. I know she hit you, but that was a while ago and I thought you'd forgiven her. Has something else happened recently that I should have known about? Has she said or done something to make you think she doesn't like you?'

There was another long pause before Paula said, 'It's not what she's done but the way she looks at us. It's like she's telling us off with her look, without saying anything.'

I paused and considered this. 'Can you explain a bit more, or show me the look?' I didn't dismiss what Paula said as childish sensitivity because I was well aware that control could come in many shapes and forms, and once the seeds of control (or fear) have been sown, a look can reinforce it as much as any words. Parents use the technique as a normal part of child rearing: the look, the warning that the child has done something that has overstepped the mark, and they'd better not do it again – a censorious expression. Although I had been very vigilant, I now wondered if I had missed something. Was Donna trying to control Paula and Adrian by a look? Perhaps along the lines her mother had done at home (and was possibly still doing at contact)?

'I can't make the face she does,' Paula said. 'It's in her eyes, the way she looks, like this.' She widened her eyes and glared at me in an expression of 'I'm warning you: I know what you're up to, and you'd better watch out or else.' 'Adrian can tell you better,' Paula said. 'It's not nice, it frightens me and I don't want to go to her party.'

'All right love,' I said. 'Thanks for telling me. I'll talk to Adrian, and then I'll work out a way to put it right. I just wish you had told me sooner. Next time something bothers you, tell me: don't brood on it.'

She nodded. I lay on the bed next to her and read her a bedtime story; then, reassuring her again that I would put it right, I kissed her goodnight and came out. Donna was in her room, getting ready for bed. I could hear her moving around; it always took her a while before she settled. I went into Adrian's room. He was propped up in bed, reading.

'It's not time to say goodnight yet,' he said.

'No, love, I know. But I need to talk to you about something Paula has just told me.' Once again, I sat on the edge of the bed. Adrian put down his book, and I repeated what

Paula had said. By the time I'd finished, Adrian was nodding furiously. 'She does this,' he said, and widening his eyes, he glared at me with a really angry, accusing, threatening expression; whether it was exaggerated or not I didn't know.

'So why didn't you tell me?' I said. 'You're older than Paula. I would have thought you could have come and told me.'

'You're always so busy with Donna,' he said, echoing Paula's words. 'I was going to, but when I thought about what I could say – "I don't like the way Donna looks at me" – it sounded silly. So I stick my tongue out when she does it to me. But it frightens Paula.'

I looked at him as his gaze fell to his open book. How many times since I had started fostering had I reminded myself to make sure my time was divided equally between all my children – continuously? It was something that was always on my mind. But if I was honest, I could see that when I looked after a child with a high level of needs, as in Donna's case, I had to give the fostered child more than their fair share of attention, to welcome and settle them into our family and ensure all their needs were met – apparently to the detriment of Adrian and Paula.

'Sorry,' I said.

Adrian looked up and shrugged. 'It doesn't matter.'

'It does matter,' I said firmly. 'I realise now how much time I have been putting into Donna. I just assumed you two were all right but now I know, I shall be able to do something about it.' Adrian nodded. 'I will be keeping a close eye on Donna. I like her a lot, but she has been treated very badly by her family. I think she is copying the way she was treated at home. She doesn't know any different, and part of our job is to show her a different way. But I'm not having you and Paula upset. It makes me sad, Adrian. I love you both so much.'

'I know,' he said quietly. 'We love you too.'

'So will you work with me on this? And tell me if anything else crops up in the future?' I couldn't have a sub-plot running in the family, with Adrian and Paula in collusion and not telling me. A foster family is a unit where all members pull together, including natural and foster children, with no double standards; otherwise it's impossible to make it work.

'Yes,' he said.

'Good boy. Thanks, Adrian. I'll leave you to your book now. Hopefully in a week's time, when it's Donna's party, you and Paula will feel comfortable enough to join in, and enjoy it. There's only us, her brothers and Emily going.'

He nodded and picked up his book. I kissed his forehead. 'It's eight thirty. I'll come up again in half an hour to say goodnight.' I left him once more immersed in Roald Dahl's *Revolting Rhymes*, which apparently they were studying at school.

I didn't raise the matter with Donna that night, for when I thought about it, what could I have reasonably said? 'Donna, Paula and Adrian don't like the way you are looking at them. Could you stop it, please?' Such a complaint seemed as 'silly' to my ears as it had done to Adrian's, and also I wanted to see at first hand what exactly they were talking about before I said anything to Donna.

I didn't have to wait long.

The following morning at breakfast I was presented with a classic example. Paula was sitting opposite Donna at the table, with Adrian to her side. The three children were eating, and I had just made some fresh toast and was carrying it through to take my place at the end of the table. A cornflake dropped off Paula's spoon on to the table and I saw Paula immediately look up at Donna, as though expecting censure. She was well rewarded: Donna's eyes widened and she stared at Paula – an all-in-one package of anger, chastisement and a warning that it shouldn't happen again, or else!

'It's only a cornflake,' I said to Donna, 'and there's no need for you to tell her off.'

Donna looked at me, shocked and surprised by my sudden insight. 'I didn't say anything,' she said.

'No, you didn't have to. Does your mother look at you like that?'

Donna looked doubly shocked by my second stab of insight and stopped eating her wheat flakes.

'Does she?' I asked. 'Because if so it's not nice.'

She didn't say anything but remained very quiet and still, as did Paula and Adrian. I didn't think that Donna was particularly concerned about the cornflake being dropped and making a (small) mess; it was that she was reverting to learned behaviour, seizing any opportunity to discipline, blame and punish a family member as had happened to her at home.

My voice was even but firm, as I buttered my toast and continued, 'Harsh words are bad, but harsh looks are equally bad,' I said. 'They can make you feel uncomfortable and threatened. There is a saying – a picture paints a thousand words, and your look just now, Donna, painted a picture of anger with a punishment to follow.' I looked around the table. 'We are a family here – all four of us,' I said, 'and we work together as a family. If anyone has a problem they come to me, and I will try to put it right. I am the adult, the parent here, and if any one of my children – Adrian, Paula or you, Donna – needs correcting in any way, I shall do it. I will not have anyone else trying to tell another family member what to do, either through words or looks. It's a form of bullying. And no one bullies anyone in this family, or anyone outside it.' They were quiet and I felt the atmosphere weigh heavy, for rarely did I speak so harshly, and to everyone. Normally I dealt with the little incidents that arose individually, but clearly this was a whole family matter and needed direct, collective and immediate input.

'So now we will finish our breakfast and get ready for school,' I said. 'And I don't want to see any more looks or tongue poking from anyone. Do I make myself clear?'

Adrian and Paula nodded, very subdued. Donna remained quiet and still. I picked up my toast and continued eating. Adrian finished first and left the table to go to the bathroom and brush his teeth. I looked between Donna and Paula.

'You know, Donna,' I said more gently. 'Paula could be like a little sister to you. You never had a younger sister at home and she's dying to play with you.'

Paula looked hopefully at Donna, and we both waited, but still feeling bruised by my lecture, Donna wasn't about to give anything away just yet. After a moment she shrugged and then picked up her spoon and began eating again. When Paula had finished she left the table to take her turn in the bathroom. I looked at Donna again. 'That look you have been giving Paula and Adrian – is that what your mother has been giving you at contact? I know your mum can't say horrible things to you at contact because Edna stops her, but a look is easy to hide and just as hurtful. Particularly if it has a history and makes you remember hurtful things that happened in the past.'

Donna gave a small nod. 'She always does it.'

'OK, I'll speak to Edna. You should have told me. Your mum shouldn't behave like that, and you mustn't do it here any more. Now go into the bathroom when Paula has finished and do your teeth. We're going to give out your invitations to Emily, Warren and Jason today,' I added brightly.

Donna left the table without saying anything, and sulking. But now that I'd spoken directly and firmly the matter was dealt with and would be put behind us, although obviously I would still be vigilant. Old habits die hard and Donna had spent all her life learning this behaviour, so it wasn't going to disappear overnight.

After I had taken the children to school I telephoned Edna and explained what had happened. Edna treated the matter with the seriousness I had done, well aware that fear and control come in many forms. She said she would watch Rita closely, and asked me to tell her immediately if Donna said she had experienced the look again at contact. I also told Edna that Donna was giving out party invitations today – to Warren, Jason and Emily – but in view of the Guardian's advice we wouldn't be giving one to Chelsea, with which Edna agreed.

'Donna's birthday is on a Monday,' Edna said, 'so I'll do a special tea at contact that evening, and I'll remind Rita and Chelsea to buy a present. In fact I think I'll buy presents for them to give to Donna, because Rita will say she hasn't any money. If I give her money it's sure to go on something else – drink. Have you got any suggestions for presents?'

'Donna likes making things,' I said. 'How about some sort of craft set? A jewellery-making set or basket weaving? We've bought her a bike. She's never owned a bike before.'

'That's very generous of you, Cathy,' Edna said. 'Is the birthday money enough to cover it?' She was referring to the allowance that is paid to foster carers towards the cost of the looked-after child's birthday present and party. It wasn't enough to cover it, but if foster carers kept only to the allowance, children would have pretty meagre birthdays.

'No problem,' I said. 'It has helped towards the cost.'

By the time I collected Donna from school that afternoon the heavy atmosphere of the morning had lifted, and she told me she had given out her invitations and Emily had immediately said she could definitely come.

The following day, without the quick turnaround necessary for contact, I made a point of seeing Emily's mother, Mandy, and confirmed the arrangements for Sunday. Emily hadn't been to tea yet – I had left an open invitation with Mandy – and Mandy was very pleased that Emily would be going to Donna's party, for like Donna, Emily found it difficult to make friends. I told Mandy who would be going to the party, and she said she would drop Emily off at the bowling alley at 2.30 p.m., and then collect her at the end at 5.00. She also asked what Donna would like for a present. I said I'd give it some thought, but I was sure Emily could suggest something; as her best friend she would know what Donna liked.

* * *

The week as usual ran away with us, and very quickly it was Friday and Donna's party was two days away. However, this took a back seat on Friday morning when Donna went into school to be tested on her three times table. We had been practising the three times all week, as we had done the previous week with the two times table, and I wished her luck, as did Adrian and Paula. We'd had only two incidents of Donna giving that 'look' to Paula, and I'd dealt with it by saying a firm 'No' to Donna. Adrian and Paula seemed more relaxed in her company now that they were aware I was dealing with the situation. Donna had accepted my 'No' and spent only a short while sulking, for she was too excited about her party to sulk for long.

It was only when I arrived home on Friday morning, having dropped the children off at school, that I realised I hadn't had confirmation from Mary and Ray that Warren and Jason would be coming to Donna's party, although I'd assumed they would be. Occasionally I saw Mary and Ray going in or coming out of school, but not often, and I wouldn't have the chance to seek them out in the after-noon because I had to do the quick turnaround for contact. I thought I would give them a ring, just to confirm that the boys had shown them the invitations and would be at the bowling alley at 2.30 p.m. for Donna's party. I phoned at lunchtime, Mary answered, and I knew immediately something was wrong.

Chapter Thirteen

The Birthday Party

'Cathy,' Mary said slowly, as though gathering her thoughts. 'I was going to phone you. I have been putting if off, in the hope that the boys could be persuaded to change their minds.' I didn't say anything, and waited as Mary paused again before continuing. 'I'm sorry, Cathy, but Warren and Jason are saying they won't come to Donna's party. I have been trying to persuade them all week, but they are stubbornly refusing.' She stopped, and I could tell she was as uncomfortable and disappointed to be giving me the news as I was to be receiving it.

'Why not?' I asked. 'There's only Warren, Jason, Emily and us going. There's nothing for them to be worried about. You can stay with them if they want you to.'

'No, it's not that,' she said, and she paused again. I thought, what on earth is it then? This is the boys' sister's birthday we're talking about! 'Look, Cathy, I don't know if the boys have been got at by their mother or whether it's a continuation of their behaviour towards Donna from the past. But they are both saying they won't come to the party, and have rightly pointed out that Ray and I can't force them to go. I told Edna yesterday, and she asked me to talk to them again to see if I could find out what the problem was, and if I could get them to change their minds. I can't. Edna said she was going to speak to you later today.' Mary stopped and there was a very awkward silence.

'Donna will be very disappointed,' I said at last. 'She has been planning this party all week. It's all she talks about. It won't be much of a party with just Emily and us there.'

'I know,' Mary said sadly. 'That's what I told the boys, but they just shook their heads and wouldn't budge.'

'And they haven't said why they don't want to come?'

'Not exactly, although Warren said, "Mum wouldn't like it," which is why I'm pretty certain it's come from Rita. The boys went to a friend's birthday party last Sunday with no problem; they're not shy. I'm sure Rita has told them not to go.'

'That's dreadful,' I said, appalled. 'If that is so, then Rita is still managing to victimise Donna, even from a distance! It could only have happened at contact. Somehow Rita has got at them.'

'I know. That's what Edna said. Although she's no idea how. I didn't push it with her, because she's such a dear and I know she feels it personally. Edna never leaves them alone at contact, but of course she only has to turn her back for a second and Rita could have easily whispered in Warren's ear. Jason does as his older brother says.' I thought that with this, and the looks she had been slyly giving Donna, Rita was running rings around Edna at contact.

'All right,' I said, sad and deflated. 'I'll have to try to think of a way to tell Donna, although goodness knows what I'm going to say.'

'Do you want to tell her the boys are ill?' Mary asked. 'I wouldn't normally suggest lying, but I can't think of anything else.'

'I don't know. I'll phone Edna and see what she thinks. If the boys do change their minds, will you let me know?'

'Yes, of course, but I don't think they will. They are adamant. I'm so sorry, Cathy. I know how you must be feeling. I have bought a nice present for the boys to give to Donna, and also one from Ray and me. I'll send them with the boys to contact on Monday.'

'Thanks,' I said, no less disappointed. 'Let me know if they do change their minds, even if it's on Sunday morning.'

'I will do, but honestly Cathy, they wouldn't dare go against their mother, even now.'

'No,' I said. 'I know.'

We said goodbye and I put the phone down, my heart heavy and my plans for Donna's party falling apart. What mother does that to their daughter, I thought? It was vindictive to an unprecedented extent. Not only had Rita made Donna's life a misery for all the years she had been at home but she was now finding ways to continue doing so. By stopping the boys going, Rita was not only reinforcing her rejection and control, but also continuing to reinforce Donna's brothers' rejection of her. It was unbelievable. Rita must have known how much Donna's party would mean to her, particularly as it was the first one she'd ever had, and now she was sabotaging it! It was only ever going to have been a small affair because Donna only had one proper friend, and Rita couldn't even allow her that. I silently cursed the woman who, as far as I was concerned, had absolutely no claim to the title of mother apart from that of having given birth to her. I sincerely hoped she got her comeuppance one day.

I hovered by the phone, my mind frantically searching for any way to salvage Donna's party. There was no one else in her class she wanted to ask, and it was probably too late anyway to start issuing more invitations now. I considered phoning around my friends who fostered and inviting them and their children to the party, but what would have been the point in that? A party of strangers was hardly likely going to recompense Donna for her brothers' refusal to go. No, we were just going to have to do our best and make the most of it.

Just as I walked away from the phone it rang again and for a moment I thought it might be Mary, phoning back to say she'd thought of a way to persuade the boys to go.

'Hello?' I said, my spirits briefly rising. They fell again instantly. It was my ex-husband, John.

'Hello, Cathy,' he said, suitably subdued, aware that I hadn't fully appreciated his running off with a woman half his age three years previously. 'How are you?'

'Fine,' I said, which was what I usually said.

'I was due to see the children Sunday week,' he continued, 'but something's come up. Could I bring my visit forward to this Sunday?' That's all I need, I thought!

'I'm sorry,' I said. 'Adrian and Paula are going to a birthday party this Sunday. They are free on Saturday, though.'

'No can do Saturday. I've got tickets for the theatre in the evening – it would be too much of a rush.' Suit yourself, I thought, but didn't say. 'Couldn't they miss the party?'

'No, I'm afraid not. It's someone close.' He didn't have to know the details; he knew I still fostered, but my business was none of his concern now, unless it was related directly to Adrian and Paula.

'OK,' he said. 'I'll have to shift my visit back. I'm on holiday for a couple of weeks, so I'll see them a month on Sunday.'

'Fine,' I said. 'I'll put it in the diary. I'll tell Adrian and Paula you phoned.'

'Thanks.'

Curt possibly, but I hadn't been rude. I put down the phone and wondered what other bad omen was going to blow my way this Friday. It was just as well it wasn't Friday the 13th or else I could have been persuaded into feeling superstitious. Not only did I now have to tell Donna that her brothers wouldn't be coming to her party, but I also had to tell Adrian and Paula that their father was postponing his visit and wouldn't be coming for another month. They looked forward to seeing him, and although I had my own thoughts about his irresponsibility in deserting his family, I had kept them to myself and not let them get in the way of the children's relationship with him. The time they spent with their father was limited – one day a month (his decision) – and Adrian and Paula looked forward to his visits. The last time he had post-poned, Adrian in particular had seen it as a personal rejec-tion – 'He doesn't have to come at all if he doesn't want to,' he'd said moodily. It had taken me some while to persuade Adrian that his father did want to see him and that the postponement had been unavoidable.

Edna phoned five minutes before I was due to leave the house to collect the children from school.

'I'm sorry,' she said. 'I didn't realise the time.' She apolo-gised again for the boys not wanting to go to Donna's party, feeling that it was her fault that the boys had been 'got at', as she put it. 'Cathy,' she said, 'I'm going to try to find a colleague to help me supervise the contact in future. You need eyes in the back of your head when Rita and Chelsea are together. They're a devious pair, and I know how cruel they can be to Donna, but I'm shocked they have stooped this low. Trouble is I'm finding it difficult to get someone to commit to staying until six thirty three nights a week.'

I could see her problem; I doubted many of her colleagues would want to extend their working days into the evening, one of the evenings being a Friday. In my experience Edna's commitment was well beyond the norm, and proof of her dedication and love of her work.

'What will you tell Donna?' she asked.

'I really don't know yet. I think it might be the truth. If I lie to Donna and tell her the boys are ill, and she finds out they aren't, it's going to undermine her trust in me. I'm not sure yet what to say. I'll give it some more thought. I'm sorry, Edna, I'm going to have to go now or I'll be late collecting the children from school.'

'Yes, of course. Sorry, Cathy,' she said, finishing as she had started.

I left Adrian and Paula in the car in the staff car park while I went in to collect Donna from school. It was pouring down and the rain had a cold biting edge to it, which said winter was just around the corner. I was so preoccupied with the bad news of the day that I had completely forgotten about the three times table test, and I wondered why Donna was bounding towards me, and why Beth Adams was close behind her, clearly wanting to see me.

'I remembered them all!' Donna exclaimed. 'And got all the test right!'

'She did,' Beth Adams confirmed.

It took me a moment to realise what they were talking about. 'Excellent,' I said. 'That's fantastic news. Well done, love.'

'I have earned another two team points,' Donna said, beaming.

'She deserves it,' Beth Adams said. 'The three times table is a tricky one, and only half the class got all the test right. Donna was one of them!'

I congratulated Donna again, and thanked Beth Adams. It was the best news I'd had all day, and also proved that with time and a lot of hard work Donna could learn as well as anyone. I thought that Beth Adams was going to have to readjust her expectations of what Donna could achieve, for if this was an indication of what Donna was capable of, then she had only just begun!

That evening when Donna was in the bath I told Paula and Adrian that I needed to talk to them. Without making a big issue of it, and thereby hopefully minimising their disappointment, I told them that unfortunately their father had had to postpone his visit planned for the following Sunday. Paula didn't say anything, which didn't surprise me, for if I was honest she had less of a bond with her father than Adrian did; she'd been only three when John had left and didn't remember a time when he'd lived with us. Adrian had been seven, and remembered a different family where his father had been present, and perhaps also because he was a boy, he had suffered more when his father had suddenly gone. Predictably, now Adrian was the one who made the comment 'What is more important than seeing us?' And as I was put in the position of having to defend my ex for the sake of Adrian maintaining a positive image of his father, I felt that familiar stab of irritation.

'He didn't say exactly why he couldn't come,' I said. 'But he made a special point of asking me to tell you that he is sorry. And that he misses you both and loves you very much.' Which softened the blow a little, as it had done in the past when he'd postponed a visit. I moved swiftly on. 'I'm afraid there is another piece of disappointing news,' I said. 'And I'm going to need your help on this one. Both of you.' They looked at me questioningly. 'It's not about your father,' I added quickly. 'But I have learnt this afternoon that Donna's brothers won't be coming to her party.'

'Why?' they asked together.

'It's something to do with her mother,' I hedged.

'What?' Adrian said. 'We'll look after them if that's what she's worried about.'

I wish, I thought. 'No, I'm afraid it's more to do with the bad way she treated Donna at home, and her not wanting Donna to have a good time.'

'That's horrible,' Paula said.

'It won't be much of a party if no one's coming,' Adrian said. 'I had twelve at mine.'

'I know, love. And that is why I'm going to need your help. I'm not going to say anything to Donna yet: I'm still hoping her brothers' carers can persuade them to change their minds. But if they can't, then the three of us and Emily must make sure Donna has a wonderful time. I'm sure we can do it.'

Paula nodded and Adrian said, 'I could ask some of my friends to come?'

I smiled. 'That's sweet of you, and I had thought of that, but I don't think it will be the same for Donna. She doesn't really know them, does she?'

'But why doesn't Donna's mum want her to have a good time?' Paula asked, her naïve and unsullied innocence making it impossible for her to grasp the concept of such nastiness from a mother to a daughter.

'Donna's mother treated Donna very badly,' I said, 'which is why she came into care. I think she's still trying to do it from a distance. By making her feel rejected and unloved.'

'I love Donna,' Paula said, looking very sad, and my heart gave that little lurch. 'We'll make sure she has a good time. You don't need lots of people. It's the ones close to you who count.'

'Exactly,' I said, smiling at Paula. 'I couldn't have put it better myself.'

Over the weekend, when we weren't learning the four times table, Adrian and Paula paid Donna extra attention, and went out of their way to talk to her and suggest games she might like to join in. They clearly felt the rejection that Donna would be feeling if her brothers didn't change their minds and come to the party. It was at times like this that I was most proud of Adrian and Paula: I was always proud of them, but the tenderness and concern they showed for Donna highlighted their empathy and insight into Donna's plight, feeling as most children from normal families would have done. However, in making these friendly advances towards Donna, Paula and Adrian had left themselves wide open, and I had to remind Donna a few times over the weekend not to try to boss Adrian and

Paula or discipline them. It wasn't Donna's fault; she was simply reverting to the example of how her family had treated her in the previous ten years. Adrian and Paula, now more aware of what Donna had been through, and with her party looming, were even more forgiving.

By 12.00 noon on Sunday, when I hadn't heard anything from Mary and Ray, I had to finally admit that Warren and Jason wouldn't be coming, and I braced myself to tell Donna.

She was in her bedroom, already sorting through her wardrobe of clothes, trying to choose what to wear for the party, although there was plenty of time – we didn't have to get ready until 1.00 p.m. at the earliest, to leave the house at 2.00. Her bedroom door was open and, giving my usual knock, I went in. Donna turned to look at me, new trousers in one hand and pink sweatshirt in the other.

'I think I'll wear these,' she said, holding them up. 'I was going to wear a skirt. But when I bend over to bowl I might show my knickers in a skirt.' She gave a small laugh.

'I think that's a good choice, and you haven't worn either of them yet. It's nice to wear something new for a party.' I hesitated, as Donna again looked at the clothes, clearly considering if this was going to be her final decision. Best get on with what I had to say, I thought. 'Donna, I'm afraid that Warren and Jason won't be coming today, so you'll celebrate your birthday with them tomorrow at contact.'

She moved towards the wardrobe and looked in again. 'No, I will wear these. I'm not going to change my mind again,' she said.

'I think they are fine,' I said again, and paused. 'Donna, did you hear what I said, love? The boys can't make it this afternoon.'

'I heard. I expect Mum told them not to come.'

I was taken aback, and also quietly relieved that I'd been saved the awful job of telling her the reason, although I wasn't going to make it worse by confirming it with detail. 'It's possible.' I said. 'Mary doesn't know for sure.' I paused, waiting for some kind of reaction as the information sunk in.

'It's their loss,' she said after a moment. 'They are the ones missing out, not me.' And so saying, Donna put the clothes she had chosen on her bed and closed the wardrobe door. 'Will you help me do my hair when I've changed? I want it to look nice for the party.'

'Of course, love,' I said. 'Give me a shout when you're ready. We'll use those new hair braids I bought, shall we?'

She nodded, her face lighting up.

'Come here and give me a hug,' I said. 'You're a lovely person.'

She came over and I put my arms round her and gave her a big hug. For the first time since she had arrived I felt her arms tighten around my waist as she returned it. After a moment she eased away. 'I'm going to get changed now,' she said. 'I'm so excited. This is going to be my best birthday ever! Thanks for giving me the party, Cathy. I can't wait to get there!'

I smiled, and felt my eyes well. 'You're welcome, love.'

While I had spent the entire weekend angsting over our depleted numbers, aware how Adrian and Paula would have felt if they'd been in Donna's position with having only one friend and us attend, Donna, bless her, having never had a birthday party before and therefore having no expectations, had simply accepted the non-attendance of her brothers in her usual stoical manner.

I left Donna to change and went downstairs.

'Donna's fine,' I said to Adrian and Paula, who were in the lounge looking very concerned, aware that I had gone upstairs to break the 'bad' news.

'Good on her!' Adrian said.

'I told you,' Paula said. 'It's not how many who go to your party, but who.'

I nodded, and hugged them both, my spirits lighter than they had been since I'd received the news on Friday. And as I acknowledged the sensible rationale of all three children, I felt that as an adult I could probably learn a lot from them.

By 1.45 p.m. the four of us were changed into our party best and in the hall ready to leave. I had braided Donna's hair; she'd inherited dark brown and slightly curly hair from her father and with the new braids she looked very pretty. I arranged the children in a semi-circle in the hall and took a photograph of them before we left, and then another as they got into the car. I wanted a record of Donna's party and birthday; there would be a copy for her and one for my album. I had no idea if Donna would be with us for her next birthday; that would depend on the outcome of the court case.

I took another photograph of the three children going into the bowling alley, and then two more as we went inside. Adrian was getting embarrassed by now – having to stand still and pose between the girls. It was 2.15 p.m., but we weren't the only ones who had arrived early, for as

I tucked my camera into my handbag Emily appeared with her mother.

'Happy birthday!' Mandy called as they came over. Donna smiled sheepishly. 'You look nice, all of you.' Mandy had met Paula and Adrian in the playground on the occasions when they had come into the school with me.

Emily gave Donna a small box-shaped present, gaily wrapped and tied with ribbon. 'Happy birthday,' she said, giving her a kiss on the cheek.

'Thanks,' Donna said. She took the present and then held it as if it was the first one she'd ever received in her life, which it might well have been. She would be having her presents from us on her actual birthday the following morning.

Emily and Donna began chatting and laughing excitedly, glancing at the bowling lanes and pointing. It was lovely to see Donna so relaxed, and happy, and with her friend.

'There's just going to be us,' I said quietly to Mandy. 'Donna's brothers can't come.'

'Oh dear,' she said. 'That's a pity, but I'm sure Donna will have a good time. Emily hasn't stopped talking about this party all weekend. She was changed and ready by twelve thirty.'

I laughed. 'Same with Donna.' And we both glanced at the girls, giggling and whispering excitedly. 'Emily must come to tea, if she feels ready now,' I said, renewing my invitation.

'Yes, I'm sure she'll be fine now,' Mandy said. 'And Donna must come to us too. We'll arrange something next week.' Mandy confirmed she would return to collect Emily at 5.30 p.m., and we said goodbye. 'Have a lovely time!' she called to the children as she left, and Emily gave a little wave.

Leaving the children in a small group, I went over to the reception desk a couple of yards away and gave my name. 'I've booked for seven including me,' I said. 'But there will only be five of us, four children. Unfortunately two can't come.'

'No problem,' the girl on reception said. 'I'll introduce you to your party organiser. Lisa,' she called to a girl who was tidying the bowling shoes at the far end of reception. 'Lisa, this is Cathy Glass,' she introduced. 'The party is for Donna, who will be eleven.'

Lisa smiled brightly at me. She was about eighteen and had a light and fun manner. 'Is everyone here?' she said glancing at the clock. 'Because if so we can make a start.'

'Yes, unfortunately two children can't come,' I confirmed again.

'So it's four children and yourself?'

'That's right.'

'We'll have lots of fun. First we'll bowl, and then we'll have some games, then the party tea and then another game of bowling. How does that sound?'

'Sounds good to me,' I said.

'If you could bring the children over, I'll sort out their bowling shoes first.'

I waved to the children to come over, and they ran to my side; from then on Lisa took charge, and I did as I was told. She asked us what shoe size we were and handed us each a pair of bowling shoes, storing our own shoes in a rack at the end of the reception area. Then she gave us each a large name badge. It was about three inches across and decorated with pictures of multi-coloured balloons, with the name of the person printed in red in the centre. As Lisa led us over to lane twenty, which was set aside for the party, my anxieties about Donna having less than the best party finally evaporated. Large balloons in every colour imaginable hung in bunches from the ceiling the entire length of the bowling lane, and a massive banner declaring 'HAPPY BIRTHDAY' stretched from one side to the other.

'Look!' Donna exclaimed as we approached the lane. 'That's for me!'

'It is,' Lisa said, 'especially for you! It's your special day.'

We grouped at the end of the lane as Lisa gave us a brief talk on how to bowl safely – that is, without dropping the bowl on our toes, falling over it or getting our fingers stuck in the holes. 'I hope you're listening to this,' Adrian said to me with a laugh.

Then, with Donna naturally going first, we began the game. There was a lot of cheering and jumping up and down as Donna's ball swerved and rolled down the lane towards its target, knocking three pins over with the first ball and two with the second. Emily went next, then Adrian and Paula, and I went last. And it was pure fluke, for I am the world's worst at bowling, but somehow my ball went on target (probably helped by the sides being up), and I scored nine with my first ball and then felled the tenth with my second. Everyone clapped and cheered, and Adrian good-humouredly yelled, 'Fixed!'

Lisa didn't bowl but gave an exciting running commentary as we took our turns, and also helped Paula, who was struggling, even with the lighter children's ball. Our excitement grew as the game continued and the scores mounted on the display board, until there was only a few points' difference between the two leaders – Donna and Adrian. I saw the family who were playing on the lane next to ours glance across; so too did Donna, and she beamed. Possibly for the first time in her life she was the centre of attention in a positive way, and she was loving every minute of it. And while Adrian was the stronger bowler (having had lots of practice in the past) I noticed that his skill suddenly fell away with the final round, so that Donna was the winner. 'That was nice of you,' I said quietly, and he shrugged with a boy's embarrassment. In truth, though, I didn't think it would have mattered to Donna whether she won or lost, for the whole experience was so new and exciting to her, it was a winner in itself.

After we had congratulated Donna on her win, Lisa led us through to the party room for drinks and some games. The party room was gaily decorated with a large mural of clowns running round the walls, more bunches of balloons and another large 'HAPPY BIRTHDAY' banner strung across the ceiling. We played musical chairs and then various guessing games, designed to quieten the children down before their tea. Tea was a choice of pizza, chicken nuggets or burger, all with chips; then there was jelly and ice cream – as much as anyone could eat – and a birthday cake with eleven candles. I had bought another birthday cake to have at home on Donna's actual birthday the following day.

We finished with another game of bowling, which Donna won again; then Mandy arrived to collect Emily, and Lisa gave all the children a party bag. I thanked Lisa for all she had done and tipped her £5. She wasn't going to accept it to begin with, but I insisted. 'You've made the party a great success,' I said. 'I'm very grateful. Thank you.'

We exchanged our bowling shoes for our own and, with more thanks, finally said goodbye to Lisa. Outside I reminded Donna to thank Emily and Mandy for the present; she was still clutching it protectively and had carried it everywhere with her, only putting it down to bowl and eat her tea. She hadn't yet opened it, wanting to save it for her actual birthday. 'Thanks,' I added to Donna's, as we said goodbye to Emily and Mandy in the car park outside.

There was silence in the car as I drove us home and also, I thought, a small anti-climax as happens at the end of a good time. Donna was sitting with Emily's present cupped on her lap, and as I glanced in the rear-view mirror I saw Paula rest her head on Donna's shoulder and begin to doze.

That night I said everyone had to be in bed exactly at their bedtimes, as I would wake them early so that Donna had time to open her presents in the morning before we went to school. All three children were asleep within ten minutes of going to bed, exhausted by the day's excitement. Paula had gone to sleep with her thumb in her mouth, Adrian with his book open on his bed and Donna with her hand under her pillow clutching Emily's unopened present.

Chapter Fourteen

No Dirty Washing

I had been touched by Donna's innocent and accepting pleasure of all aspects of her little party, and I was doubly touched the following morning when she began to open her presents. Before I had gone to bed I had taken her presents into her room and placed them on the floor beside her bed so that she would see them as soon as she woke. There was the bike from me, which I had wrapped in yards and yards of wrapping paper, a cycle helmet from Adrian and Paula, a present from my parents, and another from my brother and his wife; and of course there was the present from Emily, which was still tucked under Donna's pillow.

As soon as I heard Donna stir, I went to her room. 'Happy birthday,' I said, kissing her forehead. I woke Adrian and Paula so that they too could watch Donna open her presents – it was a family tradition that we all grouped around the person's bed on the morning of their birthday to watch them open their presents. This was a whole new experience for Donna and, as I looked at her, I became increasingly convinced that she had never opened presents in her life before.

She stared at the large gift-wrapped frame of the bike. 'I wonder what it is?' she said, not daring to believe her eyes, although its shape made identification pretty obvious.

'You'll have to open it to find out,' I said, encouraging her. Donna appeared to want to savour being surrounded by the brightly wrapped presents and I knew we hadn't got unlimited time – at some point we had to get washed and dressed, ready for school.

Finally Donna sat on the edge of her bed and, sliding Emily's present from under the pillow, she carefully and very slowly began untying the ribbon. She picked off the sticky tape even more slowly, then peeled off the paper, not ripping it off as Adrian and Paula would have done. It was a jeweller's box. 'I wonder what it is,' she said again, and Adrian and Paula watched in awe as she slowly lifted the lid. Donna's eyes widened, and her whole face shone as she looked inside, but didn't remove the gold necklace with a pendant in the shape of the letter D.

'Isn't that lovely?' I said, as Adrian and Paula moved closer for a better look. 'What a beautiful present!' It was very generous of Mandy. Donna gazed at the necklace and touched it, clearly believing that at any second it might disappear.

'Shall I put it over here, while you open the rest?' I said, again mindful of the time. She carefully closed the lid on the box and handed it to me. I placed it on top of the chest of drawers. She gazed at the other presents, finding it impossible to choose which one to open next. 'How about this one?' I suggested, passing her the large box from my brother and his wife. Donna was now sitting on the floor, with Adrian and Paula kneeling either side of her. Once again she started picking at the sticky tape; then very slowly and carefully, she unwrapped the present. It was a large boxed compendium of games – Snakes and Ladders, Ludo, playing cards, dice for performing tricks and so on.

'Cor, that looks good,' Adrian said. Donna glowed from being the owner of something valued and admired by Adrian.

She opened the present from my parents next, which I knew was a fashionable denim skirt – my mother had asked me Donna's size and sent the receipt so that Donna could change it if it didn't fit or she didn't like it. There was no need to worry on the last score: her face beamed, and standing, she held it up against herself. 'Just what I always wanted,' she said. Paula and I admired the skirt while Adrian was more interested in Donna opening the next two presents.

'Here,' he said, passing her the present from him and Paula. 'It's from us. Happy birthday.'

'Happy birthday,' Paula said.

With the same painstaking precision Donna peeled off the sticky tape and unwrapped the present – a bright pink very fashionable cycle helmet. 'Now I wonder why you have been given that?' I said, smiling.

Donna grinned, and, setting the box on her bed, knelt down and began steadily unwrapping the bike. It had taken me ages to wrap it; I had wound the gift paper around the crossbars and handlebars, and fully over both wheels, so that the whole bike was entirely covered. It took Donna equally long to unwrap it as, trying not to tear the paper, she picked off the sticky tape a little at a time and unwound the paper. Although it had been obvious from the bike's shape what it was even before she'd begun unveiling it, it wasn't until she had completely removed the last piece of paper, folded it, and placed it on top of the pile of other wrapping paper that she allowed her excitement to show.

'Is it mine to keep?' she asked, looking at me.

'Of course, love. All the presents are. You can ride it in the garden after contact tonight. Then at the weekend when we have more time, we'll go to the park for a long ride.' I knew Donna could ride a bike because she'd used an outgrown one of Adrian's in the garden in the summer.

Donna looked wistfully at the bike and then ran her hand over the length of it, almost caressing the shiny metal bars, black leather seat and handlebar covers. The trimmings and wheel guards were in two-tone pink and the bike was the latest Raleigh model for girls; I had wanted Donna to have the best. It had a bell on the handlebars, and also a small saddlebag at the back in matching pink.

'And I can keep it for always?' she asked again.

'Yes, love, it's your present. Of course you can keep it. I'm not going to take it back, am I?' I saw her face tighten and register pain.

'Mum gave me a present once,' she said slowly, still running her hands over the bike as if at any moment it might disappear. 'It was a doll.'

'Oh yes?' I said.

'But when it was Ruby's birthday, she was the girl next door, Mum took it back and gave it to Ruby as a present. It was brand new and I never saw it again.'

Adrian and Paula looked at me, absolutely horrified, and I fought to hide my own shock as my eyes misted. 'Donna, the bike is yours to keep, love, as are all the presents. They are yours and only yours. People don't give presents and take them back – well, not nice people, anyway.'

Apparently there was no depth Rita hadn't stooped to in order to make Donna feel worthless and unloved. I thought that emotional sadism like this was more hurtful and damaging than any beating: the scars ran deeper and lasted longer. Who knew what else Donna had suffered? She'd said very little really.

Another of our little family traditions is to sing 'happy birthday' in the morning after the presents have been opened, usually to the person's embarrassment. We would sing it again to Donna in the evening when the birthday cake was lit and before she blew out the candles. I now struck up the first note, and Adrian and Paula joined in. It sounded like the alleycats' tea party, but Donna didn't mind. 'Thanks,' she said as we finished (not all at the same time). 'Thanks for giving me a birthday. I've never had a birthday before.'

I think at that point Adrian and Paula realised that what they had enjoyed and had assumed to be the norm in respect of birthdays clearly wasn't, and unfortunately didn't apply to everyone. It was as much a shock to them as it would have been for the average child, and it served as a stern reminder that even in our country some children are deprived of what we assume to be a basic ingredient in every child's life.

I had to encourage everyone to get washed, dressed and ready for school, as we were running late. In fact we arrived at Donna's school fifteen minutes late – at 8.30 a.m. instead of 8.15. I went with her into the dining room where the breakfast club was held to explain the reason for our lateness. But there was no need. Miss Warren, who ran the breakfast club, apparently had known it was

Donna's birthday and guessed she might be late. 'Happy birthday!' she called in front of all the children as we went in. Donna smiled, embarrassed. I kissed Donna goodbye and told her to have a good day, and passed her the carrier bag of variety chocolate bars, which I'd bought for her to give to her class to mark her birthday.

'Do you think Donna's mum really gave her present to the girl next door?' Adrian asked as I returned to the car.

'Yes,' I said.

'But that's evil,' he said.

'Very, but Donna is having a good birthday with us now.'

However, I had grave reservations about the contact that night, for even with Edna there, I knew with sly underhand comments and evil looks Rita could still easily sabotage Donna's birthday.

Edna phoned just after 10.00 a.m. to ask how the party had gone on Sunday, and I told her. 'I'll be keeping a close watch on Rita tonight,' she said, 'and I have managed to enlist a colleague to help. She can't stay to every contact but she's available this evening. I've bought the presents for Rita and Chelsea to give to Donna, and wrapped them. All they have to do is to sign the gift card and give Donna the presents. Rita isn't going to get the better of me or Donna tonight, that's for sure.'

As it turned out, Rita did get the better of Edna and Donna, or so she thought: she didn't turn up for contact, and neither did Chelsea. What mother doesn't see her daughter on her birthday? It said it all. But if Rita thought she was causing Donna any suffering she was wrong.

Donna was wearing the new denim skirt my parents had bought her and a pale blue blouse for contact. She was looking forward to what she called her 'second birthday party'. When I dropped her off Edna quietly told me that the boys had arrived a few minutes before us, with their presents, but Rita and Chelsea hadn't arrived yet. Edna said she had tried phoning Rita's mobile but it was switched off. She assumed they were running late and she was expecting them at any moment, which was my expectation too. Donna's father would not be attending, as he was still in hospital; however, his mother, Donna's grandma, was waiting inside as a surprise. Edna had gone into the contact room early and, armed with sandwiches, biscuits and cake, had laid out a party tea.

When I collected Donna at 6.30 p.m., Edna, her colleague, Mrs Bajan and the boys all came out to the car, helping Donna carry her presents. They were in high spirits and I said hello to Mrs Bajan and Edna's colleague. I opened the car boot for the presents, and Edna quietly told me that Rita and Chelsea had boycotted the birthday contact; they hadn't sent a message, and couldn't be contacted. 'Wait until I see them,' Edna hissed under her breath. 'That Rita had better have a damn good excuse,' although Edna thought, as I did, that Rita's absence had been intentional; we would have both been very surprised if she'd had a genuine reason for her and Chelsea not coming.

'Not that Donna appeared very bothered by their absence,' Edna added as I closed the car boot. 'She's had a good time. I organised games for her and the boys. My colleague, Kate, and I joined in. I tell you, Cathy, we're both exhausted.'

I smiled at Edna and Kate. 'That was nice of you,' I said. 'And so many presents! I'm sure all in all it's been Donna's best birthday ever.'

Edna nodded. 'That's what Donna said, and she thanked me, bless her, for making it happen.' I could see that Edna was deeply touched by Donna's gratitude.

It took a good five minutes for everyone to say goodbye to each other. Donna kissed and thanked Edna again, then her gran, her brothers and Edna's colleague, Kate. The escort car to return the boys to their carers drew up on to the forecourt beside us, and then had to wait as the boys wanted to give Donna a final kiss on her birthday, and also wave her off. Left to their own devices, away from the influence of their mother, Warren and Jason seemed completely different – reasonably loving and affectionate towards Donna. Eventually we were all in the car. With the windows down and arms waving, and to the shouts of 'Happy birthday' and 'Bye', I slowly drove off the forecourt and up the road, finally raising the windows when we were out of view.

'You've had a smashing time,' I said, glancing in the rear-view mirror at Donna. 'What a lovely surprise to see your gran there! I know it's a long way for her to travel on the bus.'

'I love my gran,' Donna said. 'She told me she'd seen Dad and he's doing well.'

'Excellent. I said the doctors would make him better, didn't I?'

'Did you have another birthday cake?' Adrian asked.

Donna nodded.

'We've got one for you at home as well. That makes three you've had,' Adrian said admiringly.

'I know,' said Donna. 'Aren't I lucky?'

Adrian and Paula agreed, not at all begrudging, as they knew how much the birthday meant to Donna, and what dreadful ones she'd had in the past.

I wasn't going to raise the subject of Rita and Chelsea's absence with Donna, but I felt that it hung in the air. Donna had obviously had a really good time without them, and I wasn't going to sully it by mentioning them unless Donna did. Her face, her whole body language reflected pure enjoyment and delight, and like yesterday at her party when her brothers hadn't come, she had simply and unreservedly made the most of every moment without any preconceived expectations.

'It was nice of Edna to do me a party tea,' Donna said after a while. 'And I've got so many presents. I've even got one from Mum and Chelsea. They've never bought me a present before.' No, I thought, and little do they know that they have now.

Donna must have reflected on this during the journey home, or possibly she had entertained suspicions from the outset as to who the actual buyer of the presents was, for when we arrived home and were unloading the presents from the boot, she suddenly said, 'Cathy, I don't think Mum and Chelsea bought the presents, although the card had their names on.'

I closed the front door and hoped this was an observation rather than a question, but a minute later as we sat in the lounge and admired her presents, Donna said, 'I wonder if Mum and Chelsea really bought the presents? They're very good presents.'

I guessed they were too good. The present Edna had bought for Rita to give was a table tennis set. When I had first seen it I thought that it was a clever choice, designed to encourage Donna to play with others rather than alone – you can't play table tennis by yourself. Now I was faced with the dilemma of either lying to Donna, or telling her the truth and undermining Edna's good intentions of making sure Donna had a present from her mother and sister.

'Mum's never bought me a present before,' Donna said again reflectively, while I was still considering what to say. 'Neither has Chelsea. I think Edna or Gran had something to do with it.'

I paused from reading her cards and looked straight at her. 'Donna, I think Edna is such a kind person that she wanted to make sure you had the best birthday ever. If she did have something to do with it, then I think that makes your present even more special, doesn't it?'

Donna nodded, and then a smile lit up her whole face.

'What is it, love?' I asked. Adrian and Paula were looking too, wondering, as I was, why Donna was smiling if she believed her mother hadn't even managed to buy her a present.

'I'm glad Edna chose it,' Donna said. 'Otherwise my present might have been another load of dirty washing.'

I laughed. Despite everything Donna's humour had surfaced again. 'Absolutely!' I said.

The four of us continued to admire Donna's presents. Apart from the table tennis set there was a jewellery-making set from Chelsea, a fashionable girl's handbag with a matching purse from Warren, a large boxed set of scented and coloured bubble baths from Jason, a beautiful silver bracelet from Mary and Ray, a basket-making set from Edna, and a £10 note in a card that was signed 'Gran and Dad'.

Leaving the children in the lounge gloating over Donna's presents, I went into the kitchen and lit the candles on the chocolate birthday cake. I carefully carried it through, and Adrian, Paula and I sang 'happy birthday' again (no more in tune than the first time). I took another photograph of Donna blowing out the candles. She was becoming quite proficient at blowing out candles now and blew out all eleven candles with one breath. I handed her the knife and she carefully cut the cake and served us each with a slice on a plate. It was raining now and dark at 7.00 p.m., so I suggested to Donna that she left trying out her bike in the garden until the following day, when hopefully it would be dry and, without contact, we would be home earlier.

'You can take your bike into the garden as soon as we get home from school tomorrow,' I said.

'Is it still there?' she asked.

'Your bike? Of course. It's in your bedroom where you left it this morning, with your other presents.' Even now Donna didn't fully believe me when I said that her presents were hers to keep. I had arranged her cards on the mantelpiece in the lounge, but I had left the presents in her room. Adrian and Paula always liked to keep their presents in their bedrooms for a week or so after their birthdays so that they could see them each morning when they woke.

After we had eaten the cake and had a glass of lemonade we had a few games of table tennis. Then it was time for bed. Paula, Adrian and I helped Donna carry her presents upstairs to join the others in her room. Like Adrian and Paula, she liked the idea of having her presents close to her.

'My bike!' she exclaimed as we walked into her bedroom, apparently surprised to see it still here.

* * *

'Donna,' I said after Adrian and Paula had gone to wash and change, ready for bed, 'I know your mum didn't buy you presents when you were living with her, but didn't Granny Bajan ever give you something on your birthday? Or send you a card? She seems a lovely lady.'

Donna was again slowly running her hands over the length of the bike, apparently still not fully convinced it wouldn't evaporate into thin air. 'She tried to,' she said, 'but Mum stopped her.'

'What do you mean, "stopped her"?'

'Mum told Gran not to send me anything, and Gran didn't like to upset Mum 'cos she took it out on Dad.'

I looked at her carefully. 'How did your mum take it out on your dad? He's a big man and your mum isn't any taller than me.'

'She hid his tablets and wouldn't let him have them. So he would lose his mind and be locked up. Gran worried about that.'

I stared at her, amazed and shocked. 'How do you know this?'

'Mum told me, and so did Gran. Mum said Gran was an interfering bitch because she talked to Edna about our family. If Mum wanted to get at Gran or Dad, she stopped him from having his tablets, so he went mad. Sometimes I found the tablets again when Mum was drunk or asleep, and I gave them to Dad. But Gran worried what Mum would do if she disobeyed her, so she didn't send me any presents. I didn't mind. I just wanted Dad to be well.'

'Yes,' I said, absently, contemplating this new disclosure of deviousness. 'I'm sure your dad will be well soon, now he is in hospital. I'm going to let Edna know what you said about his tablets; then perhaps she can think of a way of making sure he has his medicine.

'Thanks, Cathy,' Donna said. 'It would be great if Edna could help him. And thanks for my birthday. It's been lovely. And no dirty washing!' We both laughed.

Chapter Fifteen

Mummy Christmas

A week later Donna put the yards of gift paper I had used to wrap her bike to good use. Together with the other sheets of wrapping paper and an old magazine, she tore it up and littered her entire bedroom. Hundreds and hundreds of tiny pieces were once again strewn on every available surface. She did this less often now; it used to be three times a week but recently it had been about every ten days. As usual Donna had spent a productive and silent thirty minutes tearing up the paper and then sprinkling it over her room, ready to clear up later.

'Very pretty,' I said dryly as I went into her room. 'It looks as though it has been snowing coloured paper.' I could be fairly relaxed about this behaviour now, and even joke about it with Donna. I was aware that this was her way of acting out, and dealing with, her role of cleaner and general dogsbody when at home, and I knew that eventually it would be addressed in therapy.

What I wasn't so relaxed about was Donna's ongoing need to try to dominate and chastise Adrian and Paula, and also trash her bedroom. Her treatment of Adrian and Paula was slowly improving, but despite my earlier optimism, I found that if I relaxed my vigilance and didn't remind Donna not to speak to Adrian and Paula so harshly, her earlier behaviour quickly resurfaced, and she reverted to chastising them in imitation of the vicious pecking order that had existed at her house. Both Jill and Edna had witnessed Donna 'sniping' at and trying to control Adrian and Paula on their visits, and agreed that it was something that would take a long time to go and was something else that should be addressed in therapy after the final court hearing. But the final court hearing wasn't until May, and even then I wasn't expecting a miracle cure. Children can be in therapy for years before there is any sign of improvement.

Trashing her bedroom was something else that I really needed quicker results with, and Jill and Edna both advised me that I should start applying sanctions. Donna had trashed her room four times by the beginning of December and on each occasion it was after contact. Apart from the mess, which I now insisted Donna helped clear up, she had torn down the curtains each time and they were now irreparably ripped, as was a new duvet cover. Anything that could be smashed was, and on the last occasion Donna had thrown the portable CD player so hard against the window that it had chipped the glass; had it been thrown with much more force it would have shattered the window. It was also frightening to witness Donna's loss of control, not only for me but for Adrian and Paula. I always told them to stay downstairs when it happened, but they could still hear Donna shouting and screaming, and the sound of things breaking as they were hurtled against the walls. Donna was so out of control at these times that had her anger turned towards a person instead of property she could have done them real harm. I always waited by her bedroom door, gently talking to her and persuading her out of the anger before I went in.

Jill had suggested that, as well as making Donna help clear up (which was no great punishment, given her need to clean), I stopped her pocket money to help towards some of the cost of replacing the items that she had destroyed or damaged. I'd had to get Edna's permission to stop Donna's pocket money because there was a small amount included in the foster carer's allowance for pocket money; it was designated as the child's and could not be withheld without the permission of the social worker. Edna fully concurred with Jill's suggestion and we agreed that I would stop two weeks' pocket money each time Donna trashed her bedroom. The small weekly amount was hardly likely to cover the damage she'd done, but its withdrawal was designed to give Donna the message that her actions had a knock-on effect, and that she was culpable and therefore had to take responsibility for her actions and learn to control them.

Having trashed her room twice in a four-week period, she went for a month without any pocket money, but I'm not sure how much good stopping it did. A sanction is more effective if it is applied immediately, but if Donna trashed her room on a Wednesday (as had happened on the previous occasions), she didn't feel the loss of her money until Saturday, which was pocket money day. Also, since her destruction of her room always happened after contact, I felt it was directly related to seeing her mother and having all the bad things that had happened in the past reinforced. But stopping contact wasn't an option, and even reducing it wasn't going to be considered until nearer the final court hearing.

I therefore reverted to the approach I had tried on the first occasion she'd vented her anger on her room: I tried talking her out of it, and then suggested she try to channel her anger in something less destructive, like thumping a cushion or running round the garden shouting. But although Donna was amenable to my suggestions, and when she was calm agreed to try them, when she came in from contact bursting with anger she was invariably in her room, screaming and throwing things, before I had time to intervene and direct her to something else. Once she was out of control it was too late. I could only hope that in time this behaviour might also improve, although I thought the only real improvement would come if contact was stopped.

As far as I was aware, Donna hadn't tried to rub off her skin again when washing, although I knew she retained a poor self-image in respect of her dual heritage. She loved her dad, who was mixed race, and, despite his odd behaviour when he hadn't taken his medication, Donna was proud of him, and of her gran, who was black. But Donna couldn't translate this positive view of their colour to herself. Her mother had been so negative and demeaning of her racial origins that the damage ran deep.

The four of us went shopping together to spend the £10 that her gran and dad had sent her for her birthday, and Donna wanted to go to Boots the chemist to spend it. I assumed she wanted to buy some perfume or even some make-up, as girls of her age often start experimenting with a bit of lipgloss or eye shadow – they were advertised in all the girlie magazines. But once inside the chemist Donna spent ages wandering up and down the aisles without actually telling me what she was looking for. Eventually

we stopped at the display of hair removal creams – depila-
tories as they are called – and she began examining the
various boxed tubes.

'What are you looking for, Donna?' I asked. She didn't
have excessive hair, and hair removal wasn't something a
girl of eleven would normally have contemplated. She
shrugged and appeared to be studying the ingredients
listed on the boxes, although her level of reading wouldn't
have allowed her to make much sense of the long names of
the chemicals used in the products. I couldn't even
pronounce some of them, let alone identify what they were
used for – calcium thioglycolate, lithium hydroxide,
disodium lauryl sulfate, to name but three.

'Does it have bleach in it?' she asked after some
moments. Adrian and Paula were now becoming restless at
this lengthy and unproductive shopping trip.

I looked at the ingredients on the box Donna held,
containing the tube of cream designed to 'efficiently and
gently remove unwanted hair'.

'Not as far as I can see,' I said. 'But you don't need this.
It's for ladies to remove hair from their legs.'

She returned the product to the shelf and picked up a
similar one but with a different brand name and manufac-
turer. 'Does this have bleach in it?' she asked again.

'I don't know,' I said, not looking at the ingredients. 'But
you're not going to buy hair-removing cream, Donna. You
don't need it at your age.'

'Chelsea uses it,' she said.

'Well, she's older than you. I guess at fifteen she might
be removing the hair from her legs, but you haven't got
any hair on your legs to remove.' Even at fifteen I would
have supervised a girl using these products, as they are

very strong and there was a long list of warnings and contraindications on the packet, and details of when and how one should or should not use them.

'It's not for her hair,' Donna said after some moments. Adrian and Paula were really fidgeting now.

I glanced again at the box. 'This product is for hair removal, Donna. What else could she use it for?'

'Whitening,' she said.

I looked up. 'Whitening? Whitening what?'

'Some of the hair-removing creams have bleach in them and it can whiten your skin. Chelsea uses it on her face. It makes her lighter.'

Dear God, I thought! Whatever next? 'Does your mother know she uses it for that?' The answer to which I could have reasonably guessed.

'Mum told her to. I want to buy some. Then I can be lighter like Chelsea.'

Chelsea had a different father and therefore different genes to Donna, but that was hardly the issue. 'Absolutely not,' I said and, returning the box to the shelf, I moved away from the display. 'Donna, there is no way you are going to try to lighten your skin. You have inherited some of your looks from your dad and Granny Bajan, and you look lovely just as you are. Whatever would your dad and gran say if they knew? They'd have a fit, and so too would Edna. No way, Donna. You can spend your money another day on something else.'

I led the way out of the shop with Donna trailing behind, sulking. Adrian and Paula asked me what the matter was, and I said I would explain later. Had I been a black carer it would have been easier to try to persuade Donna to a better self-image because she would have had an immediate and positive example to follow. This is one of the reasons children coming into care are placed with carers who reflect their ethnicity. But there is a permanent shortage of carers from 'ethnic minorities' where I live, despite repeated advertising campaigns. In the past I had successfully fostered black children and those with dual heritage but it was in cases like Donna's, where she had such a negative view of her skin colour, that I had the biggest challenge.

I decided that something I could do was to buy some magazines that were aimed at black women and teenagers, and would show Donna positive images of black women and girls. Donna often bought magazines with her pocket money but she usually chose *Girl Talk*, *Amy* or *Go Girl*, in which the pictures were mainly of white girls. She could still buy these magazines, but together with what I had in mind there would be a better balance.

Having left the chemist, we went up the high street and into the newsagent's, where I sifted through the shelves of magazines. Adrian stood smirking at the magazines on the top shelf, which showed pictures of women with their breasts exposed. I couldn't find any magazines catering specifically for black girls of her age, so I took down and looked through *Ebony*, which was aimed at black women, and *Young Voices* and *Right On*, which were aimed at black teenagers. Although the actual articles were a bit old for Donna, there was nothing inappropriate in them, and they contained lots of pictures and feature articles on black women and teenagers, all very positive. I decided to buy *Ebony* and *Young Voice*, and then I let Paula and Adrian choose a magazine each for themselves (though not from the top shelf), and Donna also wanted the latest edition of *Girl Talk*.

In the car going home Donna had got over her sulk, and all three children were looking at their magazines, and also glancing at each other's. I would explain later to Adrian and Paula why I'd bought Donna two extra magazines, and why they featured only black women and girls, although I doubt they had even noticed. They were unaware of the issue of Donna's colour – to them she was their foster sister and they appeared to take for granted that she had a slightly darker skin tone and hair.

I had a good friend, Rose, who is dual heritage and that evening I phoned her and told her what Donna had wanted to buy in the chemist. 'I didn't even know hair-removing cream had bleach in it,' I said. 'Did you, Rose?'

'Yes. And unfortunately I know some women do use it to lighten their skin. There are also products on the market specifically to lighten skin tone, although I've never seen them in the shops around here. I think they're mail order.'

'Really?' I said, taken aback. 'You don't use them, do you?'

'No, of course not.' She laughed. 'Look, we're overdue for a coffee and a chat. Why don't you and the kids come over on Saturday? Daniel was saying only the other day he hadn't seen Adrian for a while, and Libby can educate Donna; they're about the same age.'

'That would be great,' I said, for obviously Daniel and Libby were well adjusted and proud of who they were and would be a good example to Donna. But I could only do so much, and the rest was a matter of time and giving Donna ongoing praise and encouragement.

* * *

Christmas was fast approaching, and by the end of the second week in December I had done most of the present buying and the four of us had decorated the house. Given what Donna's birthdays with her mother had been like, I hadn't dared ask her about her last Christmas.

Paula asked, though. 'What did you have for Christmas last year?' she said, as they wrote their Christmas cards for their school friends; Adrian had finished his and had left the table where we were working.

'Nothing,' Donna said.

'Nothing?' Paula repeated disbelievingly, although I think even she now understood enough of Donna's life to know that 'nothing' might be possible. 'Didn't you have presents from Father Christmas?' she tried again.

'No,' Donna said.

'What about your dad?' Paula persisted. 'We have presents from Father Christmas and ones from our dad.'

Actually it's Mummy Christmas in this house, I thought, but Donna was shaking her head. 'Edna gave me a present. It was a teddy bear, the one I take to bed.'

Paula was still looking at Donna, her little mouth open and her eyes round in disbelief. I motioned to her not to pursue the questioning. Edna's Christmas present was clearly the only one Donna had received, and I now knew that her gran had probably been stopped from sending Donna a present. I thought that receiving nothing from her mother was at least preferable to the pile of dirty washing she'd received on her birthday.

School broke up the week before Christmas and we relaxed into the festive season. With the three children together for the greater part of each day I renewed my vigilance.

And possibly because Christmas was coming, or perhaps because she was improving anyway, I noticed that when Donna spoke to Paula and Adrian it was with less severity and she appeared to be joining in more. Donna was looking forward to Christmas, and I guessed it would be her first proper Christmas, as it was with so many of the children I had looked after.

Christmas Day was on Sunday and Donna had her usual contact on the Friday before. I had found with the previous children I had fostered that this last contact before Christmas (unless they were seeing each other over Christmas) was used to celebrate Christmas, and presents were exchanged.

Donna had chosen and wrapped presents for her mother, father, gran, Chelsea and brothers, and took them to contact. I had added a present and card for Edna from us all. I knew that Donna's gran wouldn't be at contact because she had gone to stay (as she usually did) with her family in Barbados for a month. Donna's dad was still in hospital, but Edna had said she would make sure that he and her gran got their presents from Donna as soon as was possible after Christmas. Buying all these presents, together with my own shopping, had taken quite a lot of time and organisation, but it is part of a foster carer's role to arrange presents for the looked-after child to give to their family on birthdays and at Christmas, and quite rightly so.

When I collected Donna from contact at 6.30 p.m. I was relieved to see she was carrying a number of presents, all of which were still wrapped and would be put under the tree for her to open on Christmas Day. There was a present from Edna, one each from Warren and Jason, one from

Donna's dad and her gran, which Edna said her gran had sent to her office before she'd gone away, and also one each from her mum and Chelsea. 'I took Rita and Chelsea Christmas shopping,' Edna said to me quietly, as I placed the presents in the car boot. 'I made sure they bought Donna something this year.'

'That's so sweet of you, Edna,' I said. 'You have a lovely Christmas, and a well-deserved rest.'

'And you,' she said. 'And thank you for my present and card.'

'You're very welcome.' Edna was truly an angel. With all her workload, she'd found the time to take Rita and Chelsea shopping to ensure that Donna had a Christmas present from them. And doubtless the money for this had come from the social services budget, for Rita appeared to be permanently broke.

Adrian and Paula saw their father for the day on Christmas Eve, and returned with presents from him to go under the tree. This would be their third Christmas without their father and it still touched a raw nerve with me, as I'm sure it does for any family that isn't complete. But I wished John a merry Christmas and he did me. Paula and Adrian gave him an extra hug and a kiss before they said goodbye, and he returned to spend Christmas with his partner.

Our Christmas followed its usual tradition and on Christmas Eve we went to the family service at our local church. It's a very informal short service and centres around the crib scene and what the Christmas story is all about. We returned home for a late supper, after which the children put a glass of milk in the porch for Santa, together with a carrot for the reindeer (one to be shared between nine because I needed the rest for Christmas dinner). Then Donna, Paula and Adrian hung their pillow-cases on the inside of the front door in anticipation of Father Christmas's visit that night, while I took a photo-graph. The pillowcases would be magically filled during the early hours and appear by their beds in morning. It had never actually been stated in our house how this happened; Paula and Adrian happily accepted, as Donna now did, that it was just part of the 'magic' of Christmas. Aged six, Paula still believed in Father Christmas, and I had asked Adrian a couple of years previously, when he'd started expressing doubts, to keep them to himself, for no child likes to be told that Father Christmas doesn't exist; they want to hang on to the fantasy for as long as possible. Donna embraced the whole concept of Father Christmas unreservedly, although obviously being the same age as Adrian (and aware that Santa hadn't existed in previous years) she must have known the truth.

It was 9.30 p.m. before I finally had the children in bed, and another half an hour before they were asleep. Mummy Christmas then sat up until nearly midnight with a couple of glasses of sherry and a mince pie, watching a late-night film. Only when she was certain that the children were really fast asleep did she resist another glass of sherry and unhook the empty pillowcases from the front door. She then tiptoed up the stairs and into her bedroom, where she took the wrapped presents from her locked wardrobe and packed them into the correct pillowcases. Then, very quietly, she trod round the landing, carefully avoiding the squeaking floorboard, and into the children's bedrooms, hoping they wouldn't wake and see her. She carefully rested the overflowing pillowcases against the bed of each child, then stole from the last bedroom and into her own bed.

And it seemed to her that she had only just gone to sleep when she was woken by the sounds of excited squeals. She opened one bleary eye to look at the clock and saw it was 5.55 a.m.

'Merry Christmas!' came the cries from the landing. 'Can we come in?'

'Yes. Merry Christmas,' Mummy Christmas returned.

And as all three children dragged their pillowcases into her room, as tradition required, then sat on her bed and opened their presents, she saw the look on their faces, and knew that all the hard work and expense had been completely and wondrously worthwhile.

My parents, and my brother and his wife, arrived within five minutes of each other at 11.00 a.m. on Christmas morning, and put their presents under the tree to join the huge pile. We had drinks, nibbles and mince pies, and then played some games – Twister and an old favourite, Hunt the Thimble. We spent over an hour unwrapping Christmas presents, with my father reading the names on the gift tags one at a time and handing them out. We had another drink before I served dinner at 3.00 p.m., and my brother carved the turkey. After the main course we had a break from eating and I organised some 'sitting down' games in the lounge while we digested our meal. We returned to the dining table in the front room for pudding, and my brother poured copious amounts of brandy over the pudding and set fire to it. I had made a trifle because I knew that Adrian and Paula didn't like the rich Christmas pudding, and Donna had a bit of everything. She'd done very well joining in, and although she had been quiet she'd taken part in all the games, and also spent some time talking to my mother, to whom children easily warm. I presented the cheese board in the lounge at 7.00, and although everyone groaned and claimed they 'couldn't possibly eat another thing', either they did, or we'd had a nasty invasion of mice.

We finally said goodbye around 10.00 p.m., and everyone agreed it was the 'best Christmas ever', but then we say that every year. However, for Donna I thought it was probably true, and most likely her only Christmas to date. As the four of us grouped on the doorstep and waved off my parents and my brother and his wife, it crossed my mind what my ex had missed with just him and his partner and no children. I also wondered what Rita and Chelsea had done, for while Donna and her brothers had enjoyed a Christmas with all the trimmings, Rita and Chelsea had presumably spent it by themselves, and I imagined it had been a pretty dismal one. Despite everything Rita had done to Donna, I felt sorry for her and Chelsea, particularly for Chelsea, who had been denied the pleasure and excitement of a child's Christmas for life.

Chapter Sixteen

Winter Break

The children returned to school on 4 January, and when I arrived home I took down the decorations with a severe case of post-Christmas blues. I felt like this every year; I'm sure a lot of people do. There is all the excitement and build-up to the festive season and then January falls flat and cold, with short days, overcast skies and spring seeming a long way off. Adrian's and Paula's birthdays were the next family celebration – 30 March and 7 April – but until then there was a bit of a void. What we really needed was a holiday, a change of scenery, in the February half-term break. Somewhere hot and sunny, I thought, in a hotel where I was waited on hand and foot! We hadn't had a holiday abroad since my husband had left. How much would a holiday for four in February cost, I wondered as I packed away the last of the decorations? There was only one way to find out, and on the whim of the moment I took my coat from the hall stand, picked up my bag, and with that buzz that comes from throwing caution to the wind, I drove to the shopping mall, where I parked in the multi-storey car park and walked to the travel agent's.

Two hours later I came away with the brochure and booking form – proof that the children and I would be spending half term in Morocco, and with my winter blues banished and my savings account just about coping. I'd phoned Edna from the travel agent's, before booking and had obtained her permission to take Donna. She'd given it without hesitation 'What a lovely opportunity for Donna,' she'd said. 'Thank you so much. I'll arrange a passport for her straight away and also check that her vaccinations are up to date.'

It was 2.30 p.m. by the time I was in the car again and I drove straight to collect Paula and Adrian from school. I was bursting to tell them, but I stopped myself: I wanted to wait until we were all together at home. It was Thursday, so without the quick turnaround necessary when Donna had contact, as soon as we arrived home I told the children to go into the lounge because I had something important to say. They were subdued and wide-eyed when I went in, sitting in a line on the sofa and wondering what was so important, and if they had done something wrong.

'I've booked us a holiday,' I announced, producing the brochure and squatting on the floor in front of them. 'At half term we're going on a plane to Morocco!'

'Wow!' Adrian said, and he immediately slid off the sofa and joined me on the floor for a closer look. 'Cor,' he said. 'What type of plane is it?' I hadn't thought to ask. 'I bet it's a Boeing 747,' he said, bubbling over with excitement. 'It's one of the biggest planes in the world – that's why it's called a jumbo jet. It's got four engines and can seat over five hundred passengers!'

'Yes,' Paula knowledgeably agreed, joining him on the floor for a closer look at the brochure.

Donna hadn't said anything.

'Well, what do you think?' I asked. 'Are you happy to go?'

She stared at me in utter amazement. 'Are you taking me?' she asked.

'Yes, of course.' I had thought it would be obvious but apparently it hadn't been. 'Donna, you are part of this family. Of course you are coming with us.'

She too now left the sofa and joined us on the floor, and with the brochure open at the page showing the hotel I read out the details of this luxurious and family-orientated resort. To say they were excited was an understatement; if Christmas had taken Donna's breath away then this left her absolutely speechless.

'Are you all right? Donna,' I asked, for even now she wasn't saying anything. 'There's nothing for you to worry about on the plane. I'll look after you. It will be one big adventure for us all.'

'I don't think Mum will let me go,' she said sombrely.

'I've spoken to Edna and she is going to ask your mother, but if she says no then Edna can make the decision. Edna wants you to come, so you will be coming, I promise you that.'

But later when Edna told me what Rita had said I was still shocked. 'Good riddance to bad rubbish. I hope the plane crashes,' Donna's mother had said.

'Why does Rita hate Donna so much?' I asked Edna, for I had come to believe that 'hate' wasn't too strong a word.

'I really don't know,' Edna said. 'But I have come across cases before where one child in the family is victimised, sometimes when the other children are reasonably well cared for, although that wasn't so here.' No one really knew why Rita hated Donna, but it was very, very sad.

* * *

The weeks flew by to our holiday and before we knew it, it was the last day of the half term and we were going the next morning. When I collected Adrian and Paula from school it appeared that most of their classes were aware of our holiday, and we left the playground to the cries of 'Have a good time!'

When I met Donna from school, the head, Donna's teacher, Emily and her mother, Mary, Ray and the boys all made a point of seeing us and wishing us a happy holiday. Mary and Ray were taking the boys for a few days out over the half-term break, including a trip to the zoo, and I wished them a good time. 'It's a lovely opportunity for Donna,' Mrs Bristow said to me. 'We'll look forward to hearing all about it, and make sure you show us the photos, Donna.'

Beth Adams added that the class had been tested on their twelve times table and, as with the others, Donna had got them all right and received two team points. I was obviously pleased and praised Donna, as I had in all the previous weeks, but I was also quietly relieved that we had finally come to the end of the times tables and that learning them would no longer dominate our car journeys, evenings and weekends. But the result of all the weeks of hard work and repetition was not only that Donna now knew her times tables but that she had proved to herself and her teacher that she could learn as well as anyone, given time. I had high hopes for Donna in the future.

It was a very noisy crew that I drove home that afternoon, and also a very cold one. The temperature had dropped, and although we hadn't had snow, 'flurries' had been forecast and the skies looked full of it. I prayed that nothing would happen over night that could disrupt our travel plans.

As it was Friday, Donna had contact, so we weren't out of the routine yet. I had plated up Donna's dinner as I usually did, and she ate it and then changed out of her school uniform. At 4.30 p.m. we were in the car again, taking her to contact. When I collected her at 6.30, Edna brought Donna out to the car and made a point of wishing us all a good holiday. Edna always took the opportunity at the end of contact to let me know how contact had gone and update me, and tonight was no exception.

Once Donna was in the car with the door closed and out of earshot, Edna said, 'Rita has told the boys that she will take them on a plane to Morocco when they go home to live with her!' Edna raised her eyes, for clearly making unrealistic promises to young children was unfair and could only lead to disappointment. However, on a purely personal and selfish level I felt that if that was all that had been said, then Donna had escaped very lightly.

That evening my parents and my brother phoned to wish us bon voyage, and so too did Paula and Adrian's father, which I thought was decent of him. By the time everyone had had a bath and was changed, it was 8.30 p.m. 'In twelve hours' time,' I announced, 'we shall be in the taxi going to the airport!' They all cheered.

It was difficult to say who was more excited that evening, the children or me; certainly it took me the longest to get off to sleep. Apart from the anticipation of a long overdue holiday, I kept running through a mental checklist of anything I could conceivably have forgotten. I was still tossing and turning at 1.00 a.m., and eventually I got out of bed and double checked that the plane tickets and passports were still in my handbag, which of course they were. At 7 o'clock the alarm went off and I was up, washed and dressed within fifteen minutes. I woke the children and they performed the same feat in ten minutes!

I love take-off – the speed and exhilaration that flattens you into your seat, as you hurtle down the runway, going the fastest you are ever likely to go on land in your life. Then there's that euphoric moment as the wheels lift from the tarmac and you are airborne, actually flying! As at the end of a good ride at the fair, I feel I want to go back and do it again. Just one more go, please! I glanced across at the children and knew they were feeling it too, although Donna and Paula with a little trepidation. The children occupied the three seats that stretched out from the window, while I was on the end of the row directly across the aisle. They were going to take turns to sit by the window. I looked at their happy smiling faces, on the biggest adventure of their lives to date, and I knew I had made the right decision to throw caution to the wind and come on holiday. And just as Christmas had been the best one ever, I felt this holiday would follow suit, and also help confirm to Donna that she was truly an integrated member of the family.

Chapter Seventeen
Final Rejection

My only criticism of the holiday was that it wasn't long enough and before we knew it we were at the airport again for the return flight. But as well as giving us all a wonderful break, the holiday had helped to strengthen our bond as a family. There had been no major disagreement or incidents, despite us all being together for the most part of seven days. I'd only had to tell Donna once not to boss Paula, when I'd asked Paula to get out of the pool, as it was time to get changed for dinner, and Donna had shouted, 'Get out of the pool now!' But she had quickly apologised.

I felt Donna was more accepting of her role as simply that of a child and I didn't anticipate having to continually watch her any more when she was with Paula and Adrian as I had done in the past. I also hoped there would be no more of the violent outbursts of anger which had culminated in Donna trashing her room. I wasn't expecting an angel, for Donna had suffered a lot in her past, but she was making more attempt to talk to me, and I hoped she would therefore be able to verbalise her anger rather than taking it out on her room.

* * *

The following Monday saw us back in the routine, and me with a suitcase full of washing to be done. The children had wrapped the model camels they were going to give their friends as presents, and we took them with us to school. The children looked incredibly healthy: their faces glowed from the sun and fresh air, and we were all a shade darker. The weather wasn't quite as cold as it had been when we had left England, but we wrapped up warmly on that first morning – it was taking a while for us to acclimatise. I saw Donna into the breakfast club, and Mrs Bristow, the head, was waiting for her.

'Come here and tell me all about your holiday,' she said, and she gave Donna a big hug. 'You do look well!'

I didn't have time to chat with Mrs Bristow, as I had to take Adrian and Paula to school, so I left it to Donna to tell the head all about our holiday, which she'd started to do immediately. 'We had loads to eat,' I heard her say as I left the breakfast club, 'and a camel ride, and swimming in the pool and sea.'

A similar reception greeted Adrian and Paula, first from their friends, all wanting to know if they'd had a good time, and then, when the bell rang and the staff came out into the playground, from their class teachers. I said goodbye, and returned home, where I set the washing machine going. I sorted the mail, which I'd opened but hadn't dealt with, then finished unpacking the cases. Edna and Jill phoned to ask how the holiday had gone, and I was able to tell them that it had truly been a holiday for us all.

In the afternoon, half an hour before I was due to leave to collect the children from school, Edna phoned again. And unlike her previous call when she'd asked brightly about our holiday, her voice now sounded strained and anxious.

'Cathy, Donna has contact tonight,' she said, going straight into what she had to say. 'And I've just had a phone call from Rita, telling me she's pregnant.' She paused and, whereas I would normally have offered congratulations on hearing the news of an expected baby, now I didn't know what to say. 'It's due in August,' Edna said. 'Two months after Chelsea's baby is due. I've told Rita not to say anything to the children tonight at contact, but she might.'

'So you don't want me to tell Donna before we go?' I asked.

'No. Hopefully Rita will do as I've asked. I've tried to explain to her how traumatic the news will be to the children, particularly to Donna. She's likely to see it as the final rejection.' I knew what Edna meant: Rita's children had been taken into care and now she had set about replacing them, like a worn-out pair of shoes. 'I want time to prepare Donna for this,' Edna said again. 'And also to be certain that Rita is pregnant. She's phoned me before with these "phantom pregnancies".'

'Has Chelsea's pregnancy been confirmed then?' I asked. 'It hadn't when the Guardian told me.'

'Yes, last week. I'm trying to persuade Chelsea to listen to my advice so that there's a chance she'll be able to keep the baby.'

'Good.'

'Mrs Bajan will find out at some point about Rita, assuming she is pregnant. I know she will be upset. I might tell Mrs Bajan myself before Rita does.' I assumed Edna meant that Donna's gran would be upset because the baby might be mistreated as her other grandchildren had been, but there was a different reason for Edna's comment. 'Mr Bajan can't be the father because he is still in hospital,' Edna said. 'Rita hasn't been anywhere near him all the time he's been in.'

'Oh, I see.'

'There's a strong possibility,' Edna continued, 'that Rita's baby (if there is one) has the same father as Chelsea's. There's a man living on the estate who sees himself as some sort of Casanova and goes round impregnating single women. He's been seen going in and out of Rita's house.' I didn't know whether to laugh or cry. 'Anyway, Cathy, once Rita's pregnancy is confirmed, I'll talk to Donna. There's no point in upsetting her if there is no need.'

'Thank you, Edna. Is Chelsea still attending contact? Donna never talks about contact when she comes home.'

'Sometimes. When Rita has run out of money. She knows that because Chelsea is still a minor I can give her additional allowances, and I'm not likely to refuse to. When Rita is broke, Chelsea appears at contact and asks for money.' She paused and I heard her sigh. 'What a mess! All the support I have put into that family and it's come to this. Sometimes I wonder how efficient I am at my job.' I thought Edna sounded tired and worn out, which was hardly surprising given her workload. She would probably be dealing with another fourteen child protection cases, and being so conscientious, it was obviously taking its toll.

'You do an excellent job, Edna,' I said. 'I'm sure you have made a big difference to a lot of people. I couldn't begin to imagine what Donna's life would have been like had she not come into care. And her brothers are doing well, aren't they?'

'Yes, I suppose so, put like that.' But her voice still sounded flat. 'Perhaps I'm getting too old for this job,' she said. 'Or possibly I'm in need of a holiday. I haven't had a proper one in years. When I take time off from work, I end up writing reports. My hubby is always going on at me to take a holiday. Perhaps I should follow your example.'

'You should, Edna. It wasn't until I got back, feeling so relaxed, that I realised how much I had needed one. Book it tonight!'

She laughed. 'OK, Cathy. I'll speak to my hubby. See you later at contact.'

Chapter Eighteen

Don't stop Loving Me

Thrust straight back into our routine, I collected the children from school, gave Donna her evening meal and then took her to contact. The children were still talking about our holiday, reliving the highlights and looking forward to seeing the photographs, which I'd yet to send off to be developed. I hoped that Donna would have the chance to talk about her holiday at contact. I knew Edna would obviously be interested, but it was highly doubtful that Rita would. I had worked with parents in the past who'd derived much pleasure from their children being taken on holiday while in care, and selflessly enjoyed hearing about something that they'd never had the opportunity to experience. However, this wasn't to be so here.

When I collected Donna from contact, Edna came up to me and said quietly, 'Rita ignored Donna for the whole evening, apart from telling her news!' I glanced at Donna, who was sitting in the back of the car with Adrian and Paula; unsurprisingly, she looked dejected and morose.

'Not only did Rita tell her that she was pregnant,' Edna said, shaking her head sadly, 'but she told the boys, so that Donna could hear, that the baby would be beautiful, not like Donna.'

I cringed, shocked and appalled, and I looked seriously at Edna. 'Edna, I really think it's time to be reducing contact. I'm sure it's doing Donna more harm than good. How is she supposed to improve when she is subjected to this type of comment three times a week?' I stopped myself from saying more because I could see that Edna was blaming herself.

'I know,' Edna said, looking as dejected as Donna. 'I'm going to speak to the Guardian and see about an application to court.' Because Donna was in care under an ICO Edna couldn't change the level of contact that had been set by the judge without making an application to the court, which meant appearing before the judge and giving good reasons why the contact should be reduced. Parental rights in respect of contact are taken very seriously by the court, sometimes, I feel, to the detriment of the child, who may be trying to move on from the past. There was no point in saying anything further. Edna was as aware as I was of the negative impact contact was having on Donna; whether or not the judge agreed remained to be seen.

I said goodbye to Edna and got into the car. Edna usually spoke to Adrian and Paula, but now she was too preoccupied to ask about their holiday.

'All right?' I asked Donna, turning in my seat to look at her. She shrugged and, with her head down, wrung her hands in her lap. Adrian looked at me questioningly, for the contrast in the Donna who had gone into contact bubbling with her news of the holiday and the dejected child who now sat next to him was obvious to all. Donna still yearned for, and sought, her mother's praise and acceptance, and Edna had told me more than once that it was crucifying to watch Donna trying to ingratiate herself to her mother.

I started the car and headed for home. Adrian and Paula were silent during the journey, sensing and respecting Donna's unhappiness. I had decided that once I had Paula in bed I would try talking to Donna about what her mother had said this evening, and also about some of the issues from her past. I had tried talking to Donna before when she'd returned from contact obviously upset, but I'd come to realise that she preferred to be left alone, and she usually sat in her room for half an hour to unwind. Sometimes she tore up paper, and on four previous occasions she'd trashed her room. But since the bonding of our holiday I felt more confident in approaching her and hoped she would feel able to confide in me.

I parked the car on the driveway, got out and opened the child-locked rear doors. The children followed me up the path to the front door and I unlocked it and let us in. Paula squatted in the hall to take off her shoes. Then suddenly, without any warning Donna let out an almighty roar and thumped Paula in the chest. Paula fell backwards and banged her head on the edge of the partially open front-room door.

'Donna!' I yelled as I went to Paula, who was struggling to right herself. 'My God, are you all right?' I drew Paula to me. Her eyes were watering and she had one hand clutching her head and the other on her chest. I took her onto my lap as Donna ran upstairs. Adrian closed the front door and then stood, looking horrified, his face white. Donna's bedroom door slammed shut; then there was quiet.

I quickly examined Paula's head. There was an angry red lump on the back of it where it had hit the edge of the door, but thankfully the skin wasn't broken. I gently eased up her jumper to reveal a red mark where Donna had thumped her in the chest. As I comforted her, my heart pounded and my anger rose. Donna had hit Paula with such force that she could have easily broken a bone, and I knew at that moment that such an incident must never be allowed to happen again, and I cursed myself that it had happened at all.

I held Paula to me and soothed her. Suddenly the silence in Donna's room was replaced by banging and crashing as she started trashing her room.

'Adrian, will you look after Paula for a moment, please,' I said tightly. 'I need to see Donna.' Adrian took Paula by the hand, and easing her off my lap, led her along the hall and towards the lounge.

I went upstairs, my heart thudding and my body tense. I was furious with Donna. What the hell did she think she was doing! Damage to property was one thing, but damage to my child was something else! I went round the landing to Donna's room. The sound of her screaming and breaking things grew louder. Without knocking, I threw open the door and went straight in. She had her back to me and was throwing everything that came to hand.

'Donna!' I yelled at the top of my voice. 'What the hell do you think you're doing? How dare you! How dare you hit Paula! Stop that now!' My chest tightened and my pulse raced as my voice drowned out Donna's screaming. 'I won't have you doing that!' I shouted. 'Do you hear me? I won't have you hitting Paula! How dare you!' I was right in her room now, only a couple of feet in front of her. I was hot and shaking with anger. I had never been so angry in my life. 'Do you hear me, Donna?' I yelled again. 'How dare you hurt Paula!'

She suddenly stopped screaming and throwing things, and turned to look at me, shocked by my outburst.

'How dare you!' I cried again. 'She's only little! You have hurt her. I won't have it, Donna! Do you understand me! I won't have it in this house!'

She stood very still and stared at me.

I stared back. 'You didn't like it when your brothers hit you. And now you've done it to Paula! I've had enough, Donna. We've just returned from holiday and you've done this! You've gone too far now! You've overstepped the mark!' Fuming, I came out and slammed the door. I needed to put some distance between us before I said something I would regret.

I stood on the landing, my heart pounding and my breath coming fast and shallow. I felt hot and sick. I'd never shouted at anyone like that, ever, let alone a child. Foster carers aren't supposed to shout at the children they look after, and I hadn't, not in all the years I had been fostering, until now.

All manner of things went through my mind as I moved away from Donna's door and round the landing and began going downstairs. How could she have taken it out on Paula like that? Why wasn't I getting through to her? Why couldn't she talk to me instead of unleashing her anger on a child of six? Could I really continue looking after her with the possibility of Paula being hurt again? Was there something wrong in the way I was treating Donna? Why hadn't she made the progress I'd anticipated? I had been so hopeful that we'd turned a corner during our week away, and now this had taken us back to square one, or further. I would have to tell Jill and Edna what had happened, and admit to my outburst, and perhaps also admit defeat. For if this was the point we had come to after eight months, I didn't see how I could be the right carer for Donna. What she needed I didn't know, but clearly it was more than I could offer.

I arrived at the bottom of the stairs, still shaking and with tears forming at the back of my eyes. I went along the hall and into the lounge. Adrian and Paula were sitting together on the sofa, Adrian with his arm round Paula. They were both very pale and looked frightened; they had never seen me so angry or shout like that. I went over and made room between them on the sofa. I put an arm round each of their shoulders and we sat in silence, while I slowly calmed down.

They were as shocked as I was by my shouting, and it is for this reason that foster carers shouldn't shout. It is frightening for a child to witness an adult out of control (and in the case of foster children, very likely replicating the behaviour they've been moved from at home). The fostering family is supposed to set a good example of what family life should be like; if foster carers lose the plot and started ranting and raving, what sort of message does that send out? But I was only human, and I had been furious, not only because of Donna's treatment of Paula, but that after all this time of looking after Donna it appeared I'd done her no good whatsoever.

We sat in silence for some moments as I cuddled Paula and Adrian, and my thoughts slowly settled. It was still quiet upstairs, and I wondered what Donna was doing. I would have to go up and check on her soon, in case her anger turned inwards and she tried to harm herself.

'Are you all right now?' I asked Paula gently. 'Your head isn't cut, but there is a lump. It will be sore for a few days.'

'I'm all right,' she said quietly. 'Are you?'

'Yes, love.' I slid my arms from their shoulders, and again parted her hair and examined her head. The red lump hadn't swollen any larger, but it had obviously hurt a lot. I eased up her jumper again and saw that the red mark on her chest was fading. Donna's attack could have been a lot worse, I told myself, but that was no consolation at all.

'What's the matter with Donna?' Paula asked in a small voice.

'She's angry with her mother and unfortunately she's taking it out on us. I'm sorry, love.'

'It's not your fault,' Paula said.

'I should have realised she was so angry when we came in. I am wondering if Donna wouldn't be better off living with another family.' But even as I said it I knew that wasn't the answer, though what the answer was I'd no idea. I had tried my best, tried to integrate her into the family, and used my well-tested strategies to help her come to terms with her past and hopefully move her on to a better future, and apparently I'd failed.

'Is Donna all right?' Paula asked, her concern for her foster sister outweighing her own hurt.

'I'm going to check,' I said. 'Will you be OK here for a minute, while I try to talk to her?'

Paula nodded. 'Good girl. And thanks, Adrian.' I moved to the edge of the sofa and stood, but before I got any further we heard Donna's bedroom door open, followed by her footsteps on the stairs. I glanced at Paula, who was looking anxious, clearly thinking that if Donna was still angry she might hit her again. 'It's all right,' I reassured her. 'You stay on the sofa with Adrian.' I walked to the lounge door and stood in the entrance, where I waited as Donna appeared. She came slowly towards me along the hall, her shoulders slumped forward and head hung down. Her slow lumbering gate reminded me of when she'd first arrived, when she appeared to carry the weight of the world on her shoulders and even breathing was too much effort.

She stopped a little way in front of me and slowly raised her head. Adrian and Paula were silent in the room behind me. Donna looked at me with large woeful eyes, so full of pain and suffering that the sight of them made my heart sting, despite what she'd done. Yet although I now felt desperately sorry for Donna my concern lay with Paula, who sat on the sofa behind me, hurting from the pain Donna had inflicted, and with her trust in Donna gone.

'Yes?' I said to Donna.

She opened her mouth to speak, and slowly, laboriously the words came out. 'I need to say sorry to Paula,' she said, her gaze falling from me to the floor. 'I need to say sorry. I want to say sorry to Paula so she will love me again. I don't want her to hate me like my family does. I want you all to love me. Please don't stop loving me, Cathy. I need you to love me.'

Tears immediately stung the back of my eyes, and I heard Paula leave the sofa behind me. I was still in the doorway to the lounge, blocking Donna's entrance, and protecting Adrian and Paula, although there seemed no need to now. Donna's anger was spent and I knew Paula was in no danger. Paula came past me and put both her arms around Donna's waist and hugged her tight.

'I still love you, Donna,' she said. I looked at Paula, that much smaller than Donna, with her arms clasped tightly around Donna's waist. 'Don't worry, Donna,' Paula said. 'We won't stop loving you. This family isn't like that.'

If ever I'd needed an example from a child, it was now, and Paula had given one. No, I thought, our family isn't like that. I glanced at Adrian, who, like me, was watching Paula and Donna framed in the doorway, holding onto each other.

'Come and sit down, both of you,' I said at last, 'and then we can talk.'

I saw Paula give Donna a final squeeze; then, taking her hand, she led her to the sofa, exactly as she had done when Donna had first visited and Paula had led her down the garden to the swings.

Emotional scenes happen in any loving family, but even more so in a family that fosters, where dealing with distressing issues is a part of everyday life. Yet as I looked at Paula, so small beside Donna, but taking the lead and comforting her, I didn't think I had ever felt so emotional. Paula, vulnerable by her unreserved and childish love, and Donna, rendered as vulnerable by her desperate need to be forgiven and loved.

'I'm sorry, Paula,' Donna said again, her head resting on Paula's, and tears on her cheeks, as Paula cuddled up to her.

'Don't cry, Donna,' Paula said. 'You hurt my head but I forgive you. I still love you.'

I saw Adrian's face cloud over, even though he was trying to do what he saw as the 'man thing' and view this female emotion with dispassion. Yet while my heart lurched, and I was deeply touched by both Donna's and Paula's words – and I could have gone over and encircled them both and told them that everything would be all right – I knew that if we were to continue as a family I would have to make sure Donna's rage didn't touch Paula again. Paula was a child and couldn't see further than Donna's present apology and unhappiness, as I could.

I crossed to Paula and Donna, who were side by side on the sofa, and drawing up the footstool, I perched on it, just in front of them. Donna had her eyes lowered, her head still resting on Paula's as they hugged each other tightly. I gently eased Paula's arm away.

'Donna, I need to talk to you.' Paula sat back and took one of Donna's hands in hers. Slowly Donna raised her head and looked at me, her cheeks and eyelashes wet from crying. 'Dry your eyes, love,' I said, passing her the tissues. I waited while she took a tissue from the box, wiped her eyes and blew her nose. Paula followed suit. I took hold of Donna's other hand. 'Donna,' I said, gently but firmly, 'I know you're sorry now, and I'm pleased you have apologised to Paula. But love, we have to make sure it never happens again.'

'I won't hit Paula again, I promise.' She sniffed and wiped her tears.

'I know you won't, not while you're like this. But your anger can get the better of you, and then you don't know what you're doing and you're out of control. This evening you were very angry with your mother, but instead of telling me, or letting it out somehow, it all built up until it had to come out like an explosion. I was very angry with you just now, Donna, but I didn't hit you. Something stopped me getting close to that, and that something would always stop me from striking someone. We have to help you do that.'

'I didn't mean to hit Paula,' Donna said, her face crumpling.

'No, I know. That's what I am saying. You were very angry and she was the first person you saw.' I paused. 'Donna, can you think of a way that would allow you to control your anger and stop it from happening again?'

Donna was quiet, thinking about what I'd said. Adrian and Paula were quiet too.

'I will have to try to talk to you,' Donna said at last.

'Yes, that's important, and talking before it builds up. Also letting your anger out in other ways like those we have talked about helps. I know you're hurting inside, because you have been treated badly. Edna has talked to you about finding a counsellor, but it won't be until after the court case in May. Donna, do you think it makes it worse by seeing your mother three times a week?' It wasn't a question I would have asked a very young child because it would have been asking them to make a value judgement about their family, which wasn't right. But I felt Donna was old enough, and had enough insight, to give her opinion. Indeed the Guardian had already asked Donna about her feelings towards her family, although I hadn't been in the room to hear her answers.

Donna shrugged.

'Edna thinks, as I do, that it might be better if the contact was reduced. You would still see your mother and

Chelsea but not so often. You see your brothers every day at school. Mrs Bristow says you have lunch with them in the canteen.'

'I'd rather see my dad,' she said.

'Your dad is still in hospital, but as soon as he comes out I'm sure Edna will arrange for you to see him, perhaps on another evening, separately from your mother.' I paused, scanning my thoughts for what to say next. It was diffi-cult. The truth was that Donna badly needed therapy to help her to come to terms with her anger and her past, and I was no therapist.

Suddenly she looked at me, as though seeing something for the first time, or perhaps viewing it from a different angle. 'Cathy, I think it would help me if I stopped wanting my mum to love me so much. I get angry because I try so hard to get her to love me, and when she doesn't, it hurts and makes me angry. I don't know why Mum doesn't love me. I haven't done anything wrong. I was the one who did all the housework at home, and I tried to stop us going into care. But I was blamed for everything, even those things that weren't my fault. I think there is no point in loving my mum any more. She hates me and she will always hate me. I am right, Cathy, aren't I?'

What could I say? How could I agree with a child that her mother hated her, apparently had always done so and was very likely to continue doing so in the future, and for reasons that no one understood? But in some ways that was what Donna needed to hear, put less severely, so that she could start to come to terms with her past and hope-fully move on to a better future.

'Donna, love, you are a good person and your mother has treated you very badly. I don't know why, and neither does Edna. Sometimes in families it happens, though fortunately not very often. Your mother didn't treat your brothers very well, nor Chelsea, but her treatment of you was far worse. Your brothers love you, and so do your dad and gran. You need to remember that: it is important. Some children I look after have never had anyone love them. Your mother is very silly for not loving you as much as she could. It was bad of her to treat you as she did. But it has nothing to do with you as a person, or anything you did or didn't do. It could just have easily have been Warren, Jason or Chelsea she picked on. Sadly it was you. Her comments tonight about the baby were part of all that. I don't know whether she will ever change. But you have your whole life ahead of you, and it will be a good life because you are a good person, Donna.' I finished as I had started, for festering within Donna was the feeling that she was bad and to blame, and her badness had brought it all on. Although my simplification of the situation was grossly inadequate, it was the best I could offer.

Donna slowly nodded. 'I'm sorry, Paula,' she said again. 'I'm really sorry for hurting you. Do you still love me?'

Paula's little voice came out from where she was snuggled into Donna's side. 'Yes, I love you, Donna.'

'I'm sorry, Adrian,' she said, looking at him as he squirmed slightly at the surfeit of emotion. 'Do you still love me?'

He nodded and grunted.

Donna looked at me. 'And you, Cathy? Can you love me like my mum should have done? I love you like a daughter.'

I swallowed the lump in my throat and blinked back my tears. 'Yes, love. I'm sure we can all put this behind us and move on.' We had to. I couldn't give up on Donna now, and I was sure Adrian and Paula wouldn't have wanted me to either.

Chapter Nineteen

Paula's Present

Donna didn't suddenly and miraculously recover from all the trauma of her past, but we did slowly and gradually turn the corner. I was sure it was that recognition Donna had had, that flash of insight which had allowed her to view her mother objectively that was responsible, rather than anything I had said or done. How dreadful was it that a child had to admit that their mother didn't love her, had never done so and probably hated her, before she could start to like herself?

My assertion to Donna, my promise to love her as a daughter was true: I did, while she was with me, but her future was still undecided. The final court hearing was two months away and I couldn't know what the judge's decision would be, or what the care plan drawn up by Edna in conjunction with the Guardian would outline for Donna while she was a child in care, although I knew enough to be certain Donna wouldn't be returning to live with her mother, and neither would the boys. For, apart from the boys being severely neglected, they had begun to say things about their mother to their carers.

Warren and Jason had told their carers that they'd been made to go into their mother's bed when they'd been naughty, but the punishment they began to describe to

Mary and Ray wasn't a smack or even a beating but of a sexual nature. I wasn't told the details by Edna: there was no reason for me to know. It wouldn't have helped my care of Donna to know, and I certainly wasn't going to ask. As a foster carer I hear enough details of degradation and abuse (including sexual abuse) from the children I foster to last me a lifetime; I didn't want more horror stories to plague me at night.

Edna discussed the possibility of reducing Donna's contact (and also that of the boys) with the Guardian, Cheryl Samson, but they decided that with the final court hearing less than two months away, after which contact would be reduced, there wasn't much to be gained. By the time the application had been compiled and gone before the judge there would probably be only about a month left. But Edna suggested that I start arriving late for contact and also collect Donna early for the next couple of months. This arrangement gave Donna about forty-five minutes there. I sat in the car with Adrian and Paula, reading or listening to the radio while Donna was at contact. There was no point in returning home for the ten minutes it would have given us. We all had our evening meal together on our return just after 6.00 p.m.

Aware that Donna seeing her mother had been a catalyst for many of her angry outbursts, I told Donna that I didn't want her going to her bedroom or sitting by herself and brooding immediately after contact. I gave her little jobs to do as I prepared dinner, which redirected her thoughts and also allowed me to keep an eye on her. Donna was a child who internalised her pain and anger to the point where it eventually exploded. I spent a lot of time talking to her and encouraged her to tell me what she was feeling, rather than letting it build up. I would like to say that Donna's self-image dramatically improved, but it didn't: her progress was very slow and piecemeal, for the scars ran deep.

Emily finally came to tea the second week in March and returned the invitation the following week. When I collected Donna from Emily's, her mother, Mandy, said that the girls had played nicely and remarked how polite Donna was. 'I had to tell Emily off, though,' Mandy added. 'I thought I would mention it, as Donna looked very worried.'

'OK, thanks,' I said lightly, not thinking anything of it. But going home in the car, Donna seemed quieter than I would have expected after spending an enjoyable evening at her best friend's.

'Is everything all right?' I asked.

She shrugged, and then, remembering my repeated warnings about not letting worries build up and to tell me instead, she said, 'I got Emily into trouble.'

I glanced at her in the rear-view mirror. 'Did you? How?'

'I showed her how to tear up paper into little bits. And we threw them all over her bedroom. Her mum came in before we cleared it up and Emily got into trouble.'

'I see,' I said. 'Thank you for telling me. Shall I explain to Mandy that it wasn't really Emily's fault?'

'Yes please. Or else Emily might not want to be my friend any more.'

'Don't worry. I'll put it right.'

I had to smile to myself, for what I had come to view as an innocent and harmless way for Donna to release and act out her role from the past Mandy had seen as unacceptable. If I had been a mother without the experience of fostering, and had invited a child to tea and doubtless cleared up and made sure my daughter's bedroom was tidy, I wouldn't have been very pleased either to find it littered with hundreds, possibly thousands, of bits of paper. But as a foster carer I had seen such bizarre and extreme behaviour from the children I'd looked after that I had adapted and modified my judgement of what was a wrongdoing.

The following day I had a quiet word with Mandy in the playground when I collected Donna from school. I thanked her again for having Donna to tea and said how much she had enjoyed it. I then apologised, and said that the mess the girls had made in Emily's room wasn't really Emily's fault. Without breaking confidentiality I briefly explained that this was Donna's way of acting out some of her past, and that I had now told Donna it wasn't acceptable to do it in someone else's house. Mandy thanked me for telling her and said she would square it with Emily, and that Emily had already asked when Donna could come again to tea. But as we said goodbye I wondered what Mandy really thought, for ours must have seemed a strange house to her. Not only did I appear to tolerate such odd behaviour but I accepted it almost as the norm, which it was for Donna. And, I thought, Mandy didn't know the half of it: shredding paper was nothing compared to some of the behaviour I had seen from children who had had to rid themselves of their trauma in any way they could.

Adrian's and Paula's birthdays were two weeks away. I had planned their parties, and they had given out their invitations. Although their birthdays were only a week apart –

30 March and 7 April – as usual they were going to have separate parties, on consecutive Sundays. Adrian wanted a football party that would be organised by, and hosted at, our local football club. Paula wanted her party at home, with jellies and ice cream, and games organised by yours truly. Donna had said to me that she wanted to buy Adrian and Paula a birthday present each, and she had set aside two weeks' pocket money to do this, which was very thoughtful of her. The opportunity for us to go shopping without Adrian and Paula arose the following Saturday, when they were out with their father for the day.

Once I had said goodbye and seen them off at the door, Donna and I went into town to find the gifts, and also for me to buy some wrapping paper and order their birthday cakes. Much to the dismay of Adrian and Paula, I didn't have the cake-making skills of some of their friends' mothers, who annually produced the most amazing scenes of Superman, castles and Winnie-the-Pooh, out of sponge, coloured icing and Smarties (and, I suspected, sorcery).

Donna and I were browsing in the 'pound shop' in the arcade. It was a shop selling low-priced goods including children's toys and games, books and ornaments. I had told Donna that I would add to her pocket money so that she could afford whatever gifts she chose for Adrian and Paula, but she was adamant that she wanted to buy them herself, so that they were 'really' from her. 'I've never been able to buy presents before with my own money,' she said. For like most children who come into care she'd never had pocket money: there simply hadn't been enough in the household budget.

We had been in the pound shop for about ten minutes, and Donna was looking at a little gaily painted jewellery

box, which she thought Paula would like, and I agreed. I
became aware of someone standing close behind us and I
thought they were trying to get past. The shop was
crowded on Saturday; it was always popular with those
wanting small gifts that were reasonably priced. I took a
step forward to allow the people behind us to get by, and
continued looking at the box, which Donna was now opening to examine the inside. A woman's voice suddenly came
from behind.

'Well! Look what we have 'ere!' The voice was harsh and
scathing, and I immediately turned. Rita and Chelsea were
standing side by side, hands on hips in a mirror image of
each other, glaring at us.

I felt my stomach tighten. Donna didn't turn but
remained, head lowered, looking at the jewellery box,
although obviously she'd heard her mother.

'Hello, Rita, Chelsea,' I said evenly. 'Nice to see you
again.' I hadn't seen either of them since that first day at
school in September, and although 'nice' wasn't the term I
would have used given what I now knew of the way Rita
had treated Donna, I had to remain polite. They were as
poorly turned out as before, with very worn matching
black nylon jogging bottoms, and stained nylon tops now
stretched over their bumps. Chelsea, six months pregnant,
had the larger bump, and Rita (who I'd learned from Edna
was definitely pregnant) was catching up fast, assisted by
already being badly overweight. They were both watching
Donna intently, although not in a friendly way. Donna still
hadn't turned; she was actually trying to ignore them.

'How are you both?' I asked, trying to deflect their interest from Donna. 'Congratulations,' I added. I wasn't being
hypercritical; it was the polite and decent thing to say.

'We're good,' Rita said, while Chelsea chewed on her gum. 'Be better if that nosy parker Edna minded her own bleedin' business.'

I gave a half smile and glanced at Donna. She still had her back to them, and was now nervously fiddling with the jewellery box, opening and closing the lid.

'Ain't ya gonna say hello to your mother and sister?' Rita demanded loudly, and she prodded Donna sharply in the back. I saw a woman standing further up the aisle glance at us.

Donna shrugged but still didn't turn. I felt my pulse rate begin to rise. I could see that this could quickly develop into an ugly scene. I had run into foster children's parents before while shopping and the outcomes had been variable – sometimes a brief 'hi' was enough and we went on our way, sometimes if the parents were amicable I stopped for longer and chatted, but neither of these approaches fitted the present encounter.

'Donna is choosing a present for my daughter's birth-day,' I offered, hoping to defuse the situation.

'Is she?' Rita sneered sarcastically. 'D'you 'ear that, Chels? Your sister is buying a present for someone else's kid. Ain't bought us nofing, 'as she?'

Chelsea shook her head and continued chewing her gum. Damn, I thought, now what?

'And why d'you keep bringing her late for contact?' Rita said, turning her attention to me. 'Ain't that bleedin' social worker told ya what time you supposed to be there?' Given that Rita ignored Donna at contact unless she wanted to say something spiteful, I didn't think she could be missing her.

'Edna thought this arrangement would suit everyone better,' I said evenly, swallowing what I would really have liked to have said.

'Did she now?' Rita said sarcastically. 'Wait till I see her. I'll show her what suits me.'

The conversation was going from bad to worse, and I didn't see how it was going to get any better with Donna ignoring them and Rita openly hostile. I was feeling very hot, and as uncomfortable as Donna looked. Rita and Chelsea were making no move to go and seemed to be basking in Donna's nervousness. I thought the only way out was for us to leave the shop, hopefully not followed by Rita and Chelsea.

'Donna,' I said. 'Would you like to say hello to your mother and Chelsea and then we must go.'

Donna shrugged, and still didn't turn. Rita prodded her sharply again in the back. 'D'you hear what your carer said? Say hello to your mother and your sister, you little shit.'

That was it: I'd had enough. Politeness and diplomacy were never going to help Donna when it came to her mother. We needed to just get out of the shop, and fast. 'Come on, Donna,' I said more firmly. 'We're going now.' I touched her arm, and took a step to go, but Donna didn't move. She remained staring at the jewellery box she still held in her hand.

'There!' Rita exclaimed. 'She don't even do what you tell her. Waste of fucking space, that kid! Come on, Chels, don't waste your time on that turd.' Giving Donna another, harder, prod in the back, Rita lumbered off, followed by Chelsea, who threw Donna a look of hate and disgust.

I stood beside Donna and watched the pair of them leave the shop, then I sighed with relief. My heart pounded and I felt upset by what had happened, and Donna must have been feeling far worse than me.

'Are you all right, love?' I asked quietly.

She nodded and carried on examining the jewellery box, once again hiding and internalising her pain and sense of rejection.

'I think Paula will like this,' she said after a moment, turning the box over to look at the base.

I took a breath and looked at her. 'Yes, Donna, I'm sure she will. But we've just had an awful scene with your mother and you are not saying a word. I know what you must be feeling. I feel some of it too. You must be very upset, angry and also, I think, a bit frightened.' I spoke quietly, for there were shoppers all around us, moving down the aisle in the space Rita and Chelsea had left.

Donna slowly closed the lid on the jewellery box and turned and met my eyes. 'I am, Cathy. They make me upset and angry, but they won't change. I'm having fun choosing a present for Paula with my money, and I won't let them spoil it. I won't let them spoil my fun any more.'

I held her gaze and my heart went out to her. She was worth a thousand Ritas, and her response to her mother of not letting her upset her had proved it, and touched me deeply. Donna had been able to rise above her mother in integrity, compassion and everything that makes us socialised human beings, and I felt very humble beside her. 'All right, love. I understand.' I said. 'That's very sensible of you.'

We continued shopping and Donna bought the jewellery box for Paula, and then a book for Adrian, both of which she wrapped with great excitement when we arrived home. If Donna could hold on to her philosophy and rationalise her mother's words and actions, then her future looked a lot brighter. So often abuse in childhood goes on to blight the adult, souring and diminishing anything they achieve. It took a very courageous person to put the past behind and move on, and I hoped Donna had what it took.

Chapter Twenty

The Question

Adrian's and Paula's birthday parties were a great success. Adrian's was all boys and they spent an hour and a half playing football, organised by the coach, had a party tea provided as part of the package, then finished with games, also organised by the coach. Donna, Paula and I watched the football, although Donna could have joined in if she'd wanted to; Paula was a bit too young. We all sat down and joined in the tea, and afterwards Donna and Paula joined in the games. Paula's party was a more sedate affair and required a lot more organisation on my part than Adrian's had, where all that had been required of me was to arrive, watch and enjoy, then pay.

For Paula's I made sandwiches with the crusts cut off, cooked mini pizzas, arranged cocktail sausages on sticks, squirted cream on the individual jellies I had made, and limited the number of chocolate biscuits the children ate so that no one went home feeling sick. I organised games with prizes – Squeak Piggy Squeak, Pin the Tail on the Donkey, Musical Chairs (or rather pillows and cushions, because we didn't have ten dining-room chairs), and then followed this with a sing-along – 'Old MacDonald Had a Farm' and 'The Farmer's in his Den' – before lighting the candles and bringing in the cake. Donna joined in as best she could, for although her ability to play had improved, she still couldn't completely throw herself into games with a child's uninhibited pleasure. She came to me more than once during the party worried about the mess that was being made – 'There's a drink been spilt,' she said anxiously, or 'There's popcorn on the carpet.'

'Don't worry,' I reassured her, as I always did. 'I'll clear it up later. It's a party and I'm not worried about a bit of mess.' I wasn't, for compared to Adrian's party the previous year, which he'd had at home, I was getting off lightly: I had found pieces from the party-poppers lodged in corners of the bookshelves and behind sofas for weeks afterwards; one hadn't been discovered until I'd moved a cabinet to make room for the Christmas tree, eight months later. But Donna's anxiety about mess stemmed from her role of domestic drudge at home, and the guilt that had been heaped on her by her mother, who had made her feel that it was because Donna had failed in her duties she and her brothers had been taken into care. Not that Donna viewed being taken into care as a bad thing now – far from it – but the guilt remained, and would do for a long time to come.

Donna's school work improved dramatically in the summer term. Her reading age went up by two years, from seven to nine. She was still four years behind the average child of eleven, but relieved of the burden that she'd carried at home with its continual degradation, she'd gained confidence in her ability to learn and was going from strength to strength. Mrs Bristow, the head, and Donna's class teacher, Beth Adams, were delighted, and I think surprised – more so than I was. I had looked after children before who had been badly underachieving at school simply because of their appalling home lives. There's nothing left over for studying and learning if you're worried about where your next meal is coming from or when you'll receive the next beating, or worse.

The final court hearing was expected to last for five days and was scheduled to begin on 25 May. Although Donna was aware of the date, largely because her mother was cursing about it at contact, Donna appeared unaffected by its approach. Edna had explained to Donna, as I had, that the hearing would be when the judge made his decision in respect of the best place for her and her brothers to live while they were children. Chelsea was also part of the care proceedings, but I didn't have any details other than that Edna and the Guardian wanted her away from Rita and living in a mother and baby unit. In practice, however, given Chelsea's age and opposition to anything Edna suggested, this was going to be highly unlikely, unless Chelsea had a change of heart and cooperated, for clearly no one could force her to move, even if it was for her own good.

The Friday before the court hearing was due to begin was a dramatic one for news. Edna phoned in the morning to advise me of two developments. Firstly, that Rita had withdrawn her application to the court to have the boys returned to her, so she was no longer contesting the case. She had never made an application for Donna to be returned, but for whatever reason had now decided she no longer wanted to 'fight' for the boys return.

'I would like to think that Rita has finally seen good sense,' Edna said. 'I have spent months talking to her, trying to persuade her that it was best for the boys to remain in care. Perhaps I succeeded, or perhaps she realised there was too much evidence against her and has finally listened to her solicitor.' Or perhaps, I thought uncharitably, with the baby due in three months she's lost all interest in the boys, who were now hard work and not as immediately appealing as a vulnerable baby.

'And Cathy,' Edna continued, 'I have a piece of news of my own that I want to tell you before you hear it from anyone else.' She can't be pregnant too, I thought, for Edna was in her late fifties! 'I've decided that when I've finished with this case I shall be taking early retirement.'

'Oh Edna! I am sorry.'

She laughed. 'I'm not.'

'No, I didn't mean … I'm just sorry to be losing you.'

'Thank you, Cathy. But I've been a social worker for twenty-eight years and I think I've done my bit. Things have changed so much, and I'm getting too old to be up to midnight writing reports. My husband retires this year – he's a bit older than me. We want to enjoy our retirement and spend time with our children and grandchildren in Scotland. Do you know, Cathy, I haven't seen them in over a year?'

'I understand perfectly, Edna. But it will be a great loss.'

'That's nice of you. I will see Donna and the boys through to permanency before I fully retire. I've got a couple of other cases that are nearing the end, so I'll be coming in part-time for a few months.' Conscientious to the last; I could see only too well why Edna was taking early retirement. But I did wonder how easy she would find it to adapt, for social work had been her life, as looking after children had been the greater part of mine. 'And,

Cathy,' Edna continued, 'I've stopped contact for tonight
and next week. It will be too much for Rita to handle with
the court case. I don't want her anger spilling over. Will
you tell Donna, please?'

'Yes, of course.'

'I'll phone you with the outcome as soon the court's made
its decision and approved the Care Plan; then I'll come
round and see you. I don't think the hearing will last the five
days set aside now that Rita isn't opposing the case.'

We said goodbye, and I wasn't expecting to hear from
Edna again until the following week. However, she phoned
again at 6.00 that evening.

'Chelsea has had her baby, early,' Edna said. 'A little girl.
Could you tell Donna, please? She's an aunty now.' I could
hear warmth in Edna's voice, for although the social situation the baby had been born into was far from perfect, the
birth of a baby is special and always welcomed, whatever
else may be going on.

'Yes, of course,' I said. 'Are Chelsea and the baby well?'

'They are now. They're in hospital.' Edna paused. 'Don't
tell Donna these details, please, but Chelsea gave birth at
home. I didn't hear about it until the police phoned me. A
neighbour heard Chelsea screaming early this morning
and thought she was being assaulted. She called the police,
and when the police and ambulance crew arrived they
found Chelsea on the kitchen floor with the baby, still
attached by the umbilical cord.'

'Good grief! Poor kid,' I said, horrified. 'Chelsea must
have been very frightened. Where was Rita?'

'Upstairs in bed, sleeping off last night's drink.'

My heart went out to Chelsea, who at fifteen had given
birth to her first child alone and on the cold kitchen floor.

'I'll try to visit Chelsea after court on Monday,' Edna said. 'I've told the hospital to keep her and the baby there for as long as possible. They've said they won't discharge her while the baby is so small. It was just five pounds. It will give me a chance to persuade Chelsea to go into a mother and baby unit. I've reserved a place for her. Chelsea can't return home with the baby: the place is filthy. The police said there was cat pooh all over the downstairs, even in the kitchen where Chelsea had given birth!'

I cringed. 'How absolutely dreadful! Do you want me to take Donna to visit Chelsea and the baby in hospital?'

Edna paused. 'Not yet. Let's get the court case over with, and then I'll set up a separate contact for Donna to see Chelsea and the baby. If you were to go to the hospital in visiting hours with Donna, Rita is sure to be there, so I think it's better to wait.'

'OK, Edna. Shall I buy a card for Donna to send?'

'Yes, that would be nice. Chelsea is on Maple Ward at the General.'

I jotted it on the notepad by the phone. 'I'll tell Donna the news, and when you see Chelsea, please pass on my best wishes.'

'I will, Cathy. Take care and I'll phone you next week.'

A new baby, a new life, but what a way to start it – born on a filthy kitchen floor! If Chelsea went into a mother and baby unit, then she would stand some chance of being able to look after the baby and keep her. Mother and baby units teach mothers (and fathers if they are parenting) to change nappies, bath the baby, make up bottles and generally look after the baby, as well as how to play with and nurture them. The staff are always on hand to give assistance, as well as monitor the young mother's progress. Only when they are satisfied that the mother knows how to parent the baby safely does the girl leave. The girls are usually found a council flat if there is no suitable home for them to return to, and the staff from the unit, as well as the social worker, continue to visit and monitor mother and baby for as long as is necessary.

It was difficult to know how to pitch the news to Donna, as it was likely to produce conflicting emotions. While the birth of a baby is a joyous event, given the way Chelsea had treated and rejected Donna I was half expecting Donna to be angry. I should have had more faith in Donna, for when I told her, she took the news with stoicism. 'That's nice,' she said, briefly pausing from the jigsaw she was helping Paula to complete. 'I hope Chelsea will be happy now and look after the baby well.'

'She will do,' I said, and I explained to Donna that Chelsea would be receiving a lot of help, both in hospital and then on her discharge, at a mother and baby unit. 'If you want to see Chelsea and the baby, Edna will arrange it in a couple of weeks. In the meantime you can send a congratulations card.'

'OK, Cathy,' Donna said, glancing up again. 'I'll think about that. Thank you for telling me.'

I sat on the sofa and picked up the newspaper, which as usual had remained unread during the day. As I scanned the front page for any news that wasn't doom and gloom, Donna added succinctly (and I could have said with great insight), 'She's a bit of a tart, that Chelsea. I always thought she'd end up in trouble with the boys.'

'Hmm,' I said as I raised the paper to cover my smile. 'I'm pleased you won't be following in her footsteps then.'

'What's a tart?' Paula asked.

'A pastry with jam in,' I said.

'And it can also mean a girl who is free with the boys, and doesn't respect her own body,' Donna added. And I thought that Donna had come a long way in the time she'd been with us; I couldn't have imagined Rita or Chelsea phrasing it so delicately.

We'd had no more incidents of Donna chastising, bossing, bullying or in any way trying to hurt Adrian and Paula, and I was once again finding that I could safely leave the three of them in a room without having to be continually vigilant. Donna was trying to find other outlets for her anger: she sometimes pummelled a cushion when frustrated, and she was also talking to me more. With no contact for the whole week there was less reason for her anger to build up and then explode. All of which was beginning to confirm my thoughts of offering to foster Donna long term – that is, to suggest she become a permanent member of our family.

One of the documents before the judge was the Care Plan, and this would detail the arrangements the social services were planning if the Full Care Order was granted: that is, where and with whom Donna and her brothers would live. If the Care Plan was upheld by the Guardian it was likely the judge would agree to it. Sometimes the Guardian's recommendations were different from those of the social services, and in some cases the children were returned home against the advice of their social worker. But I knew this wouldn't be so here. Both Edna and Cheryl Samson had agreed that the children should not return to Rita's care because, put simply, Rita couldn't look after them, had neglected and abused them, and in all probability would continue to do so.

What I didn't know was what the long-term plans were for where Donna would live. She was eleven and would be in foster care until she was eighteen; so too would the boys, although being that much younger there was a chance that they might be found adoptive parents. Donna was too old to be considered for adoption – most adopters want young children, who are less likely to be emotionally damaged. Sometimes relatives come forward and offer a permanent home to the child, and they are assessed as to their suitability. If they are suitable then this is usually considered the best option for the child – that is, to live with a member of the extended family; it is known as kinship caring.

But as far as I knew no one had come forward to look after either Donna or the boys. Donna's father unfortunately wasn't in any position to look after her, although when he was well he appeared to have a lot of love for Donna, as she did for him. Likewise Donna's gran, Mrs Bajan, was a kind and loving person, but she was not in the best of health, and also spent long periods during the winter with her family in Barbados. Edna had already said that Mrs Bajan didn't feel she could look after any of the children permanently but wanted them to stay with her during some of their school holidays. There was an aunt, whom I had only met once on that first morning at school, but Donna and the boys hadn't seen her since, and no mention had been made of her, so I guessed she wasn't a candidate to look after any of the children. I was almost certain that the court would say the boys should stay together and that Donna should continue to be fostered separately long term. If they were reunited and fostered as a sibling group there was a strong possibility that the problems that there'd been initially between them would resurface. Donna was settled and was achieving, as were the boys.

The question that I considered, therefore, was that if Edna asked if I could look after Donna permanently (which I thought she might) would I agree? And I already knew my answer. I'd always felt very protective of Donna, and in recent months that protectiveness had turned into a strong bond which was quickly turning to love. I was very proud of Donna and what she had achieved, and I wanted to be there for her as she continued her journey through childhood to become an adult. Obviously I would have to ask Adrian and Paula, as it was a life-changing decision and would affect us all. And of course. Donna would be asked, but I was pretty certain I knew what her answer would be. But all this rested on the outcome of the court case and the judge's decision in the final hearing.

Chapter Twenty-one
A Kind Person

The court case ended after two days and the judge gave his decision on the morning of the third. Edna phoned from outside court and said the judgement was as they'd expected, and Donna and her brothers would be staying in foster care.

'Good. Well done,' I said, which was in recognition of the hard work Edna had put in to secure the children's futures.

Edna said she'd like to see Donna and me later in the day, and also that she'd taken a photograph of Chelsea and her baby, Cindy, to give to Donna. 'Will it be all right if I visit at five thirty?' she asked.

'Yes, absolutely.' And my heart skipped a beat at the thought of the question I was sure Edna was going to ask.

Having collected the children from school, I made our evening meal earlier than usual. I knew that what Edna had to say wouldn't take five minutes, and everyone would be hungry if I waited until after she'd gone. I hadn't said anything to Adrian and Paula about the outcome of the court case (or my hopes of Donna staying with us), for Edna should speak to Donna first.

Uncharacteristically Edna arrived nearly half an hour late. 'Sorry, Cathy,' she said, hurrying in out of breath. 'It's been non-stop, all day.'

I offered her a drink and she gratefully accepted a cup of tea. 'I'd like to speak to you before I speak to Donna,' she said. 'Can we go somewhere alone?'

I could guess why.

Edna called 'Hello,' to Donna and Paula who were playing in the front room, and I showed her through to the lounge. Adrian was upstairs, doing his homework in his bedroom.

'Thank you very much,' she said as I handed her the tea. 'It was after three o'clock by the time I got back to the office, and there were two emergencies needing my attention. Roll on retirement!'

I nodded, and, sitting in the chair opposite, waited for the important news she brought.

Edna took a few sips of her tea and then returned the cup to the saucer in her lap. 'So, Cathy,' she said with a small sigh and looking at me. 'We have the Full Care Order on Donna and the boys. The case for Chelsea has been adjourned so that I can assess her with the baby. I've got to go back to court in two months with that.' I nodded. 'I was able to tell the judge how well Donna and the boys have settled, and how much improvement the children have made since coming into care. The judge has upheld my plans for them. We are going to try to find adoptive parents for Warren and Jason, who will be placed together. Failing that it will be a long-term foster placement, but I'm hopeful we can find them an adoptive family. They are young enough to adjust.'

'Yes, indeed. And how nice for them to have a fresh start,' I said, willing her to move on to Donna.

'Absolutely. I want to get that going as soon as possible.' Edna paused and took another sip of her tea, and I wasn't sure if it was my imagination but I thought she looked as though she was hesitating, or perhaps summoning up the courage to tell me something. She returned her cup to the saucer with a small chink, and then looked up and smiled at me reassuringly. 'Donna will remain in long-term foster care, Cathy. And after a lengthy discussion with my manager, we feel that it would be best if she was placed with a black carer or a couple who reflect her ethnicity.'

'Oh,' I said. 'Oh, I see.'

Edna smiled kindly. 'I know, Cathy. Donna has done incredibly well since she's been with you. I'm so grateful to you and your family, but the issue of her cultural identity remains. It wasn't a decision we took lightly, but we really do feel Donna should be found a family who can help her with her cultural identity. You remember when she was trying to rub her skin off?'

'Yes, but she hasn't done that for a long time,' I said, almost as a plea for her to stay.

'No, I know, thanks to you. But I think you will agree that Donna is still struggling with her self-image. Only last week her teacher overheard her telling Emily that she wished she was white like her.'

'Did she?' I asked, taken aback. 'I didn't know.'

Edna nodded. 'You have done so much for Donna and I can't thank you enough, but in respect of her cultural needs the scars inflicted by her mother run deep. The Guardian and judge agreed this would be best addressed in a black or dual-heritage family. I realise this will mean another move for Donna when she is so settled with you, but it's thought it's for the best. I hope I've made the right decision, Cathy. You will of course keep in touch with her; it's important that you do.'

'Yes,' I said, finally coming to terms with what Edna was saying. 'Yes, of course we will. We're going to miss her very much.'

'I know you will, and she'll miss you.'

Although the news wasn't what I'd anticipated, or wanted to hear, I could see the truth in what Edna had said, and if I was honest I suppose part of me had wondered if Donna's cultural identity would come into Edna's plans for Donna's future.

'I shall also be looking for a family where there are no younger children,' Edna added. 'You have coped remarkably well, but I don't want a repetition of what happened here with Paula and Adrian.'

'Donna wouldn't do that again,' I said defensively. 'That's all under control now.'

'I know, and Adrian and Paula have been so accepting of Donna, but Donna does need a lot of attention. I'm hoping to find her a family where the carers' own children are older, or have even left home. Donna is an absolute credit to you, as are Adrian and Paula.'

'Thank you, Edna,' I said, although the praise did nothing to soften my disappointment. 'I'll have to let Adrian and Paula down gently,' I said reflectively.

Edna nodded, then finished the last of her tea while I remained quietly watching her.

'In a minute when I see Donna,' Edna said, 'I'll tell her the outcome of the case, but I'm not going to say anything yet about the proposed move. I have a meeting with the Family Finders team later this week, but as you

know it could take months to find a suitable family. I
don't want Donna becoming unsettled here. Once we
have identified suitable carers I will speak to her and
explain.'

'All right,' I said. It was a sensible decision. It wouldn't
have helped Donna to know at this point.

'Now to the matter of contact,' Edna said. 'We will be
reducing it to once a month straight away for Donna and
the boys to see their mother.'

'Good,' I said.

'It will still be supervised, but I will be handing over the
supervision to someone else. Once Donna and the boys go
on to permanency it will be three times a year.'

I nodded. This was usual for children who wouldn't be
returning home. Otherwise, if they were continually seeing
their natural parents there was less chance of them settling
and bonding with their 'forever families', as they are
known.

'Once the children have moved I shall be arranging
extra sibling contact,' Edna continued. 'It's not necessary
now, as Donna and the boys see each other every day at
school. Does Donna want to see Chelsea and the baby?'

'I'm not sure. I told her the news and suggested we
bought a card, but Donna said she would think about it.
She's still thinking about it as far as I know.'

Edna smiled. 'OK. I'll talk to her about that in a minute.
I've brought the photograph.' She placed her cup and
saucer on the coffee table and, opening her briefcase,
passed me the photograph.

Chelsea was sitting in a chair beside her hospital bed;
the iron bedhead and white cotton pillows were to the left
of the photo. Baby Cindy, wrapped in a white blanket, was

asleep on Chelsea's lap with her head resting on Chelsea's arm. Chelsea wasn't looking down at the baby as many new mothers do but stared into the camera. Her young, vulnerable face seemed to say it all: a mixture of surprise, shock and distance, as though she was struggling to come to terms with what had happened. She looked so lost that my heart went out to her. If ever a girl had needed looking after it was Chelsea.

'She's agreed to go into a mother and baby unit,' Edna said.

'Good,' I said, handing back the photograph. 'Hopefully Chelsea will be able to keep her baby.'

'Hopefully,' Edna repeated. 'I'll see Donna now then, please, Cathy.'

I went through to the front room and told Donna that Edna wanted to see her, and I also told the girls to say goodnight to each other, as it was Paula's bedtime. Leaving Edna with Donna in the lounge, I took Paula upstairs.

'Is Donna staying?' Paula whispered as we turned the landing, for even Paula, at her age, knew that the final court hearing meant decisions.

'Yes, for now,' I said. 'The judge has decided she won't be returning home.'

'Good,' Paula said. 'Her mum is horrible.'

I perched on the edge of the bath and looked at Paula as she washed her face. 'You know, love, Donna's mother wasn't born horrible. I know she's done bad things to Donna but she hasn't always been like that. Perhaps her mother wasn't nice to her. Since Donna has been with us we've shown her a different way to behave so that if she has children one day, she'll know how to treat them and love them properly.'

'Donna will make a good mother,' Paula said, drying her face on the towel. 'She's a kind person. She doesn't get angry with me any more.'

'That's right, love. And she was never really angry with you. It just came out that way.'

'I won't get angry with my children, and Donna won't get angry with hers,' Paula said decisively.

'I know, love, you are both very kind people. And I love you!'

Giving Paula a big hug, I then went with her to her bedroom and saw her into bed. I had just started reading a bedtime story when I heard Edna call from the hall. 'I'm off now, Cathy.'

'I'll finish your story in a minute,' I said to Paula, and kissing her forehead, I went downstairs.

'Everything all right?' I asked Edna as I met her in the hall. Donna was still in the lounge.

'Yes, Donna is fine. I've explained the judge's decision, and given her the photograph. She doesn't want to see Chelsea yet, so I've told her to tell you if she changes her mind. Now I must be getting back to my hubby.'

It was after 7.30 p.m. and I doubted Edna would have finished yet; having spent all morning in court and away from her office, she would doubtless have some reports to write. I opened the front door and wished her goodnight.

'Oh yes,' she said, suddenly remembering something. 'About the therapy.' She lowered her voice so that Donna couldn't hear from the lounge. 'I feel it should wait until after her move. It would be too much for Donna to begin therapy and cope with a move to permanency.'

'Yes,' I agreed. 'And there's no urgency for therapy now. Donna is doing so well.'

'I know,' Edna said with a smile. 'Thanks to you. Goodnight and God bless, Cathy.'

'And you, Edna.'

Chapter Twenty-two

Marlene

Life continued as usual for us while the 'family finding' for Donna went on unseen in the background (and unknown to Donna, Adrian or Paula). I felt very sad sometimes as I watched Donna going about a task, or playing with Paula and Adrian, aware that at some point she would no longer be with us. Edna asked me to send her a full-face photograph of Donna, which was easy, for I had plenty to choose from. This would be used to 'advertise' Donna in fostering magazines, and also on flyers sent to approved foster carers. Beside her photograph would be a small piece about her, and the type of family that was wanted. Advertising a child is an emotive issue but has been shown to be highly effective in finding the right family for a child – for how else can prospective parents be paired with children in need of a family? – although the child is never aware they are being 'advertised'.

I expected the family finding to take some time for Donna, as the social services were looking for quite a distinctive family – black or dual heritage, and with no younger children – which would obviously limit the number of applicants. This was fine with me, for while I recognised Donna needed to be settled with her forever family as soon as possible for her own good, on a purely selfish level, I was pleased we had the extra time with her. It was the middle of September, and Donna had been with us for over a year, when Edna phoned me out of the blue to say Family Finders had found a good match for Donna, and could I attend the 'matching meeting' scheduled for the following Wednesday.

'Er, yes,' I said, quickly coming to terms with what I was being told. 'Yes, of course.' The matching meeting was to make sure the carers, or carer, who'd come forward, wanting to parent Donna, were the most appropriate, before the match was approved by the 'permanency panel' and Donna was told. Having been part of this process before, I knew how it worked, and also that it did work: mistakes were very rare.

'Her name is Marlene,' Edna said. 'She's lovely, but I'll let you be the judge of that.' Which was all I would know about Donna's new carer until I met her at the meeting.

The children had returned to school for the autumn term, the week before – Adrian was in the first year of his new grammar school, Paula had gone up a year in her junior school and Donna was in the final year of her junior school. The matching meeting was scheduled for 10.00 a.m., at the social services office, and I made my way up the various flights of stairs towards the small committee room with no small amount of trepidation. For when all was said and done I was about to meet the person who would be taking over from me and would eventually become as close to Donna as I had been.

Going into the committee room, I smiled at the assembled group, then took a chair at the large square wooden table. Joyce, from the permanency team, whom'd I'd met before, was chairing and opened the meeting by asking us to introduce ourselves. Apart from Joyce, Jill, Edna and myself, there was Marlene, her link worker Carla, and Lisa, a trainee student social worker who would be taking the minutes. Marlene was sitting directly opposite me, and I eyed her suspiciously. She was certainly an attractive and elegant-looking woman, but would she make a good mother for Donna? I tried to remain objective as I scrutinised her, without appearing rude. Her brown skin was almost the same as Donna's, and her hair was black and well oiled, as I'd tried to do for Donna. Her large dark eyes seemed warm as she looked at me and smiled. I guessed she was in her early fifties, and she wore a light pink jumper and black skirt. She sat upright, with her hands folded loosely in front of her on the table. When she spoke, she had the faintest hint of an accent, a milder version of Granny Bajan's Caribbean accent. She must have felt self-conscious, for the meeting centred on her, but she didn't show it and appeared calm and dignified.

Having introduced ourselves, Joyce explained the purpose of the meeting for the minutes, then asked Edna to give us an update on Donna. Edna would have met Marlene at least once prior to this meeting, as well as having read Marlene's details and discussing her application to foster Donna with Joyce from the permanency team. Likewise Marlene would have had the chance to read the details about Donna, and would also have had the opportunity of discussing these with Edna and Joyce. Edna was being asked to bring Marlene up to date, therefore, adding to what Marlene already knew about Donna.

Edna looked at Marlene as she talked about Donna's continued progress – during the summer holidays and now she had returned to school. She described Donna's personality, elaborated on her background before she came into care and described some of the problems we'd encountered in the early days, all of which Marlene would have had some knowledge of from her previous meeting with Edna and Joyce. 'Donna wants to be a nurse when she grows up,' Edna finished by saying.

I nodded and smiled. 'She talks of nothing else,' I said, 'and is always administering medicine to her dolls.' Everyone smiled. The mood of the meeting was relaxed and informal, for this was about the beginning of a new family where Donna had a new mother and Marlene a daughter, unlike some of the meetings I attend, which are very serious and formal and deal with abuse before a child is brought into care.

'Perhaps you would like to continue?' Joyce asked me.

I nodded and took Donna's Life Story book from my bag and passed it across the table to Marlene. I had begun the book when Donna had first arrived and it was now bulging with photographs, paper memorabilia such as cinema tickets and school merit certificates, and with a handwritten commentary from me. I compiled a Life Story book for all the children I looked after and it was an important and ongoing piece of work that the child took with them. For unlike one's own children, who are continuously surrounded by their past in the form of other family members and their shared memories, once the fostered child had left, particularly if they didn't keep in touch, the Life Story book was the only evidence they had of their time with us, together with their own memories.

Marlene turned the pages as I spoke. I began by saying, as Edna had, how much Donna had improved since she'd been with us, and how loved she was by my family. I went over the problems we'd encountered, and how I had dealt with them. It was no good giving Marlene an unrealistic account, for that would have been dishonest, and also left her ill-prepared for any problems that might arise, particularly in the early days when they were still getting to know each other. I told Marlene why I thought Donna had behaved as she had, setting it in the context of her past. So I described her bullying of Adrian and Paula as a result of the bullying and degradation Donna had endured in all the years she'd lived with her mother.

'So when my niece and nephew visit I should keep an eye on them?' Marlene asked, glancing up from the Life Story book. 'They are five and six years old.'

'To begin with, yes, I think so,' I confirmed, and Edna nodded. 'We haven't had an incident for nearly four months now, and I'm sure we won't have another one, but it's as well to be cautious to begin with.'

'Donna could become a little unsettled by the move,' Edna said, 'although I'd put money on it not happening again.'

Apart from any personal responsibility I felt to be honest with Marlene, it was exactly because of the possibility of this type of situation that Marlene had described (her niece and nephew visiting) that it was so important for Edna and me to be honest. There have been incidents recorded where information had been withheld from a carer by a social worker and injury had resulted.

'Does Donna still tear up paper?' Marlene asked with a small smile.

I returned her smile. 'Yes, and I haven't stopped her, although she knows not to do it when visiting other people's houses.'

'It's something that can be addressed at therapy,' Edna said, 'which I intend to start as soon as Donna has settled after the move. I have the funding approved for it.'

Marlene nodded. 'That should help.' She turned the last few pages of the Life Story book and passed it back across the table. 'Donna looks a lovely child and has obviously been very happy with you. I hope I can make her as happy. My family are looking forward to meeting her. I have two grown-up children, a girl and a boy in their twenties, and lots of nieces and nephews. We have large family gatherings most weekends, and I'm sure Donna will get along well with my niece Kerry, who is the same age as Donna. I visit Barbados every year. My grandfather was born in Barbados and I have aunts and cousins who still live there.'

'Really?' I said, surprised and delighted. 'Donna's grandmother is from Barbados. Will you be taking Donna when you visit?'

'Of course,' Marlene said, slightly taken aback that there could be any suggestion she wouldn't. 'Has she ever been before?'

'No,' Edna said. 'Her gran visits for some of the winter, but Donna has never been.'

'She'll love it,' Marlene said. 'We stay with my family and there's always a house full of relatives and neighbours. It's like one big party, the whole time.'

'I'd love it too,' I said, laughing. 'Can I come?'

'And me,' Edna and Joyce chorused.

I was quickly warming to Marlene. She appeared a naturally kind and open person, who had obviously carefully thought through her application to look after Donna long term and the commitment and responsibility that would entail. As Marlene spoke, I learned that she had been fostering for five years, but they had all been short-term placements and she really felt she had more to offer a child on a permanent basis. We talked about Donna's self-image in respect of her race, which Marlene was in an ideal position to address: her mother was black, and her father was white British, although both her parents were now dead. Marlene had no children at home, so she could give Donna all the attention and help she required. She worked part-time as a psychiatric nurse with flexible hours that could be adjusted, so she could take Donna to school and collect her.

Marlene lived fifteen miles from where I did, so us keeping in touch wasn't going to be a problem. Edna had already emphasised, both at the meeting and when she'd met Marlene previously, that it was important we kept in touch with Donna, particularly in the months straight after the move. 'Donna mustn't in any way feel that she has been rejected again,' Edna said. 'And obviously once this match has been approved by the permanency panel I shall speak to Donna and explain the reasons for the move to her myself.'

By the end of the meeting I was certain that Marlene was the right person for Donna. Although I would still be very sad to see Donna go, I had to admit it was a perfect match; indeed, if someone had drawn up a profile of the most suitable person to be Donna's mum, it would have been Marlene. Joyce concluded the meeting, firstly by asking everyone if they had any more questions, which no one did. Then she went round the table asking each of us if we were happy for this match to go before the permanency panel, which would sit again on 5 October. Marlene answered first and said a loud and very positive 'Yes. Absolutely. I'm looking forward to meeting Donna' (which she wouldn't do until after the panel had approved the placement). Marlene's link worker said yes, she felt it was an excellent match, as did Edna, Joyce, Jill and Lisa.

I looked across the table at Marlene as I said, 'Yes, I think Donna will be very happy with you. She's a lucky girl.'

'Thank you, Cathy,' Marlene replied, embarrassed. 'That's very kind of you.'

Joyce wound up the meeting by saying we would all meet again on 6 October, after the permanency panel had given their approval, to plan the move. This was normal procedure: the introduction of Marlene and Donna would be carefully structured. It was likely to take place over a two-week period, resulting in the move at the end of that time if everything was all right, which I felt sure it would be.

As the meeting closed and everyone began to leave, I said goodbye to Jill, who would be visiting us the following week, and I also took the opportunity of asking Edna how Chelsea was. I hadn't spoken to Edna for a couple of weeks, and the last time she had visited us, three weeks before, she'd said that Chelsea and Cindy were doing well in the mother and baby unit. Donna still hadn't wanted to visit her.

'Yes, Chelsea is doing fine,' Edna confirmed. 'Whether she can continue as she has been doing when she moves to the flat remains to be seen.'

'She's leaving the mother and baby unit then?'

'In a month. I'm not on the case now that I'm part-time and semi-retired. But my colleague has found her a nice little one-bedroom flat on View Estate, and will be closely monitoring her and the baby. She wanted to keep Chelsea in the unit for longer, but Chelsea said she would run away if they didn't find her a flat soon.'

'Hopefully Chelsea has learned enough to look after the baby,' I said.

'Hopefully. It's whether she can look after herself as well, and keep the flat clean. At sixteen I'm not sure I could.'

'No,' I agreed. 'Nor me.'

'My hubby says I have to stop worrying about her now she's no longer my responsibility. I'm continuing part-time until Donna and the boys are settled, then we're off to stay with our children in Scotland for a month.'

'Lovely,' I said. 'And what about Rita? Isn't her baby due now? It must be soon.'

Edna's face fell. 'She had it last week.' I looked surprised. 'I haven't said anything to Donna because I didn't want to worry her. Rita has disappeared.'

'What? With the baby?'

Edna nodded. 'She had a little girl. Later the same day Rita walked out of the hospital with the baby. My colleague has taken out an Emergency Protection Order, and the police are looking for her.' She sighed. 'Goodness knows where she's staying. I suppose I should tell Donna – she has a right to know.'

'Do you want me to tell her, Edna? I could keep it low key and reassure her?'

'Yes, please, Cathy, would you? Give Donna my love and tell her I'll phone when I have any news.'

'Will do. I'll put the emphasis on how well Chelsea is doing.'

'Thanks, Cathy.'

When I told Donna that evening about her mother's baby and subsequent disappearance she shrugged. 'Typical,' she said. 'I hope they find the baby soon.'

'They will,' I reassured her.

'At least I'm out of all that now,' she added, and that was all Donna said.

A week later Edna phoned to say that Rita and the baby had been found. Apparently Rita had eventually returned to her house, and a neighbour had heard a baby crying virtually non-stop for twenty-four hours and alerted the social services. The colleague of Edna's who was now dealing with the case went to the house with the police and found it filthy and cold. Rita was drunk in bed with the baby beside her. The baby's nappy was overflowing with faeces, having not been changed for days. On being admitted to hospital the baby was found to have lost weight and be dehydrated. Edna said that as soon as the baby had regained the weight and was well enough to be discharged from hospital she would go straight to a foster carer. It didn't mean there wasn't any chance of Rita having her baby back. The childcare proceeding would begin all over again, and Rita would be assessed to see if she could parent the child, which I had to admit looked far from hopeful. As

I had done so often since I'd begun fostering, I wished I could have waved a magic wand and made everything OK, so that Rita could look after her baby; but realistically only early intervention and education can stop the cycle of abuse and neglect.

Chapter Twenty-three

Lilac

The permanency panel approved Marlene's application to foster Donna, and on 6 October, Edna, Joyce, Marlene, her link worker, Jill, Lisa who was taking the minutes and I once more sat around the table in the committee room to plan Donna's introduction to Marlene, and ultimately her move. Edna had arranged to visit us at 5.30 that evening to tell Donna, and asked me not to say anything to her prior to this.

'How is Donna?' Marlene asked eagerly at the start of the meeting.

'Very well,' I said. 'Her school work has improved tremendously this term.'

Edna looked up. 'School is one of the issues I should like to discuss before we look at the dates of the introduction.'

'Go ahead,' Joyce said.

'Donna is doing so well at her school,' Edna said, 'I should like her to stay at the same school for her last year there. I realise it isn't local to you, Marlene, and the social services are prepared to provide an escort if you can't manage the school run. I appreciate it's, what, twenty miles from you?'

Marlene nodded thoughtfully. 'I would like to take Donna to school for at least some of the time so that I am in contact with the school. But it would be too much for me to take her and collect her each day, as well as my part-time job.' Which was perfectly reasonable. Marlene paused then looked at me. 'Does Donna still help at the breakfast club?'

'Yes, she really likes it. She has to be there at eight fifteen.'

'How about if I take Donna each morning,' Marlene said, looking at Edna, 'and the escort brings her home? I can go into work after I've dropped her off.'

'That's fine with me,' Edna said. 'I think it's a good arrangement.'

'Thanks,' Marlene said. 'That would help me a lot. And presumably when Donna leaves her junior school at the end of the year, you won't mind her going to a local secondary school? We have a very good one only five minutes away.'

'Not at all,' Edna confirmed. 'Indeed, it's important Donna does go to a local school, so that she can make new friends in your area.'

This was agreed, and minuted by Lisa.

'Contact,' Edna said, looking at us all. 'Since the final court hearing this has been reduced to one a month, which has been much better for Donna. From now on it will go to three times a year as per court order. Cathy,' Edna said turning to me, 'there will be no more contact while Donna is with you. The next one will be in December, after she's left you and is settled at Marlene's. Donna will still be seeing her brothers at school, and she doesn't want to see Chelsea at present.'

I nodded.

'Marlene,' Edna said, now turning to her. 'My colleague, Valerie, is taking over the case. She will arrange the date of

the next contact nearer the time. It will be supervised and
the venue may be changing. Valerie will be in touch once
the move is complete.'

Marlene nodded and made a note in her diary.

'OK, that's all from me,' Edna said. 'Other than to say
congratulations, Marlene.' Edna was congratulating
Marlene on becoming Donna's new 'mum'.

'Yes, congratulations,' everyone added, and I smiled at
Marlene.

'Thank you,' she said, embarrassed. 'I have Donna's
room ready. It's lilac, with pine bedroom furniture. You
said she liked lilac, Cathy.' Marlene looked at me.

'Yes, indeed,' I said, surprised, for it had been one small
comment I'd made at the previous meeting when I'd
described Donna's likes and dislikes. 'It sounds lovely.'

'Great,' Joyce said. 'Now all we have to do is move
Donna into her new room.' Everyone laughed. 'Marlene,
did you bring some photographs of you and your family
for Edna to show Donna?' Joyce asked.

The photographs would form part of Donna's introduction to Marlene and her family, and they were an important first step. Edna would show them to Donna that
evening, talk her through them, and then leave the album
with her, so that when the introductions began Donna
would already be partially familiar with what was to be her
new family and home.

Marlene bent down and delved into her handbag on
the floor beside her chair. She took out a little photograph wallet, which she propped open on the table so
that we could all see. 'This is my house,' she said pointing
to the first page; then, slowly turning the pages: 'my
lounge, my kitchen, my garden, and my cat, Harris. This

is Donna's bedroom, and this is my immediate family.'
The last photo was of a group of ten or more adults and
children, all smiling and waving for the photo. They were
arranged on and around the sofa in Marlene's lounge and
had obviously adopted their best poses for the camera.
'We had a bit of a laugh taking this,' Marlene said with a
smile.

'I can imagine,' Edna said. 'Can you tell me who these
people are so I can tell Donna?'

Marlene angled the album towards Edna. 'This is my
sister and her husband,' she said pointing. 'This is my
brother and his wife, and their children. These are my two
cousins and their partners, and this is Kerry, the niece I
mentioned who is the same age as Donna.' Marlene was
divorced, so there was no husband in the photo.

'What a lovely family,' I said.

'Thank you.' Marlene smiled and, closing the album,
passed it to Edna.

'Thank you very much, Marlene,' Edna said. 'This will
help me a lot when I see Donna.'

And while it was a clearly a lovely family Donna would
be going to, I felt what had become a familiar surge of
regret and sadness that my own lovely family was soon
going to be one short.

'Now,' Mary said, 'let's get down to the dates. Edna, you
are going to see Donna this evening?' Edna nodded. 'So I
suggest Marlene visits Donna and Cathy tomorrow for an
hour. It's Saturday. Is that possible?' Mary looked at
Marlene and me, and we both nodded. 'Then could Donna
and Cathy visit Marlene on Sunday for an hour?' Once the
introductory process is started it quickly gathers momentum, so that the child isn't left for days in limbo between

one home and the next, with time to worry and speculate about the partially known.

'I go to church at eleven o'clock on Sunday,' Marlene said, 'so can we avoid that time?'

I nodded. 'You say the time that would suit you. But I will have to bring Paula and Adrian with me as it's a Sunday.' I looked from Marlene to Edna. 'Is that all right?'

'That's fine with me,' Marlene said.

Edna agreed. 'I should think they will quite enjoy it, and it will be nice for Donna as well.' I was relieved. Once before I'd dealt with a social worker who hadn't wanted my children involved in the introductory visits. Not only had I had to make extensive arrangements for my parents to look after Adrian and Paula, but also the children had felt excluded from the process, which wasn't the best way to say goodbye to a child who had effectively been their brother for nearly a year.

With Edna, Marlene and me making notes in our diaries, and Lisa minuting the dates and times, we planned the rest of the introduction, including three nights when Donna would sleep at her new home, before the move two weeks later. There were days in between some of the visits to give Donna, Marlene and my family time out, and for Edna, Marlene and me to speak on the phone and discuss how the introduction was going, and make any necessary alterations to the timescale. If it went according to plan, then Donna would move on Saturday, in two weeks' time. The week after that was the half-term holiday from school and Marlene said she would take the whole week off work so that she and Donna could spend time together before the school routine began again.

An hour later the meeting ended and I drove home, reflective and a little anxious. Although Edna had recognised the need to make sure Donna didn't feel rejected by the move, it was still a monumental step for Donna. She had been with us for just over fourteen months and in many respects if felt longer, so strong was the bond we had formed with her, as I knew she had with us. And while I liked Marlene very much, and had every faith in her ability to successfully parent Donna, I knew it was likely that the move, no matter how well planned, could unsettle Donna, and rekindle some feelings of rejection (and anger) in the short term. But Marlene, Edna and I would have to deal with those as and when they arose.

I met the children from school that afternoon with a heavy heart but careful to keep my feelings to myself. I made dinner and told the children we were eating early because Edna was coming at 5.30 p.m. to see Donna, which didn't seem strange to them, as we always ate early when Edna or the Guardian visited in the evening. But secretly I felt guilty for withholding the information that only I was party to – the real reason for Edna's visit. When Edna rang the doorbell at exactly 5.30 my stomach churned, while the children remained upstairs playing in their respective bedrooms, still blissfully unaware of the true reason for Edna's visit.

'All right?' Edna said with her usual cheerful smile as I opened the front door.

I put on a brave face and nodded. 'Donna is in her room. I'll bring her down.'

'Thank you, Cathy.'

Edna went through to the lounge while I fetched Donna and saw her into the lounge. I asked Edna if she wanted a drink, which she didn't, and I came out, closing the door behind me. Edna had already told me that she wanted to talk to Donna alone first, and I returned upstairs, where I had some talking to do.

'Will you come with me into Adrian's room for a moment?' I said to Paula, poking my head round her bedroom door. 'I need to speak to you both.'

Paula looked at me, wondering what I could want, then put down the doll she'd been playing with and came with me to Adrian's room. I knocked on his bedroom door and we went in. He was still doing his homework, of which there was plenty now he was at the grammar school. 'It won't take long,' I said to him. 'But I have something important I need to tell you both.'

He laid his pen on the table which acted as a desk. 'It's good news, but also sad,' I said, bravely. 'Edna is here to tell Donna that she has found her a forever family. So I'm afraid she will be leaving us.' There was no other way to say it. 'Her new carer is called Marlene. She is very nice and will be visiting us here tomorrow.'

'Oh,' Adrian said, clearly taken aback. Paula didn't say anything but looked as though she was about to cry. I put my arm around her.

'When?' Adrian asked

'If everything goes according to plan she'll move in two weeks.'

'Oh,' Adrian said again, and, picking up his pen, he returned to his school work. This was his way of dealing with loss, and I knew he would want to talk more about it later.

Leaving Adrian to his school work, I took Paula's hand and we returned to her room. 'Shall we play with your dolls while Edna is with Donna?' I asked, thinking this might be a good distraction.

She nodded, and I sat on the floor in front of her doll's house next to Paula, and she picked up the 'mummy' doll she'd been playing with when I'd interrupted. The doll was about three inches high and one of a set of four – two adults and two children. It was the epitome of the 'perfect' mum, with hair drawn into a neat bun and a white apron covering her knee-length floral dress. In one hand she carried a rolling pin, suggesting she was a very accomplished cook, or possibly as Adrian once said (to Paula's horror) it was to 'wallop the kids' with.

'Does Donna have to go?' Paula asked presently in a little voice, walking the mummy doll into the house.

'I'm afraid so, love. You remember like Jasmine did?' Jasmine had stayed with us for six months the year before and been found adoptive parents.

'Will Donna phone and see us sometimes?' Paula asked.

'Yes, I'm sure she will. I have met her new carer, Marlene, and she will help Donna to stay in touch.' Although in truth a balance would have to be drawn between Donna keeping in contact with us and bonding with Marlene and her family.

'Can I see where she's going to live?' Paula asked, giving me the 'daddy' doll.

'Yes, you will on Sunday. We're all going for a visit.' We wouldn't be meeting any of Marlene's family on our first visit: that could have been overwhelming for Donna. The first visit was for Donna to see her new home; meeting Marlene's extended family would come later and gradually over the two weeks.

I stayed in Paula's room, playing with her and the doll's house, although in truth my heart wasn't really in it, and I didn't think Paula's was either. Paula played the 'mummy', and her perfect mummy doll washed the pans in the tiny doll's house sink, and made the little beds, while I, the less than perfect daddy doll, stood watching her, although I did take the dog for a walk and put the garbage out when asked. Every so often Paula stopped her role playing and asked if Donna was all right, and what was Edna telling her.

'I'm sure she's fine, and Edna will be telling her lots of nice things about Marlene, and Donna's new home and family.'

'We're a nicer family,' Paula said defensively, and I smiled.

Nearly an hour passed before I heard the lounge door open and Edna call from the hall, 'Cathy, could you join us now, please.'

'I won't be long,' I said to Paula. Standing, I gave her a reassuring kiss on her cheek, and I left to the sound of Paula telling the mummy doll that she was the 'nicest mummy in the world', which I hoped reflected on me.

In the lounge Edna and Donna were sitting side by side on the sofa. Donna was holding the wallet of photographs that Marlene had prepared for her and given to Edna that morning. It reminded me for a moment of when Donna had first arrived – Donna and Edna together on the sofa. Although of course now Donna wasn't sitting dejectedly, shoulders hunched forward and arms folded into her waist as though protecting herself, but was upright and confident. I sat on the other sofa.

'Donna and I have had a nice long chat,' Edna said. 'And she is looking forward to meeting Marlene when she comes here tomorrow. Donna knows that it will be a bit strange for everyone to begin with, and that she can talk to you about her feelings.'

'I'm sure we will be talking a lot,' I said, smiling at Donna. She wasn't exactly smiling, but didn't seem unhappy, more deep in thought.

'Would you like to see my photographs?' she asked me after a moment.

'Yes please, very much.'

Edna winked at me knowingly. 'I'll leave you to it then. I'll be off now and I'll phone on Monday.'

'Fine,' I said. 'Donna, I'll just see Edna out then we'll look at your photographs together.' I smiled again at Donna and she smiled back.

I went with Edna to the front door. 'It appears to have gone well,' I said quietly.

'Yes, it did, bless her. She's so eager for you to see the photographs, I didn't let on you'd already seen them. But I've told her you've met Marlene and you like her. It's important for her to know that you approve.'

'Yes, thanks, Edna.'

We said goodbye and I closed the front door. Edna was a highly experienced and dedicated social worker, and also very sensitive to children's feelings. I didn't know what exactly Edna had said to Donna, but whatever it was had left Donna in a very positive mood. When I went into the lounge she was still poring over the photographs, eager to show me.

I sat beside her and watched as she carefully turned the pages, describing what was in each picture. When we came to the photograph of her bedroom her eyes lit up. 'It's lilac,' she exclaimed, as doubtless she had done when she'd first seen the photo with Edna. 'It's my favourite colour.'

'It is,' I said, 'and what a lovely room! Aren't you lucky?'

She nodded happily. 'I'm looking forward to seeing it on Sunday. That's when we visit, isn't it?'

'Yes, love, it is.'

Donna turned to the last photograph, of Marlene's extended family, and told me the names of those people she could remember. When Paula appeared five minutes later, Donna went through the photographs again, pointing out the details in each photo with a more elaborate commentary. When Adrian, having finished his homework, came down for a drink and snack twenty minutes later, Donna went through the photo wallet again.

That night when I went into Donna's room to say goodnight, I thought she looked sad. She was in her pyjamas, sitting in bed waiting for a goodnight kiss. The photograph album was closed in her lap. I perched on the edge of the bed and she looked at me with big wondering eyes. 'This time next week, 'she said, 'I shall be sleeping in my new bed for the first time.'

'That's right, love. In your beautiful lilac room with lilac sheets and duvet.' I took her hand between mine.

She thought for a moment, then said softly, 'I'm happy Marlene wants me as a daughter, but it will be a bit strange to begin with, like when I first came here.'

'It will seem a bit strange, yes, because it will all be new, but I don't think it will be like when you first came here, love. Do you remember how you felt then?' She nodded. 'You have come a long way since then, Donna, and I am very proud of you. I know you will be just fine, although we're going to miss you loads.'

'That's what Edna said.' She gave a little wistful smile. 'And we will keep in touch, won't we, Cathy? It's important to me.'

'Of course, love. It's important to us too. We'll all stay in touch for as long as you want, Donna. I promise you.'

She put her arms around me and hugged me tightly. 'For ever, Cathy. You will be my second family when Marlene is my new mum.'

Chapter Twenty-four
Introductions

As one o'clock approached the following day, the time Marlene was due, it was difficult to say who was the more nervous: Donna, who was standing behind the net curtains in the front room watching for the first glimpse of Marlene; Paula, who was making regular trips from the front room to the kitchen to update me; or me, wiping the work surfaces as a displacement for my own nervous energy. Adrian was perfecting his 'Mr Cool' image and, aware that Marlene's visit was soon, was in his room listening to his iPod. However, at 1.10 p.m., when I heard Donna's little voice call 'She's here,' followed by Paula's louder cry of 'She's here!' and I answered the door, it was obvious who was the most nervous – Marlene.

'Do I look all right?' she asked, smoothing her hand over her floral patterned dress and adjusting the small gold chain around her neck.

'Of course. You look fine. Come in.' I smiled and touched her arm reassuringly. 'The girls have been looking out for you.'

'I'm so sorry I'm late, Cathy. The traffic was horrendous, I should have guessed it would be busy on a Saturday.'

'Don't worry. They would have been watching for you whatever time you'd come. Let's go through to the lounge.'

I led the way down the hall to the lounge, at the same time calling, 'Donna, Paula, Marlene is here.' Now the longed-for arrival had happened the girls had gone shy and were hiding in the front room.

'Do sit down,' I said to Marlene. 'Can I get you a drink?'

'No thanks, Cathy. I'm fine. It's a lovely place you have here.'

'Thank you.' I sat on the other sofa. 'Your photographs were a great success,' I said. 'Donna was so proud of them – she must have shown us all at least six times.'

'Were they all right? Thank goodness. I did wonder,' Marlene said, flustered. 'I am pleased.' Although it was a fairly cool autumn day Marlene looked hot and her forehead glistened slightly.

I began making small talk – about the weather and the traffic in the high street; then I told Marlene more about Donna's school. It was better for Donna that we carried on in a natural manner, where there was no pressure on her; she would join us when she felt able. I told Marlene of our evening routine, some of which she could adapt in the first few days after the move to help make Donna feel at home. Then Marlene told me some more about her family. Presently we heard footsteps coming along the hall and Paula and Donna entered the lounge. Paula was holding Donna's hand and leading her, just as she had once led her down the garden in what now seemed a lifetime ago.

'Donna, Paula, this is Marlene,' I said. Marlene stood, and went over and shook Paula's hand, then Donna's. Donna had her eyes trained on the floor, and for the first time since I couldn't remember when, she had her shoulders slightly hunched forward.

'Lovely to meet you both,' Marlene said, and she glanced anxiously at me.

'Come and sit down,' I said to the girls. 'We've been talking about the photographs, and the people in the family group. Marlene is going to see her niece, Kerry, later.'

Paula led Donna to the sofa and they sat beside me. Marlene returned to the other sofa, and we picked up our conversation about Marlene's family for a few minutes, so the atmosphere was relaxed. Out of the corner of my eye I saw Donna gradually raise her head and steal a glance at Marlene, then lower it again quickly. Marlene smiled and continued talking. A moment later our cat, Toscha, sauntered into the lounge.

'Hello,' Marlene said, and Donna glanced between Toscha and Marlene. 'Did you see the picture of my cat, Harris?' Marlene asked.

'Yes,' I said. 'He's quite a bit bigger than Toscha.' Donna looked up, for longer this time.

'Harris is a very lazy cat,' Marlene said. 'All he does is eat and sleep. He's part Persian, so he has long hair and needs a lot of brushing.'

'I brush Toscha,' Donna said, raising her head and speaking for the first time.

'I don't,' Paula said. 'Toscha scratched me once.'

'That's because you poked your finger in her ear, when you were little,' I said to Paula, and she giggled.

'Shall I brush Toscha now?' Donna asked quietly, daring to raise her head for longer.

We didn't normally brush the cat in the lounge because of the hair but I thought it would help 'break the ice' and give us a focal point. 'Yes, if you like. You know where the brush is.'

Donna and Paula went to the cupboard under the stairs to fetch the brush. I smiled at Marlene. 'Don't worry. Donna is slowly thawing out. It's bound to take time. I wouldn't have expected any different.'

'Do you think she likes me?' Marlene asked anxiously.

'Yes, of course. Please don't worry.'

The girls returned with the cat brush, and Donna sat on the floor beside Toscha and began grooming her, brushing her fur from the neck down towards her tail as I had shown her. She had a naturally light touch and a soothing, almost soporific manner, as though caressing the cat with each stroke of the brush. Toscha stretched out and yawned contentedly, making the most of this sudden and unscheduled attention. Paula sat a little away from them, not wholly convinced the cat wouldn't suddenly remember her poking its ear and turn and seek revenge, although I had spent a long time trying to convince Paula otherwise.

Marlene slipped from the sofa and joined Donna on the floor. 'Hello Toscha,' she said gently, then began stroking the cat's forehead while Donna continued her slow leisurely brushing. I thought the cat was going to be very spoilt after all this.

'Harris is going to love you, Donna,' Marlene said. I smiled, and so too did Donna.

Marlene and I kept the conversation going while she continued stroking Toscha's forehead as Donna brushed. I steered the conversation to Marlene's house, and said how much Donna liked the photograph of her bedroom. Marlene said she had redecorated it herself and was about to start redecorating the kitchen. Adrian appeared and I introduced him to Marlene. He went over, and she stood to shake hands.

'How is school?' she asked.

'Good, thanks,' Adrian said, then he disappeared into the kitchen to get himself a drink, before returning to his bedroom. I hoped she didn't think him rude.

'He has a lot of school work,' I offered.

Marlene nodded. 'My son is twenty-two now, and is in his last year at university. He's studying law.'

'That's a good profession,' I said.

A few minutes later I thought the cat grooming had run its course and I suggested to Donna that she did a jigsaw puzzle, with the intention of Marlene and her doing most of it, so that they could continue working together.

'I'm not very good at jigsaws,' Marlene said. 'Are you, Donna?'

'A little,' she said in a small voice.

I went to the toy cupboard and found a jigsaw that could be completed in the twenty minutes that was left of Marlene's visit. Marlene and Donna sat side by side on the floor and began sifting through the pieces, finding the corners and straight edges, with Paula helping. I continued to make light conversation. It wasn't the easiest situation, but I hadn't expected anything different with the first meeting. I hoped that Marlene wasn't disappointed and hadn't expected Donna to rush into her arms and treat her as a new mother. An hour was enough for this first visit, and once the jigsaw was complete, I confirmed the arrangements for the following day. 'Is one o'clock still all right for us to visit you?' I asked Marlene.

'Yes. Would you like me to make some lunch?'

I thought having to sit and eat lunch might be too much for Donna on her first visit to Marlene's. 'No, don't worry about lunch,' I said. 'A drink and a biscuit will be fine.'

Marlene returned to the sofa for a few minutes and Donna fell quiet again. 'OK,' Marlene said after a moment, 'I'll look forward to seeing you all again tomorrow.' She said goodbye to Donna and Paula in the lounge, and I saw her to the door.

'It will be easier tomorrow,' I reassured her, for Marlene did look quite worried.

'Do you think she likes me?' Marlene asked again, as she had done in the lounge.

'Yes, you did fine. Please don't worry. It's a huge step for Donna, and she'll need time to reflect on this meeting. I know her – meeting new people is always difficult for her. Would you like me to phone you this evening?'

'Oh, yes please,' she said, relieved. 'You will tell me if I'm doing anything wrong, won't you?'

'Yes, but I'm sure you're not. Donna is quiet at the best of times.'

'I do hope she likes me,' Marlene said again.

I renewed my assurance and we said goodbye.

For the rest of the afternoon Donna talked about nothing else apart from Marlene and her home: 'Do you think …?' she asked repeatedly. 'Will she have …? Does she like …?' Sometimes I could answer her questions but often I had to say, 'I don't know, but that's something you could ask Marlene tomorrow.' When we sat down to dinner and the questions were still coming, I said, 'Donna, Marlene is the best person to ask, and she would like it if you did ask her questions and talk to her. You might not realise it, but Marlene is just as nervous as you are. She so much wants you to like her.'

'I do like her,' she said quietly. 'It's just all a bit strange.'

'I know, love. I do understand.'

That evening I phoned Marlene while Donna was in the bath and told her that Donna hadn't stopped talking about her all afternoon. 'And she likes you already,' I said.

'Did she say so?'

'Yes, and she's going to try to talk more tomorrow.'

'Oh, that's great. Thank you for telling me. After I left you I bought some more jigsaws, and also a new doll, which I have sat on Donna's bed.' Marlene was trying so hard – I really felt for her.

'That's lovely,' I said, 'but please don't worry. I know this will work out fine. It will just take time.'

That evening after I had read Donna a bedtime story and was saying goodnight to her, she said, 'It feels so strange, Cathy. I think it's because Marlene is different to you.'

'Just as well,' I said, smiling. 'Give yourself time, love. It's strange for Marlene too. She appreciates how you must be feeling.' Donna smiled but was clearly deep in thought. I remained perched on the edge of the bed and stroked her forehead. 'You all right, love?'

She nodded. 'Cathy, do you think Marlene really does want me?'

'Yes, of course, love. Whatever made you ask?'

'My mum didn't want me.'

'Is that what you've been thinking about?'

She nodded, and looked up at me imploringly.

'Donna, love, your mum had so many problems in her life that they stopped her from seeing the beautiful things. She couldn't appreciate you, look after you or love you enough, because of her problems. Marlene and I, and most mothers, are different. You are a lovely person, and I know

Marlene already likes you. I also know that in time she will love you as we do.'

She smiled. As we had thought might happen, the introduction to Marlene had unsettled Donna and brought back the negative feelings and memories from her past. Prior to me, the other person who had been in the mothering role, far from liking Donna, had treated her appallingly. I could only offer so much reassurance; the rest would come when Donna saw for herself that Marlene behaved as I did, with the same respect and love.

As predicted, our visit to Marlene's, the following day, was a lot easier, with everyone far more relaxed. Marlene met us at the door of her three-bedroom semi with its neat front garden, and began a tour of the house. Harris, her large (and lazy) cat, was sprawled on the sofa in the lounge and living up to his reputation. Adrian sat on the sofa next to the cat and stayed downstairs, while Marlene showed the girls and me upstairs. Donna was keen to see her bedroom, and it was even more luxurious than the photograph had suggested. The smell of fresh paint still hung in the air, and the crisp cotton lilac curtains and matching duvet cover were brand new. There were lots of little matching accessories – a pale lilac shaded lamp, a lilac velvet-topped dressing-table stool and the new doll in a lavender-colour dress that Marlene had bought specially sitting on the bed. I hoped Donna appreciated just how much trouble Marlene had gone to.

'Isn't it lovely?' I said to Donna. 'You are a lucky girl.'

Donna smiled, and looked as though she did appreciate it. She and Paula sat on the bed and began playing with the doll. The doll was about twelve inches high and dressed in

Victorian costume with layers of petticoats topped with the lavender-coloured satin dress. It was a lovely doll and I guessed quite expensive.

'Do you want to stay here and play for a while?' Marlene asked the girls. 'Cathy and I can go downstairs.' The girls nodded. 'We'll be in the lounge when you've finished,' Marlene added.

Downstairs Marlene set up the PlayStation for Adrian, and she and I sat in the armchairs at one end of the lounge-cum-dining room and chatted, while Adrian amused himself at the other end. Marlene told me that she had moved to the house three years previously and had had to extensively modernise, and redecorate every room. An elderly couple had lived in the house before her, for most of their lives, and the upkeep of the house had become too much for them. Marlene said that although the house was structurally sound she had been working on it continuously since moving in. I admired Marlene's handiwork and told her of my own decorating.

'When you live by yourself,' she said, 'it's surprising what you can do if you have to. I have even plumbed in the new kitchen sink.'

'Really?' I said, impressed.

The kitchen was the last room that needed work doing to it, Marlene said, and she wanted to show me how far she had got. 'My family give me a hand sometimes,' she said as we went into the kitchen, 'but I don't like to keep asking them.' The new gleaming stainless-steel sink stood out against a backdrop of half-removed tiles. 'They're dreadful to get off,' Marlene said. 'The news ones are over there.' She pointed to a stack of boxes by the wall. 'The next job is to replace the kitchen cupboards,' she continued, happy to have an appreciative audience. 'I've got a local man coming in to help. Then it's the flooring.' She tapped her foot on the torn and faded linoleum. 'I haven't decided what to put down yet.'

'It will be lovely when it's finished,' I said. 'I'm afraid my DIY is limited to painting and wallpapering.'

'I've had enough of it now,' she admitted with a small sigh. 'I'll be pleased when it's finished and I can just enjoy it.'

Marlene made us a cup of tea, then called the girls and Adrian for a drink and biscuits. We sat around the table in the dining area of the lounge and chatted – Adrian about the PlayStation game, and Donna and Paula about Donna's bedroom. Once we'd finished the drinks, Marlene cleared away the cups and glasses and produced one of the jigsaw puzzles she'd bought. Marlene, the girls and I sat at the table and slowly assembled it while Adrian returned to the PlayStation.

Our hour's visit ran over time but it didn't matter; Donna was clearly far more relaxed than she had been the day before, and appeared to be enjoying herself. Marlene was more relaxed too. Once the jigsaw was complete I began to take our leave. I confirmed the details of Donna's next visit, which would take place on Tuesday. I would bring Donna straight from school to Marlene's and she would stay for dinner; then I would collect her at 7.30 p.m. This was to be repeated on Thursday. Then, if everything was going all right, she would stay over on Friday and Saturday night, and I would collect her on Sunday morning. It had been decided at the planning meeting that Donna wouldn't accompany Marlene to church on this occasion as it could be too much for her so soon, and I would collect Donna at 10.00 a.m. on the Sunday. Donna was due to stay the night of the following Wednesday, and Marlene would take her to school in the morning. If everything went well, we would then have a little farewell party for Donna on the Friday, and I would move her to Marlene's on the Saturday. It was going to be a very busy two weeks: apart from the practical aspect of driving Donna to and from Marlene's, I would also be spending a lot of time talking to Donna, and generally keeping an eye on her to make sure she felt comfortable with the pace at which we were going.

The two evening visits, Tuesday and Thursday, went very well – better than I had anticipated – but a problem arose on the Saturday, although I didn't find out until I collected Donna on Sunday morning.

It had been really strange not having Donna sleeping in her bed at home, and a taste of what it would be like when she had moved. Donna's place at the meal table was glaringly empty, and suddenly three seemed a very small number. 'I wonder what Donna is doing,' Adrian and Paula asked more than once on Saturday, to which I replied, 'I expect she is getting to know Marlene,' or 'Playing,' or 'Possibly helping Marlene with her kitchen.' Marlene had already said that she'd appreciate Donna's help in finishing her kitchen. And I wondered if perhaps I hadn't let Donna help enough, and crucified myself thinking of all the things that I could have handled differently – better, if I'd had another chance. But that is the nature of fostering, and child rearing in general – you do what you think is best at the time and try not to repeat your mistakes in the future.

On Sunday morning when we arrived at 10.00 a.m. to collect Donna, Marlene met us at the door, looking very worried. Donna was nowhere to be seen downstairs.

'She's in her bedroom,' Marlene said, 'sulking, I'm afraid. Would Adrian and Paula like to play in the lounge while I speak to you in the kitchen?'

I motioned for the children to go into the lounge, where Adrian immediately picked up the controls to the PlayStation and began explaining to Paula what she had to do. I followed Marlene into the kitchen, wondering what Donna could have done. I felt my anxiety rise.

'I've dealt with it as best I could,' Marlene began. 'But I've had to tell Donna off, and she's not happy with me.' I looked at Marlene and waited as she shifted uncomfortably from one foot to the other. 'We had a really good Friday evening, and a good day yesterday,' she continued. 'When I said goodnight to Donna last night she seemed fine. But she must have got out of bed after I was asleep, and she tore up the magazines I'd bought for her yesterday. I went in this morning and found her room covered with paper. I wasn't worried, because you'd told me to expect this, and Donna said she would clear it up later. While she was in the shower I thought I would save her the bother and I got out the hoover and quickly went round her room. I thought I was doing her a favour, but when she saw what I'd done she was so angry. She shouted at me, then called me an interfering bitch.'

'Did she indeed!'

'I told her off and she's been sulking ever since. That was about an hour ago. I've tried talking to her, but she's not having any of it. I'm sorry, Cathy. I've clearly done something very wrong.'

I could see immediately what the something was but it certainly wasn't Marlene's fault. 'It's part of Donna's ritual to clear up the mess she makes,' I said gently. 'To her the clearing up is the most important part of the ritual. But that's no excuse for shouting or swearing at you.' Marlene looked at me, still upset and shaken by the whole experience, and now blaming herself. 'Because of her cleaning role at home,' I continued, 'Donna needs to clean and tidy; it's her acting it out. When she does it again, leave her to clear up the mess. But I'm not having her being rude.'

'I'm sorry,' Marlene said again. 'I should have realised.'

'No, you shouldn't. Donna could have explained to you rather than bursting into anger. She's been living with me for over fifteen months and she knows that type of behaviour isn't acceptable. Shall we go and see her together? I think it might be useful.'

Marlene readily agreed, and leaving Paula and Adrian playing on the PlayStation in the lounge, we went to Donna's bedroom. I could see that Marlene was still upset, and I guessed she'd also been frightened by Donna's anger, as I had been when she'd first come to live with me. Her rage could be very threatening.

I knocked on Donna's door and opened it. She was sitting on the edge of her bed, quite clearly sulking. Her face looked like thunder and it was so severe that it looked almost fake – an adopted pose to make Marlene suffer. Had it been me she was directing it to I would have laughed and cajoled her out of it, but it wasn't, and Marlene didn't know Donna well enough to have the confidence to risk humour. She had been frightened and compromised by Donna's outburst and it wasn't fair on her.

'Donna,' I said firmly, raising my voice slightly in indignation, 'I don't know what you think you're doing, but you
need to apologise to Marlene. Now.'

She glanced up at me, slightly taken aback, perhaps
expecting my sympathy. 'How dare you speak to Marlene
like that?' I continued in the same authoritative tone. 'You
know that type of language is unacceptable. You don't
swear in my house and you certainly don't here either.' She
lowered her head again, but the sulk wasn't as emphasised
now that she realised it wasn't going to have much effect.
'Marlene made a mistake in clearing up your bedroom,' I
said. 'She thought she was being helpful; she wasn't to
know you liked doing it. It was no reason to shout and
swear at her, was it?' Donna sat with her head lowered but
said nothing, clearly digging her heels in.

'What should you have done?' I continued. 'What have I
taught you to do if there is a problem, rather than getting
angry or sulking?'

I waited, and Marlene waited too; we were both looking
at Donna, who was still perched on the edge of the bed.

'Talk,' she said at last in a small voice.

'Exactly,' I said. 'So why didn't you talk to Marlene?
You should have explained to her that in future you would
like to clear up your mess. It would have been the adult
and sensible thing to do. It is what I have spent fifteen
months teaching you to do, Donna. Please don't forget it
all now and let me down.' But of course in the new situation of Marlene's house Donna had simply reverted to her
learned behaviour from the years before. 'Right, young
lady,' I said, finally, 'apologise to Marlene now please.'

Again, Marlene and I waited, and I knew quite a bit
hung in the balance. These two weeks were a difficult

period because Donna was slowly transferring not only her allegiance and feelings from me to Marlene, but also her trust, and the respect she had for my authority.

'Well?' I said. 'I'm waiting.'

'Sorry, Marlene,' she said slowly and in the same small voice. 'I should have talked to you. I will next time.'

'Thank you, Donna,' Marlene said. 'I hope you feel you can talk to me, as you do to Cathy.'

Donna nodded.

'Good girl,' I said. 'Now we will say goodbye and let Marlene get off to church. I bet she feels she needs it.' I glanced at Marlene and she smiled. But Donna's apology had been the best possible outcome, and I was quietly pleased. She could have burst into another furious rage and said she hated Marlene (and me) and wasn't going to come here ever again. But she hadn't, her anger had been confined to the one incident and we had dealt with it.

As we said goodbye in the hall, Donna apologised again to Marlene, 'Sorry. I've had a nice time really.'

I saw Marlene's spirits lift. 'Good. I've enjoyed it too. And I'm looking forward to seeing you again on Wednesday. I'll cook you your favourite dinner.'

Donna smiled, but I could have scowled, for it was a stark reminder that very soon Marlene would be cooking all Donna's favourite meals, and she would soon be the most important person in her life.

Later that day I reinforced to Donna how important it was for her to talk to Marlene if she felt there was a problem, and she promised me she would. Donna had progressed sufficiently since living with me to be able to rationally explain her feelings, rather than let them bottle up until they exploded as she had done in the early days. I wondered how much of Donna's anger had been simply to test Marlene's reaction.

When Edna phoned on Monday we agreed that, given the enormity of the changes Donna was having to accommodate, the incident was minor, and the introduction and move would go ahead as planned. Donna spent Wednesday night at her new home, and Marlene took Donna to school on Thursday morning and met some of the staff. When I collected Donna at the end of school Beth Adams and Mrs Bristow told me how proud Donna had been when she had introduced Marlene to them. I was pleased, but I also experienced that now very familiar sadness that my role in Donna's life was slowly being transferred to Marlene. I knew I would have to let go quicker than I had been doing, for Friday night was Donna's last with us, and on Saturday I would be moving her.

Chapter Twenty-five
Moving On

During the rest of the week I found myself stealing little glances at Donna and trying to imagine what life was going to be like without her. I thought that Adrian and Paula were doing likewise, and also making the most of the time they had left with her; Paula hardly left her side. While Donna was at school on Friday I packed most of her belongings. I had suggested to Donna that I did this, as we were going to have a little leaving party on Friday evening and there wouldn't be much time; also, packing to say goodbye was a sad business for an adult, let alone a child. Donna had readily agreed to let me do it.

When I collected Donna from school on Friday I said goodbye to all the staff and thanked them for what they had done. This would be my last visit to the school, as my involvement there had now finished, although as Mrs Bristow said, 'We might see each other again in the future with another child.' I gave her a large box of chocolates to be shared among the staff, and thanking them again, said an emotional farewell.

That evening we had our leaving party for Donna. My parents, my brother and his wife, Sue and family from next door, Emily and Mandy (they were saying goodbye to me, for they would still see Donna at school), and Jill, arrived at 6.00 p.m. They all brought presents for Donna, which she opened. 'It's like my birthday again,' she said brightly, 'or Christmas come early.' I smiled to hide my regret. Donna wouldn't be with us for Christmas, although I knew she would have a good time with Marlene. Paula, Adrian and I had bought Donna a leaving present, but we were going to give it to her on Saturday, last thing before we took her to Marlene's.

I had prepared a buffet and set it on the table in the breakfast room, and Donna's leaving party was a happy affair, despite our sadness at her going. The adults chatted, everyone helped themselves to food and I organised some games at the children's request. Our guests said goodbye just after 8.30 p.m., wishing Donna good luck and telling her to write when she had a chance. The house suddenly fell quiet and Donna thanked me for her party. 'You're more than welcome, love,' I said, and I gave her a big hug.

While the children went upstairs to change, ready for bed, I cleared away the remainder of the buffet and loaded the dishwasher. I fed Toscha, and then went up to say goodnight. Paula was nearly asleep; it was 9.30 p.m. and well past her bedtime. I kissed her goodnight then went into Adrian's room; he said he was going to read for half an hour. Donna was in bed, with her leaving presents on the floor beside her. There was a china ornament which looked like Toscha from my parents; a framed family photograph of all of us from my brother; a book from my neighbour; a pink purse from Emily; and a gift voucher from Jill.

'We'll have to remember to pack those in the morning,' I said, perching on the edge of her bed. I had taken the cases and boxes containing the rest of Donna's belongings

downstairs and stacked them in the front room, which we
hadn't used during the evening.

'And my bike,' Donna said. 'Don't forget that.'

I smiled. 'No, love, I haven't forgotten that. I've put it in
the boot of the car already. I wanted to make sure it fitted
in.'

'You think of everything,' she said with a grin.

'I wouldn't say that, love, but I try my best.' I paused
and looked at her. She was snuggled beneath the duvet, her
eyes heavy with sleep but content. 'Donna,' I said gently, 'I
want you to remember that Marlene will be trying to do
her best too. She might not always get it right, but that's
where you can help, isn't it?'

She nodded. 'I know. By talking to her and telling her
how I feel.'

'That's right. Good girl.' I continued to look at her, and
stroked away a strand of hair from her forehead. I didn't
want to get all emotional, but I was finding it difficult to
say goodnight for what would be the last time. 'And
Donna, remember it's going to be a bit strange to begin
with, until you get used to your new home. I know we've
talked about this but if you give yourself time I know
things will just get better and better for you.' I paused and
smiled, still reluctant to say goodnight and pull myself
away. 'OK, love,' I said after a moment. 'You get some
sleep. You must be exhausted. It's been a busy day.'

'Yes. And thanks again for everything, Cathy. I've loved
being here. Adrian and Paula are very lucky.'

My heart lurched. 'I feel very lucky to have known you,
Donna. It's been a privilege looking after you. But this
isn't goodbye. You promised to keep in touch, and I shall
look forward to hearing all your news. Marlene thinks

she's very lucky too.' Donna smiled, and then yawned. 'Goodnight love, sleep tight.'

'Night, Cathy.'

I kissed her forehead and, coming out, swallowed the lump in my throat. Saying goodnight to Donna for the last time was one of those heartfelt moments that I knew would stay with me for ever.

The following morning Donna was up early and very excited. 'It's like going on holiday,' she said, taking her presents downstairs and packing them in the case I had left open. Adrian and Paula were up and dressed earlier than was usual on a Saturday and joined in Donna's excitement, although I could see they were putting on brave faces to mask their sadness at Donna leaving. We had pancakes for breakfast – Donna's favourite – and I then put her nightwear and wash bag into the case and zipped it shut. The four of us loaded the car, arranging and rearranging the bags and boxes until they all fitted in. By the time we'd finished, the boot lid only just closed and the passenger seat was full, as were the foot wells. The children would also have some of the smaller bags on their laps; any more luggage and I would have had to have made two trips.

Before we set off, I checked Donna's bedroom for anything that could have been missed; then we gathered in the lounge, where I presented Donna with her present from Adrian, Paula and me. As she carefully peeled off the wrapping paper I took the final photograph – of the jeweller's box appearing, and her face lighting up.

'It's a proper watch!' she exclaimed. 'An adult one! Thank you so much. That's great!'

'You're very welcome, love,' I said. 'I thought that now you can tell the time you should have a decent watch.' It was a nice watch: I had chosen it carefully from the jeweller's, a ladies' watch not a child's, set in a silver bracelet. Donna put it on her wrist and we all admired it.

'I'm going to keep it in the box for now,' she said, carefully sliding it off and returning it to the box. 'I don't want it getting scratched.'

'You won't be able to tell the time with it in there,' Adrian teased.

'Typical boy!' Donna returned.

We piled into the car and Donna sat with the present held protectively in her lap. As I drove, I repeatedly glanced in the rear-view mirror at her. I was reminded of when she'd first arrived, clutching the present from Mary and Ray. How different she was now: brighter, more upright, more confident and happy, and much taller. She must have grown four inches in the time she'd been with us; I'd had to replace her jeans and shoes every couple of months. All three children were quiet as I drove to Marlene's, gazing out of the windows, and I saw that Paula was holding Donna's hand.

Marlene must have been looking out for us, for as soon as we drew up outside her house at 11.00 a.m., the front door opened and she came out, smiling and waving.

'Hi!' she called. 'Welcome. I hope you're hungry. I've made Donna's favourite – pancakes for us all.'

I smiled, and so too did the children. 'I'm sure you can all manage another one,' I said quietly to them.

We unloaded the car; with all five of us helping it didn't take long. We carried the boxes, cases and bags through the hall and straight up to Donna's bedroom. Marlene wheeled the bike into the conservatory. By the time we'd emptied the car, Donna's room was full.

'I know what we shall be doing today,' Marlene said to Donna.

'Unpacking,' Donna said, and she put her arms around Marlene's waist and gave her a big hug. Marlene beamed, so very pleased.

We sat around the table in the lounge and Marlene served us pancakes, with a choice of toppings – syrup, icing sugar, ice cream, honey and grated chocolate. I managed to eat one, Paula and Donna two, and Adrian three.

'These are amazing,' Adrian said, helping himself to more ice cream and chocolate. I agreed. 'They're different from the ones you make,' he added (for 'different' read 'better'), and I agreed again.

I knew it wasn't in anyone's interest to prolong our leaving, so once we'd finished our 'second breakfast', I said we had better be off. We all helped to clear the table, leaving the plates and cutlery in the kitchen sink, then we began a slow path down the hall and to the front door. Our goodbyes needed to be quick and positive, with the reminder that we would phone in two weeks. It had been decided at the planning meeting that I should allow two weeks before phoning, so that my call didn't unsettle Donna while she was still bonding with Marlene in the early days. After that it was up to Donna (and Marlene) how often she wanted to phone.

'Right then,' I said positively, as I stood by the front door with Adrian and Paula beside me. 'We'll leave you to get on with your unpacking. I'll phone in two weeks, Donna.'

Marlene smiled and nodded, while Donna gave a half nod. She was standing next to Marlene, with her eyes lowered and her shoulders slightly hunched forward.

'Come on, love,' I said. 'I want to see a big smile and have a hug before I go.'

Without raising her eyes, Donna came to me and, putting her arms around me, hugged me hard.

After a moment I gently eased her away and looked at her. 'Where's that lovely smile then?'

She looked into my eyes and managed a smile, but I could see her eyes welling.

Paula stepped forward and threw her arms around Donna's waist and gave her a big squeeze. 'I'll miss you,' Paula said.

Donna kissed her cheek. 'I'll miss you too.'

I glanced at Adrian and he pulled a face. 'I don't do girly cuddles,' he said. 'But I'll shake your hand, Donna.' Marlene and I smiled as Donna and Adrian shook hands.

'Take care,' I said to Donna and Marlene, and I opened the front door.

'And you,' Marlene said. Donna was concentrating on the floor again.

'Come on then,' I said to Adrian and Paula, for no one was moving.

I stepped out of the front door with Paula holding my hand and Adrian following a little behind. I didn't look back as I went down the path; only when we were in the car, and I had opened the windows so that we could wave, did I look at them. Marlene and Donna were framed in the doorway, standing side by side. Marlene had her arm around Donna's shoulders, and Donna was wiping the back of her hand across her eyes. I started the engine and, stifling my own tears, gave a little wave, and gradually pulled away. Paula and Adrian waved from their windows until the house was out of sight; then I raised the windows.

As I pulled to the T-junction at the end of the road, I glanced in the rear-view mirror. Adrian and Paula were silent and close to tears. I saw how empty the back seat looked without Donna in her usual place by the window. 'I've got to stop at the shops on the way home,' I said, 'then I thought we would go to the cinema.' Aware we were all going to need something to cheer us up, I'd already booked the tickets.

'Good,' Adrian said with no real enthusiasm.

'I wish Donna was coming,' Paula said. 'I miss her.'

'I know, love.'

We went home after the supermarket shopping, as the film didn't start until 5.00 p.m., and as I entered the hall, I saw that the light on the answerphone flashing, signalling a message. Paula and Adrian, still subdued, took off their shoes and coats and went into the lounge, while I pressed 'play' on the machine. The message was from Jill, timed half an hour before: 'Hi, Cathy, I hope the move went all right. I'll phone on Monday to catch up. And Cathy, we've had a referral through for a five-year-old boy. They are looking for a foster home for him in a week's time. I'll tell you more on Monday. Have a good weekend. Bye, and thanks for all you did for Donna. It's much appreciated.'

I deleted the message, and began down the hall and towards the lounge. By Monday I might be able to consider taking a new child, but not yet. Now, I just needed time with Adrian and Paula, and we all needed time to reflect on Donna. We would have to adjust to being a family of three again before we could consider welcoming a new child. I knew that for the next few days we would be sharing many fond memories of Donna and her time with us – a collective healing process, as we remembered all the good times that had made up our family life. Only then could we begin to consider the five-year-old boy, whose problems would doubtless be very different from Donna's, but no less urgent and demanding.

Wouldn't it be lovely, I thought again, if I could wave my magic wand and make every child wanted and cared for, and every parent capable of caring for and loving their child? But practically, all I could do was the best for the children I looked after, and hope I gave them something positive to take with them. And if Donna had learned something from my family, so had our lives been enriched from knowing her: to have suffered the abuse and degradation she had done and not be consumed by hate said a lot about her. I doubt I would have fared so well.

Epilogue

Eight years have gone by since Donna moved, and we are still in contact with her. She is nineteen now, a very attractive girl who braids her hair and wears a little make-up and likes fashionable clothes. When I first phoned her, after the two weeks, she was pleased to hear from me and sounded settled, and she had lots of news about her home and family. Paula and Adrian spoke to her too, mainly about school and their respective cats – Toscha and Harris. I also talked to Marlene, who confirmed that Donna was doing well, and that there had been no major problems. We said goodbye and Marlene and Donna promised to keep in touch.

It was six months before we heard from them again; Marlene made the call and spoke to me first before she passed the phone to Donna. Marlene apologised for not phoning sooner but said that they'd had a bit of a 'rocky time'. She explained that Donna had been in therapy for four months and it had unleashed a lot of painful memories, which had resulted in her becoming unsettled and angry – she had twice trashed her bedroom. Marlene said that although Donna was still in therapy (and would be for some years) she was a lot calmer now, and was slowly coming to terms with the hurt and rejection from her past.

Marlene felt that the worst was behind them. I said that I understood, and I was pleased to hear from her now, as we had often talked about Donna and wondered how she was doing. I could hear the warmth in Marlene's voice as she spoke of Donna, and also the concern about what had been a very worrying period.

When Donna came to the phone it was so lovely to hear her voice again. She sounded older, more mature and also very positive. She told me all about her home life, school and the holiday she was going on with Marlene in August to Barbados. As she spoke she referred quite naturally to Marlene as 'Mum', and her extended family as aunts, uncles and cousins. She talked a lot about Kerry, Marlene's niece who was the same age as Donna, and said Kerry had become her 'second best friend' after Emily. When we had finished speaking I passed the phone to Adrian and Paula, and between us we were on the phone for nearly two hours, catching up with all Donna's news.

After that phone call Donna (and Marlene) continued to phone us every couple of months, and we began seeing them twice a year. We took it in turns to visit each other's houses, and one Christmas we all went to a pantomime together. Now Donna is nineteen she visits us alone, although she still lives with Marlene, who always sends her warmest wishes.

Donna is a lovely girl who has now managed to let go of a lot of her anger, and much of her negative self-image, helped by therapy and Marlene. She smiles a lot, looks you in the eyes when she speaks and only occasionally hunches her shoulders forwards – when something really bothers her. Her self-effacing and placid nature has continued, though, but this has become a positive attribute. It's like a breath of fresh air to be with Donna. She is a warm, gentle and caring person who speaks slowly and takes life in her stride. Nothing seems to faze her, for as she says, 'I've seen the worst of life and now it just gets better and better.' And I think some of that is to do with her new boyfriend, Robert, whom she brought with her last time she visited. He is a tall and good-looking lad whom she met at college, where Donna is studying to be a nurse and Robert a mechanic. I liked Robert, and was touched that Donna had wanted us to meet him. He treats her with much respect and they clearly think a lot of each other. How much of her past she has told him I don't know.

And what of Donna's family – the family who were responsible for so much of her unhappiness? I know only what Donna has told me. The supervised contact three times a year was stopped when Donna was fourteen, at her request, although Donna now visits her mother, whom she refers to as Rita, once a year. Rita's baby stayed in foster care until the court process was complete, and then she was adopted by a childless couple in their thirties. Donna has never seen the child, although the adoption order stipulates that the child should be made aware of her natural family when she is of a suitable age. Chelsea's baby, Cindy, despite all the support and help, both in the mother and baby unit, and when Chelsea moved into her flat, was eventually taken into care. Chelsea couldn't parent the child alone and moved back in with her mother, where Cindy quickly became badly neglected. When the social worker went with the police to remove the baby, Cindy was nowhere to be seen. Eventually, after searching the house and garden a second time, they found Cindy hidden under a pile of filthy rags in a crumbling shed at the bottom of the garden.

A year later Chelsea was pregnant again, and then she suffered a miscarriage after being beaten up by the person she claimed was the father of the baby. She moved out from her mother's house and hasn't been seen or heard of since. Rita is still drink and drug dependent, and Donna says the house is filthy and there is never any food there because Rita drinks and doesn't eat. Donna said the last time she visited, Rita looked like an old woman. From what Donna had learnt in her nursing studies, she thought that Rita would be dead in a year if she didn't stop drinking. Donna has never taken Robert to meet Rita and has no plans to.

Donna sees her brothers once a year, around Christmas time. They were found adoptive parents together and are doing very well, both at home and at school. Donna doesn't say much about them; I think her visits are more to stay in touch rather than prompted by any deep sibling bond. Whether Warren and Jason have suffered any remorse or guilt for the way they treated Donna when they were little, I don't know, but they were old enough at the time to remember that dreadful period. It would be nice to think that at some point in their lives they apologise to Donna, although Donna doesn't bear them any grudge. She wouldn't: it would never enter her head to bear anyone a grudge, such is her gentle and forgiving disposition.

When the supervised contact stopped, Donna began visiting her dad at his flat, first accompanied by Marlene and then for the last three years going alone. Edna found Mr Bajan a council flat before she retired, and he lives by himself and has no contact with Rita. Donna visits him every two weeks, on a Sunday, and cleans and tidies his flat and cooks him dinner. He knows exactly where his tablets are in the kitchen cupboard, and remembers to take them each morning and night. He has had only two relapses in the last eight years, and he joined his mother on a trip to Barbados for one winter. Donna also visits her gran, Mrs Bajan, who is not in the best of health. Donna takes three buses every month to spend a day with her. She cleans and tidies her flat and makes sure she has enough food in the fridge. Donna loves her gran and dad; together with Marlene they are her family, and the most important people in her life.

Therapy and having Marlene as her mother have helped Donna along the path to becoming a well-adjusted and successful adult. Donna tells me that just occasionally, if she is frustrated by something or someone, she goes to her bedroom and quietly tears up a magazine, and then clears it up. She and Marlene laugh about it, and if tearing up paper helps then there is no reason for her to stop it. We all need some release from life's little downers, and on the scale of things, shredding paper is no great problem; I might try it some time.

Donna will qualify as a nurse in two years' time and is looking forward to starting work and earning a wage. She officially came out of care when she reached the age of eighteen and therefore no longer has a social worker. She still sees a therapist every so often, at her request, when she feels she needs to talk to someone outside the family. Although she has made new friends at college, she is still in contact with Emily whom, together with Kerry, she regards as her 'best buddy'. Emily left school at sixteen and works as a sales assistance in a department store. Donna, Emily and Kerry go out together in the evening and also on extended shopping expeditions; being the age they are, they love to shop. They have also discussed the idea of renting a flat together when Donna and Kerry finish their education and start earning.

Despite the years that have passed, Donna vividly remembers the time when she lived with us, and has many fond memories. She also remembers the hurt and trauma she was going through inside at that time, and how I continually encouraged her to let it go by talking. She has thanked me more than once for being so patient and understanding, and has also apologised to Paula and Adrian for being so 'horrible', as she puts it. I have reassured her that there is no need either to thank me or to apologise, and that she wasn't horrible, just a child in crisis. Paula and Adrian have only good memories of her time with us, especially of Christmas and our holiday together. We still look at the photographs, and remember – Donna, who was once the saddest girl in the world, but blossomed into a wonderful young woman. Well done, love.